HOW TO MANAGE BY OBJECTIVES

A Short Course for Managers

Paul Mali

Graduate School of Business
University of Hartford
Paul Mali & Associates

Wiley Professional Development Programs • Business Administration Series

Advisory Editor
Steven C. Wheelwright
Harvard Business School

John Wiley & Sons, Inc.   **New York • London • Sydney • Toronto**

Library of Congress Catalogue Card Number: 75-27387

ISBN 0-471-56574-1

Printed in the United States of America.

10 9 8 7 6 5 4 3 2 1

INTRODUCTION

In recent years, managing by objectives (MBO) has been one of the most striking developments in the managerial art of getting results. Hundreds upon hundreds of organizations, from small enterprises to giant corporations, report accomplishments of a most astonishing and profitable nature.

The success of these organizations has been based primarily on the effective use of managing by objectives as a management system. This effectiveness has been due in large measure to a clear understanding of the concept of managing by objectives and of how to introduce and develop it within the enterprise.

It is clear from the vast body of information and knowledge evolving around this concept that a dynamic management way of life is steadily maturing. This is probably the result of several developments. First, management practitioners themselves are increasingly concerned with improving their own effectiveness. Second, initial success in using managing by objectives has spurred additional efforts toward clarification and refinement. Third, "managing at a distance" (decentralization and delegation) is now recognized as a way of managerial life. Fourth, organizations now recognize that managerial talent is the crucial component in the perpetuation and profitability of the enterprise.

Purpose and Scope of This Course

This course is intended to accomplish several purposes: first, to set down in one place the fundamentals, principles, and procedures for a clear understanding of the concept of managing by objectives, its benefits, and its various applications; second, to serve as a practical operating guide for those who wish to introduce and develop the concept as a management system in their organization; third, to give additional insight and alternative techniques to those individuals already practicing managing by objectives but who wish to refine their skill; fourth, to assist as a resource in training programs and management seminars whose purpose is management development and skills improvement; fifth, to offer food for thought to those practitioners who are not yet convinced or committed to a managing by objective program.

The course is organized into nine chapters divided among four units. Unit I, The Strategy of Managing by Objectives, provides the fundamentals and gives an overview of the concept as a system strategy, offers benefits to be derived from its use, and indicates the type of organizational problems it best solves.

Unit II, Isolating and Setting Objectives, lays out specific procedures showing how to isolate objectives meaningful to the organization, how to formulate them, and how to measure them for the highest payoff.

Unit III, Validating and Implementing Objectives, demonstrates how to validate objectives and deals with the manner in which commitments are shared and implemented.

Unit IV, Controlling and Maintaining MBO Programs, presents techniques for maintaining the MBO practice in an organization through control and training. In addition, the unit describes a series of improvement applications as illustrations and examples of using MBO to get results.

An abundance of diagrammatic illustrations and graphic tools have been integrated into the exposition, tests, and case studies to further enhance the comprehension of basic concepts. A comprehensive list of selected readings, keyed to each unit, appears on the back of each tab page. This can serve as a useful guide for further reading in a particular area.

How to Use the Course

How to Manage by Objectives allows you to work at your own learning pace and monitor your progress on an on-going basis through exercise and review materials. Each chapter opens with definitions of the key terms in the major chapter topics and then provides a list of the learning objectives that you should be able to meet after completing the chapter material. Each chapter contains quizzes (Checkpoints) at regular intervals, and these should be used to measure your understanding and progress to that point. Finally, at the end of each chapter, there is a brief chapter summary and review section. The material in the review section includes an objective test (Doublecheck), brief essay questions, and/or a case study. This review section provides you with an opportunity to measure your mastery of the chapter material and apply it in a realistic and practical way.

The checkpoints and review materials are not designed primarily to test. Rather, used in the context of each chapter, they are a means for gaining feedback and reviewing progress in an unstructured, individualized study situation. For this reason, no formal grading scheme has been provided and the answers that are given to essay questions and case study problems should be considered as general guidelines for reviewing your answers rather than as definitive solutions. If you wish to measure your progress in a more formal way, you can devise a simple grading scheme when checking your answers with the ones given at the bottom of each of the Checkpoint pages.

The Pre- and Post-Test

Another feature of the course provides a more formal test of achievement. The Pre- and Post-Test (at the end of the course) is an objective examination graded on a formal scale (2 points for each correct answer) and designed to test your overall comprehension of the course material. It includes questions which cover the most significant points in each of the chapters.

To use the Pre- and Post-Test properly, you should take it once right after reading this introduction. Write the answers on a separate piece of paper and then compare them with the answers provided on the Answer Sheet. Then calculate your score and note it in the appropriate space on the Answer Sheet. At this point the score has no significance. *After completing the course*, follow this procedure again, exactly as described, without referring to the answers you gave on the Pre-Test or to the Answer Sheet. After you have calculated the score on the Post-Test and noted it on the Answer Sheet, you can compare the two scores for a realistic measure of your achievement. The questions and answers are keyed to chapters, and you will therefore be able to identify areas where you have significantly improved your skills and understanding, as well as areas where you should return to the course material for further review.

Acknowledgements

The material for *How to Manage by Objectives* is derived from Dr. Paul Mali's *Managing by Objectives*, published by John Wiley & Sons, Inc. The text was adapted for individual self-study through consultation with academic and professional advisors, and under the guidance of Dr. Steven C. Wheelwright, Assistant Professor, Harvard Business School and Advisory Editor for John Wiley's Professional Development Programs.

CONTENTS

I. The Strategy of Managing by Objectives ———————————

1. *Managing by Objectives: An Overview*　　3

    Managing by Objectives Defined • How MBO Works (The Five Phases) • Why MBO Works • How MBO Creates a Management System • Feeder Objectives • Summary

2. *MBO Approaches to Typical Management Problems*　　25

    The Changing Environment • Growing Dilution of Effort • Neglecting Opportunities As a Result of Crisis Management • Uncoordinated Planning Within Managerial Levels • Constant Increase of Costs • Tendency to Tolerate Mediocrity • Growing Disparity Between Employer and Employee Goals • Imbalanced Organizations • Summary

II. Isolating and Setting Objectives ———————————

3. *Isolating Objectives*　　57

    Looking Ahead for Improvements • Three Nonnumerical Forecasting Methods • The Situation Action Forecasting Method • Five Numerical Forecasting Methods • Summary

4. *Setting Objectives*　　95

    Clarity in MBO Objectives • Focus in MBO Objectives • Cost Improvement in MBO Objectives • Performance Stretch in MBO Objectives • Interlocking of MBO Objectives • Summary

III. Validating and Implementing Objectives ———————————

5. *Validating Objectives*　　129

    Decision Trees • Work Breakdown Structures • Program Evaluation and Review Technique • Model Manipulation and Review • Commitment to Deliver Results • Summary

6. *Implementing Objectives*　　153

    Planned Motivation • The Relationship of Needs to Motivation • The Role of Coaching in Planned Motivation • The Role of Persuasion in Planned Motivation • The Application of Planned Motivation • Summary

IV. Controlling and Maintaining MBO Programs ———————————

7. *Controlling and Reporting Status of Objectives*　　191

    Controlling and Reporting: Definition and Guidelines • Status Reporting • Performance Appraisals • MBO Trouble Spots and Suggested Remedies • Summary

8. *Training and Developing MBO Managers*　　221

    What Are the Basic MBO Skills? • How Are Basic MBO Skills Developed? • Reading References • Summary

9. *Improvement Applications*   *235*

    Introduction • Profit Improvement • Sales Improvement • Cost Improvement • Management Time Improvement • Communications Improvement • Methods Improvement • Training Improvement • Summary

Pre- and Post-Test   *285*

I. THE STRATEGY OF MANAGING BY OBJECTIVES

SELECTED READINGS

1. Managing by Objectives: An Overview

Carroll, Phil, *Profit Control,* McGraw-Hill Book Co., New York, 1962.

Drucker, Peter F., *The Practice of Management,* Harper and Brothers, New York, 1954.

Duncan, J. Russell, "Building and Retaining a Top Management Team," in H.B. Maynard (ed.), *Top Management Handbook,* McGraw-Hill Book Co., New York, 1960.

Managing by and with Objectives, Research Study No. 212, National Industrial Conference Board, 1968.

McConkey, Dale D., *How to Manage by Results,* American Management Association, New York, 1965.

O'Hea, J. J., "Colt Heating & Ventilation Limited," in John W. Humble (ed.), *Management by Objectives in Action,* McGraw-Hill Book Co., New York, 1970.

Parkinson, C. Northcote, *Parkinson's Law,* Houghton Mifflin, New York, 1967.

Pascoe, B. J., "Royal Naval Supply and Transport Service of the Ministry of Defense," in Humble (ed.) , *op. cit.*

Peterson, Leroy A., "Establishing Objectives," in Maynard (ed.), *op. cit.*

Riggs, James L., *Economic Decision Models,* McGraw-Hill Book Co., New York, 1968.

Shield, Lansing P., "Directing the Attainment of Objectives," in Maynard (ed.), *op. cit.*

Sloan, Alfred P., Jr., *My Years with General Motors,* MacFadden-Bartell, New York, 1965.

Smiddy, Harold F., "Deciding," in Maynard (ed.), *op. cit.*

Steinkraus, Herman W., "Motivating," in Maynard (ed.), *op. cit.*

Voich, Dan, Jr. and Daniel A. Wren, *Principles of Management-Resources and Systems,* Ronald Press, New York, 1968.

Weston, J. Fred, "Evaluating Company Performance," in H. B. Maynard (ed.), *Handbook of Business Administration,* McGraw-Hill Book Co., New York, 1967.

2. MBO Approaches to Typical Management Problems

Batten, J. D., *Beyond Management by Objectives,* American Management Association, New York, 1965.

Bennis, Warren, "Organizational Change Operating in the Temporary Society," *Innovation,* No. 1, May 1969.

Carlisle, Howard M., "Are Functional Organizations Becoming Obsolete?" *Management Review,* January 1969.

Dickie, H. Ford, "Hard-Nosed Inventory Management," in Donald G. Hall (ed.), *The Manufacturing Man and His Job,* American Management Association, New York, 1966.

Drucker, Peter F., *Managing for Results,* Harper and Row New York, 1964.

Juran, J. M., "Universals in Management Planning and Controlling," *The Management Review,* November 1954.

"How's Business? Latest Nationwide Survey," U. S. News and *World Report,* December 14, 1970.

Lewis, Ralph E., *Planning and Control for Profit,* Harper and Row, New York, 1970.

Lippitt, Gordon, and Warren H. Schmidt, "Crises in a Developing Organization," *Harvard Business Review,* November-December 1967.

Litterer, Joseph A., *The Analysis of Organizations,* John Wiley and Sons, Inc., New York, 1965.

McClelland, David C., *The Achieving Society,* Nostrand Co., Inc., New York, 1961.

Myers, M. Scott, *Every Employee a Manager,* McGraw-Hill Book Co., New York, 1970.

O'Hea, J. J., "Colt Heating & Ventilation Limited," in John W. Humble (ed.), *Management by Objectives in Action,* McGraw-Hill Book Co., New York, 1970.

Otto, Herbert A., *Guide to Developing Your Potential,* Scribner and Sons, New York, 1967.

Parkinson, C. Northcote, *Parkinson's Law,* Houghton Mifflin, New York, 1967.

Sibson, Robert E., "The Problems You Shouldn't Solve," *Management Review,* February 1969.

Smith, Richard A., *Corporations in Crisis,* Doubleday and Co., Inc., New York, 1963.

I. THE STRATEGY OF MANAGING BY OBJECTIVES

1. MANAGING BY OBJECTIVES: AN OVERVIEW ——————

Key Concepts

- *Time-Phased Objectives.* One of the keys to making objectives effective and operational is to specify them for particular periods of time. A series of time-phased objectives provides a schedule for blending the activities and operations of each manager in order to achieve both long-range and short-range organizational goals.

- *Managing the Management Resource.* Management by objectives (MBO) is really a system and philosophy for directing the efforts of an entire management team. In this regard, it can be thought of as a set of procedures for focusing, directing, and controlling the management resources of the organization.

- *Translating Objectives to Commitment.* The critical step in making management by objectives work is the transition from a formal statement of objectives to a statement of commitment. This involves validating the objectives for each of the managers involved so that the objectives become a motivational system for focusing effort and achieving desired results.

Learning Objectives

After you have completed this chapter, you should be able to

- Define managing by objectives and its principles of operation.

- Describe the five phases of the managing by objectives process.

- Explain how managing by objectives creates a management system through the concepts of strategy, tactics, and tactical-strategic interrelationships.

MANAGING BY OBJECTIVES (MBO) DEFINED

The greatest challenge to management is the necessity to reconcile, integrate, and direct human effort, resources, and facilities toward achieving common goals while avoiding discord and common disasters. Managers have tried several approaches to meeting this challenge. There are those who use the "hunch" approach. There are those who employ management fads. There are those who use the traditional processes of management. Finally, there are those who use the managing by objectives approach.

Managing by objectives is a strategy of planning and getting results in a direction that management wishes to take while meeting the goals and needs of its participants.

> In its simplest form, MBO provides unity of managerial action in achieving organizational goals. This is done by establishing for each level of management specific objectives that motivate accomplishment of results in the time period specified.

The primary purpose of this strategy is to simplify and thus clarify the managerial processes operating within an organization. There are four basic elements in the MBO concept: objectives, time strategy, total management, and individual motivation.

Objectives ►

Objectives are events or accomplishments planned and expected to happen. They are job or organizational results to be arrived at. For example:

- To achieve a net-profit to net-worth ratio of 6.25 percent is an example of a profit objective for a business firm.

- To reduce employee absenteeism from 12 to 6 percent is an example of a personnel-management objective for a government agency.

- To increase customer inquiries from 10,000 to 15,000 per year is an example of an advertising objective for a salesperson.

- To reduce material waste 50 percent is an example of a cost-improvement objective for a foreman in a machine shop.

Time Strategy ►

Time strategy refers to the schedule for blending the activities and operations of each manager to achieve long- and short-range sets of results. It is a deliberate coordination of resources with the calendar, signaling each manager to propose, act, and accomplish at designated periods of time. For example:

- Achieving a 10-percent reduction in operating costs *within the next three operating quarters* by all departments is an example of a schedule for coordinating and collecting the contribution of each manager.

- Completing development of ventilator fans, model B, *within the next 6 months* by all departments and vendors is another example of time strategy.

Total Management ►

Total management refers to a formalized effort to involve and coordinate the contributions of each manager toward a common goal. For example:

- A hospital needs an internal management system to utilize and coordinate to the fullest extent the contributions of physicians, nurses, laboratory equipment, lab technicians, operating rooms, dietitians, pharmacists, and supervisors.

- An educational institution needs an internal management system to utilize and coordinate the contributions of faculty, administrators, laboratories, computer equipment, accountants, classrooms, lecture halls, and clerks.

- A missile manufacturer requires a similar management system to coordinate metal-lurgists, stress analysts, computers, fluid dynamicists, electronic controls, fuel meters, mechanical and heat-transfer equipment, and control engineers.

Managing by objectives creates a total management system, connecting the roles and contributions of each manager and channeling them toward large-scale accomplishments.

Individual Motivation ►

Individual motivation refers to personal involvement in the objective-setting process. This involvement tends to generate a desire and willingness to achieve. Managing by objectives is a motivational strategy, since individual commitments and subsequent accomplishments lead to a higher degree of satisfaction. For example:

- The unit-restaurant manager of a large, scattered franchise chain is highly motivated when allowed to participate in all aspects of his unit operations — operations such as payroll, overhead, hiring, customer relations, advertising, and maintenance.

- A pipe-welding supervisor is motivated when allowed to participate in the many aspects of the total welding job, such as pipe weld design, welding equipment acquisition, inspection, training, qualification, and weld stress analysis.

These four elements form the basis for the four fundamental principles of managing by objectives. These principles, simply stated, are:

> 1. Unity of managerial action is more likely to occur when there is pursuit of a common objective.
>
> 2. The greater the focus and concentration on results one wants to achieve on a time scale, the greater the likelihood of achieving them.
>
> 3. The greater the participation in setting meaningful work with an accountability for a result, the greater the motivation for completing it.
>
> 4. Progress can only be measured in terms of what one is trying to make progress toward.

In many ways, the MBO concept is inseparable from such other essential management concepts as delegation of authority, division of labor, decision-making, performance appraisals, and policy making. But the management essential that has been MBO's historical taproot is *coordinated decentralization*, which is "decentralized operations with coordinated control."[1]

The term *management by objectives* first appeared in the literature as a reference to a way of building teamwork. Present-day practice of the concept ranges from applying it as an informal individual tool to applying it as a formalized management system. It is doubtful that any two organizations can practice managment by objectives in exactly the same manner. There are too many different variables operating in each situation. Since conditions vary because of differences in types of organizations, in products and services, and in employees, an eclectic approach is needed to make the concept operational. The manager needs to launch MBO within an organization as a "best fit" and to adapt it to his unique requirements. The four basic principles must be allowed to operate as unifying processes within the organizational scope and structure of specialization, diversification, and integration.

Draw a line to connect the MBO element to its description.

1. Time strategy

2. Objectives

3. Individual motivation

4. Total management

A. Planned events or accomplishments

B. Formalized effort to coordinate the contributions of each manager and direct them toward a common goal

C. Personal involvement in the objective-setting process

D. Schedule for blending the activities of each manager in order to achieve objectives when and as planned

Indicate true (T) or false (F).

5. Managing by objectives involves meeting the goals and needs of participants. ——

6. Coordinated centralization is MBO's historical taproot. ——

7. In managing by objectives, progress is measured in terms of specified goals achieved within specified time limits. ——

8. The greater the participation in setting an objective (regardless of its meaningfulness), the greater the motivation for completing it. ——

9. The greater the focus on results, the greater the likelihood of achieving them. ——

10. In managing by objectives, all the accountability is at the top. ——

—————————————————————

● Checkpoint Answers

1. D   2. A   3. C   4. B   5. T   6. F   7. T   8. F   9. T   10. F

HOW MBO WORKS (THE FIVE PHASES)

Getting results in an organization comes about through a deliberate effort of planning and organizing resources in order to meet a set of expectations. Results seldom just happen. In the past, the randomly practiced trial-and-error approach has been used with some success. However, high costs, schedule slippage, and low morale have been by-products of this approach. Managing by objectives avoids these pitfalls; it is a plan-ahead process that is made up of a series of deliberately thought out phases. This section provides an overview of the phases. The description of each phase will be expanded in the following chapters.

Managing by objectives is a five-phase process. It is an activity carried out in a sequence of steps taken in a certain order. This is similar to a manufacturing process that takes a material through a sequence of steps, each one modifying the material in some way until it emerges as a finished product. To say that MBO is essentially a five-phase process is not to exclude the many additional steps incorporated into one or another of the following five main phases:

1. Isolating the objective

2. Setting the objective

3. Validating the objective

4. Implementing the objective

5. Controlling and reporting the status of the objective

All the phases are sequentially related to give the process a cycle of start to finish. Repetitive cycles can be generated, making the process unending.

Phase 1. Isolating the Objective ►

The concept of managing by objectives begins with a deliberate and systematic identification of results needed by the organization for survival, growth, improvement, or problem solution. This identification starts with an examination of the organization as it is now constituted. All kinds of analytical situational questions are raised: Where are we? How did we get here? What is our state of affairs? Why are we deficient? What are our opportunities? Trends, projections, and indicators are examined to note situational effects on the organization. Capacity utilization and performance are measured and compared with those of other organizations. Competitive "edge" analysis is made to assess positive and negative differences. Broad areas suggesting potentially usable objectives are identified, such as product markets, improved services, new facilities, lowered costs, sales improvements, reduced turnover, work simplification, methods improvement, merger possibilities, coordinated research, productivity improvement, employee motivation, and customer satisfaction. The practitioner must give this first phase much time, analysis, and attention, since it is at this stage that drift, aimless tendencies, or incorrect directions are noted, stopped, and redirected.

> Results of phase I: list of attractive and needed potential objectives.

Phase 2. Setting the Objective ►

The broad areas of potentially usable targets identified in phase 1 provide the basis for adopting and setting the objective. This setting process involves the management team and its resources through a form of participation until a formal statement of objective emerges. This statement proposes that a commitment is to be made by an individual, a group, a department, or the entire organization. The formal statement is written, communicated, supported by top management, interlocked with other groups, and the whole organization is accountable for its implementation. Setting the objectives is a formal process of relating the resources of the organization to the involvement of those expected to deliver the results. It is based on the principle that, if you want to get maximum results from people, get them involved and accountable for these results.

```
Results of phase 2: formal statement of the objective.
```

Phase 3. Validating the Objective ▶

The formal statement of the objective developed in phase 2 is submitted to a validation procedure. This procedure determines the confidence an individual, department, or company may have that an objective can be reached within its stated time. Risks, assumptions, and changing requirements are checked and analyzed to see where faults or failures can occur in implementation. The validation procedure simulates in a "dry run" effects of errors or difficulties that may emerge. It builds within the objective contingencies to avoid potential errors. The validation procedure translates the statement of objective to a statement of commitment. This commitment is binding, since a pledge or promise is made to deliver a given set of results. The validation procedure assures that resources, facilities, materials, methods, people, and management are ready and willing to reach a desired goal. Such a procedure raises or lowers the confidence, raises or lowers the risk, raises or lowers the probability that the venture will or will not take place. It is at this point in the overall managing by objectives process that many objectives are discarded as unattainable or unworthy.

```
Results of phase 3: validated statement of commitment.
```

Phase 4. Implementing the Objective ▶

Once a validated statement of commitment has been made as a result of phase 3, a motivational system is created to implement the commitment. Setting the objective in phase 2 requires motivators to be built into the objective as an inherent ingredient. Phase 4 develops job plans and activities to begin and carry out action needed for fulfilling the commitment. There must be a connection between these two phases. Phase 2 defines the target, and phase 4 is the implementation strategy for reaching the target. This will require a more deliberate approach in motivating, coaching, and persuading.

```
Results of phase 4: implementation of activities to reach objective.
```

Phase 5. Controlling and Reporting Status of Objective ▶

Phase 5 is based on the principle, stated earlier, that progress can only be measured in terms of what one is trying to make progress toward. This phase places all activities under a schedule in order to measure and report the current status as well as progress toward completing the objective. The controlling and reporting process senses deviations of actual progress from expected progress and reports these deviations for corrective action. The concepts of *feedback* (measurement of past progress) and *feed forward* (measurement of expected future progress) give the management team an idea of their present position in relation to where they are going.

Results of phase 5: status-of-work schedule reporting progress toward established targets.

These five briefly described phases partially explain the overall process of managing by objectives. Many other features, techniques, and methods must be discussed before we can claim to have given a complete description.

Time Schedules ►

Every manager knows that our entire way of economic life involves racing against time. A new criterion for leadership is the ability to keep pace with the increasing speed of emerging complex problems and to provide, at the same pace and speed, viable solutions to those problems.

Managing by objectives is not simply getting results but getting results within a time period. The concept involves a "pace" theme of productivity. The gain in results or output is for a given period of time. The basic principle for practicing MBO is play the clock; never play it by ear.

Time is reliable, consistent, and regulatory. Managing by objectives sets expected results on the basis of the clock and the calendar to take advantage of this reliable pace setter. In so doing, MBO sets up a sequential pace that works against Parkinson's law, which states that work is elastic and will fill the time set for its completion.[2] The manager who sets realistic but tight time periods for jobs to be done acts against the elasticity of work, which results in greater productivity. He uses shorter periods of time to achieve the same amount of work. Time becomes a tool for getting greater productivity.

Obtaining results through managing by objectives within a time period is rather like playing a football game. The football goal posts are in clear view of the individual players. This is analogous to the organization's objectives. The field is marked in yards so that a player can gauge whether he is making progress toward these goal posts. This is analogous to a breakdown of the organization's objectives to milestones of progress. The offensive team as they huddle and decide on a tactic for yardage is analogous to management's planning work activities and job actions to accomplish objectives. The actual carrying of the ball and the teamwork necessary is analogous to the implementation and performance of work. The defensive team's opposing and frustrating the yardage to be gained is analogous to the constraints within and without an organization. Finally, the game goes by the tick of the clock. Just as there are only so many minutes to play, there is only so much time for the organization to get results. Consequently, the schedule is an important tool in the practice of managing by objectives.

A schedule is a list of details that must be accomplished to complete a large-scale mission. All the planned details are timed for start and finish in order to coordinate the interrelationship of these details with the clock and the calendar.

Utilization of materials is signaled with the schedule. Production of units is started and stopped with the schedule. The flow of inventory to the warehouse and to distribution centers is guided by the schedule. The hiring and working of manpower is executed by the schedule.

The time baselines shown in Figure 1 represent the amount of scheduled time required to achieve each phase in the sequential phases of the MBO process. A time baseline is a scheduled period of time in which planned work must be done. It signals all details that must be complete before passing into the next phase. It defines points of progress between interfaces of the phases. Time baselines can also provide an opportunity for managerial review of conflicts, overlaps, omissions, and difficulties before going any further with a project. For example, a practitioner who has just completed phase 3, validating the objective, discovers that a supplier cannot deliver material within a normal time because of a labor strike. The time baseline between phases 3 and 4 allows for a management review to reconsider the time expectancy of the commitment in question. This would mean either extending the time for completion, changing suppliers, or eliminating the commitment as stated. Time baselines within a schedule are used in the practice of managing by objectives for getting hundreds of details completed toward the ultimate objective. They provide plateaus for management review in the sequential phases of the process. Time baselines are indispensable in the practice of MBO.

WHY MBO WORKS

Economic life without productive work directed toward some purpose is meaningless and dull. It is the nature of man to engage in purposeful activity. It provides him with satisfaction, especially when directed toward a common good. This common good may be manifested as perpetuation of an enterprise, customer satisfaction, or employee security. Managing by objectives follows man's inherent tendencies to change disorder to order, unfinished to finished, disorganization to organization. The work situation becomes an opportunity for a person to exercise these tendencies. What makes MBO work is that it satisfies man's desire to accomplish, providing an opportunity and the process to select what is to be accomplished, how it is to be accomplished, and when. Achievement in the work situation must not be a mere possibility, but rather a certainty if economic life is to be meaningful and fulfilling.

Many organizations have set standards of accomplishment far beyond a realistic expectancy, believing that the formidable challenge will spur people to work that much harder. More often than not, this approach fails. If a person works very hard, accomplishes a great deal, but never quite reaches the formidable goal, he takes the attitude, "What's the use?" A standard he can never hope to reach loses all meaning for him. For example, the general manager of a paper mill company set a goal for his production manager of 15-percent cost reduction every year. Considering the cost of materials, supplies, labor, and overhead, this was an almost impossible task. In the first year, the production manager achieved about 10-percent reduction. Although actually a good job, it did not meet the general manager's expectancy. The next year he was asked to continue his 15-percent cost reduction. By the middle of the year, the impossibility of ever reaching the goal became apparent and discouragement set in. Three months later, the production manager quit and the general manager had to replace him with someone else. The general manager soon discovered that the replacement was not nearly as good as the previous man. In fact, the production manager who left turned out to be extremely effective and successful in another firm. It had been the general manager's notion that people would be spurred on by an extremely high goal, but he forgot that most of us need the satisfaction of achievement and an impossible goal makes it very difficult to experience this.

> Managing by objectives requires of the work situation reasonable and attainable accomplishments. It forces planning at every level.

1. The Strategy of Managing by Objectives

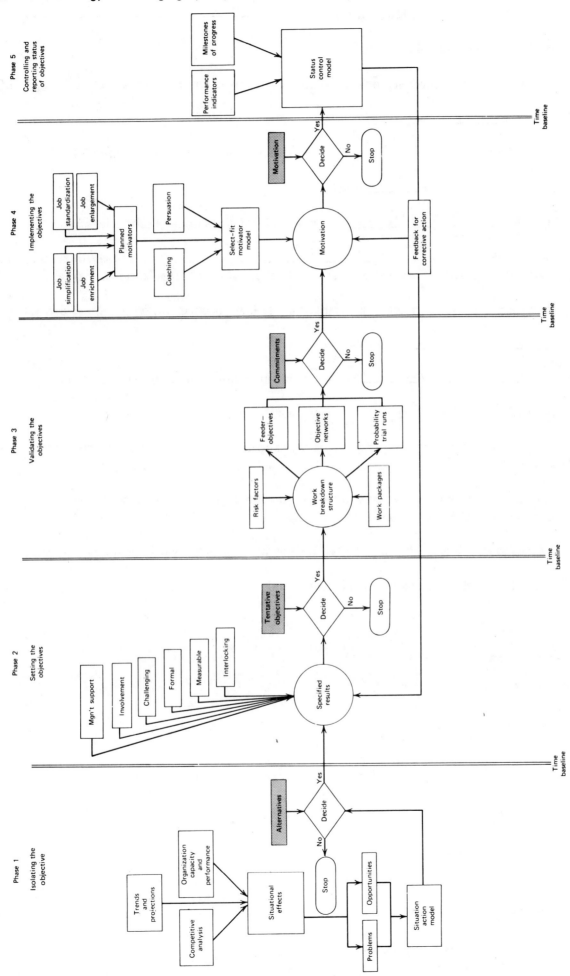

Fill in the blank to complete the statement.

1. In validating the objective, one translates a statement of objectives to a statement of

   _____ .

2. In the next phase, the latter statement is implemented through the creation of a

   _____ system.

3. Phase 5, _____ places all activities under a schedule.

4. In the MBO phase called _____ , capacity utilization and performance are measured and compared with those of other organizations.

5. Once broad areas of potentially usable targets have been identified, there is a basis for

   _____ .

6. A _____ is a list of planned details timed for start and finish.

Indicate true (T) or false (F).

7. MBO objectives should always spur managers to try to achieve more than they really can achieve. _____

8. Managing by objectives is successful because it follows man's desire to be involved in what is to be accomplished, when, and how. _____

9. A *time baseline* is a scheduled period of time in which planned work must be done. _____

10. In a well-run MBO system, no time is spent validating objectives. _____

───────────────

● Checkpoint Answers

1. commitment   2. motivational   3. controlling and reporting status of objective   4. isolating the objective
5. setting the objective   6. schedule   7. F   8. T   9. T   10. F

HOW MBO CREATES A MANAGEMENT SYSTEM

The five sequential phases described previously provide a framework within which to think about and visualize managing as an integrated whole. This framework helps to break some of the larger complexities down into simple and understandable segments, forming the foundation for a management system. The purpose of this section is to explain and illustrate how MBO creates a management system within the organization.

Management As a System ►

The story is often told about a group of blind men who were assigned the task of describing an elephant. Because each blind man felt and analyzed a different part of the body, a heated argument developed among them as to what an elephant was like. One had his hands on the tail and claimed the elephant was like a rope. Another had his hands on the body and claimed that the elephant was like a large, soft, wall. The third had his hands on a leg and claimed that the elephant was like the trunk of a tree. Each was sampling one aspect of the totality. Each failed to grasp the totality in spite of a correct description of his sample.

The ability to see the whole, the parts, and their interrelationships is the art of conceptualizing a system. A system can be defined as an organized combination of things or parts forming a complex or unitary whole.[3] The following are examples of systems:

- *Solar system.* Sun, planets, earth, moon, and asteroids orbiting in prescribed paths to give order, form, and conditions to sustain life as we know it.

- *Restaurant system.* Chefs, cooks, busboys, cashiers, waitresses, and facilities organized to convert raw food to a finished product for customer consumption and satisfaction.

- *Production system.* Machinists, toolmakers, operators, set-up men, maintenance men, janitors, machines, and facilities organized to process raw materials for finished products for inventory to be sold in markets.

In MBO systems, the manager designs and organizes all the elements so as to guide, integrate, and control all resources toward some objective. Managers take unrelated resources, disorganized facilities, and unused skills and build a framework for accomplishing a mission. The manager's ability to understand and relate individual parts to a totality gives him a conceptual overview for handling the complex parts of his job. To illustrate, imagine someone showing you, one at a time, a photograph of each part of the elephant mentioned previously. If you are not given a framework so you can arrange them correctly, you must form an image in your mind of what the elephant would look like if the parts were properly put together. You must form a conceptual overview of the picture based on just one part. The restaurant manager must "see" the impact on customer satisfaction when food does not arrive on time, the union cook is going on strike, or the waitresses are becoming angry over lack of tips. The production manager must "see" the impact on inventories when machine downtime is excessive, material reject rate is high, or established schedules are not followed. How well a manager can form a conceptual overview of his many

> Managing by objectives creates a structure that allows management a vantage point from which it can view the whole system while observing the contributions of each of its parts. The five sequential phases provide managers with links for relating the hundreds of individual contributions toward an overall large-scale accomplishment.

individual responsibilities determines to a great extent how well his contributions relate to the enterprise. How well all managers' contributions relate to the enterprise determines the extent to which a management system exists for accomplishing objectives.

MBO Strategy As a Management System►

The terms *tactics* and *strategy* are often used in management to describe maneuvers and approaches to achieving objectives. Strategy sets the long-range and broad plan, and associated tactics define the many short-range maneuvers required to implement the strategic plan. Tactical-strategic interrelations are the connections among the many short-range tactics necessary to implement a long-range and large-scale strategy. Tactical-strategic interrelations bridge individual plans to the overall larger plan. How well tactical-strategic interrelations are set up and operate determines to a large extent the development of a management system for focusing and reaching an objective. Riggs considers these interrelations in terms of managerial efficiency.[4] He defines this efficiency as the degree to which the relative value of tactical choices accomplishes the intended effort. To illustrate, the owner of a wholesale distribution center has decided that the purchase of more trucks will best satisfy his strategic objective for growth within the next five years. He wants his business to grow to a definite level within this period. He is willing to take the risk that new trucks will shorten delivery time and increase his market share. He expects the new trucks to reach new outlets and give him an attractive return on investment. His decision to buy trucks to reach a five-year growth objective, rather than to rent, lease, or subcontract them, has been a strategic one. Now he must make tactical choices to carry out his strategic decision. A few of the many tactical-strategic decisions he must make are the following: type and cost of trucks; routes of travel to potential customers; material-handling services and unloading procedures for the customer; frequency and schedule of deliveries; maintenance and insurance provisions; hiring and placement of drivers. How well the owner carries out these tactical choices will determine how closely he will meet his strategic objective. This is a measure of his managerial efficiency at systemizing the many individual tactical decisions toward his overall strategy of using new trucks for company growth.

The five cascade phases of managing by objectives illustrated in Figure 1 constitute a systems approach for integrating individual tactical planning and decision-making to an overall large-scale mission. The traditional system elements of totality, input, output, process, structure, and control are observed in this strategy.

- *A totality.* A mission, aim, or function is conceptualized when an overall, long-range, promising objective is selected from among several alternate good ones.

- *Input.* Individual resources are selected on a short- or long-range basis and related to an overall objective. These resources can be selected from within or without the enterprise.

- *Output.* Results for which the strategy was organized. A set of conditions or services yielded from the procesing of inputs.

- *Process.* Transformation required to change inputs to outputs. These are the many activities that make possible the conversion of resources.

- *Structure.* The connection of all system elements to perform the mission. Tactical-strategic interrelations are connected and blended together on a timetable to give an integrating structure to the strategy.

- *Control.* Criterion or standard of measurement that compares intended output with actual output. Quantity and quality of results of the strategy are placed on a status-reporting basis. Progress is monitored and corrections made when needed.

The process of managing by objectives facilitates a systems view of the organization as a whole (the strategy); the operations and performance of each department, section, and manager (the tactics); and the interrelated contributions among the departments, sections and managers (tactical-strategic connectors). An organization that allows these processes to operate within the heart and core of managerial work soon discovers several emerging systems overview capabilities. These capabilities provide an overview of the strategy in operation. The following table summarizes these capabilities and their value and use for management.

Systems Overview Capabilities*	Value and Use for Management	Example: Wholesale Distribution Center
1. Predictability	Foreseeing end from prescribed beginnings	Capital outlay now for 20 new trucks to improve sales 20-percent per year
2. Completeability	Foreseeing connective in-process steps to a conclusion	Annual 20-percent sales growth reaches 5-year sales volume plan
3. Reachability	Foreseeing results are attainable	20-percent annual growth from 10-percent expansion of old market and 10-percent penetration of new market
4. Visibility	Relating constituent parts into sequential whole	Decrease in delivery time by 4 hours will yield annual 20-percent growth in sales
5. Interfaceability	Conceptualizing gaps between boundaries of in-process steps	Preventive truck maintenance program reduces breakdown and idle time 50 percent
6. Reliability	Identifying strengths and weaknesses	Best delivery time in market could be offset by union unrest
7. Supportability	Relating individual plans and tactical-strategic connectors toward overall accomplishment	Increase in delivery time results from good employees, preventive maintenance, loading and unloading procedures
8. Measurability	Grasping progress indicators and timetable	Monthly sales reports by truck by route
9. Controlability	Sensing deviations within prescribed limits	Monthly sales reports acted upon by sales manager
10. Improvability	Foreseeing corrective actions to stay on course	If share of market optimized, subcontract delivery system to other wholesalers with different product line

*MBO practitioners will recognize the use of jargon to describe the systems capabilities. The use of jargon has been kept to a minimum.

Complete each statement by circling the correct letter.

1. The long-range plan is set by

   a. tactics   b. strategy   c. tactical-strategic interrelations

2. The short-range maneuvers required to implement a long-range plan are

   a. tactics   b. strategy   c. tactical-strategic interrelations

3. The traditional system element that can be defined as results for which the strategy was organized is

   a. process   b. output   c. structure

4. Transformation required to change inputs to outputs is a definition of

   a. totality   b. structure   c. process

5. The connection of all system elements to perform a mission is a definition of a

   a. totality   b. structure   c. process

6. The MBO process facilitates a systems view of

   a. the organization as a whole   b. the operations and performance of each department
   c. both of the preceding

Fill in the box with the correct systems overview capability.

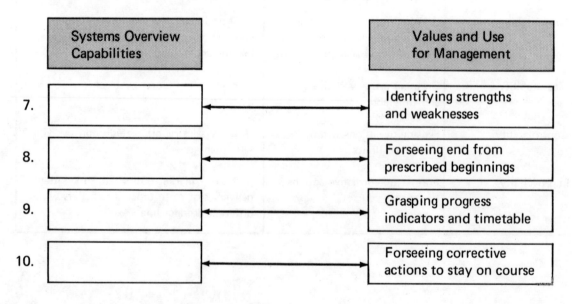

Systems Overview Capabilities		Values and Use for Management
7.	⟷	Identifying strengths and weaknesses
8.	⟷	Forseeing end from prescribed beginnings
9.	⟷	Grasping progress indicators and timetable
10.	⟷	Forseeing corrective actions to stay on course

• Checkpoint Answers

1. b   2. a   3. b   4. c   5. b   6. c   7. Reliability   8. Predictability   9. Measurability
10. Improvability

FEEDER-OBJECTIVES

Tactical-strategic interrelationships are the connectors among the various parts of a strategy that make it work. They are the individualized but coordinated action plans of a section, department, or manager. These connectors are called *feeder-objectives* to convey the idea that completion of these individualized plans by a manager or department feeds into the overall organizational plan. Each feeder-objective acts as a source of supply to the entire strategy. The supply of individual contributions "flows" or "adds" to form a total contribution, in a manner similar to tributary streams that flow and add their contributions to lakes and oceans. Examples of feeder-objectives are shown in Figure 2. Cash flow is directed toward an ultimate objective of revenue or cash position in a wholesaler distribution center but requires the collective contributions of purchasers, inventory controllers, and salesmen. Manpower flow is directed toward an ultimate objective of manpower manning level in a large corporation but requires the collective efforts of recruiters, interviewers, testers, trainers, and developers. Treatment of patients flow is directed toward an ultimate objective of patient care in a hospital but requires the collective contributions of doctors, pharmacists, nurses, and aides.

2. Feeder-Objectives Within a System's Flow Processes

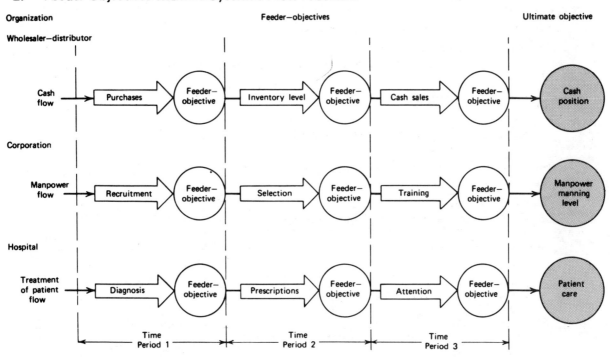

One can readily see that feeder-objectives must be formulated in every area where performance and results directly affect an organization's ultimate objective. The feeder-objective provides many useful features in the systems approach.

1. It links individual managers to the enterprise.

2. It interlocks departmental contributions with managerial levels.

3. It provides individual participation for large-scale accomplishment.

4. It signals the start and stop of individual contributors in the flow process.

5. It blends performance outputs of several flow processes.

This concept and its useful features will be illustrated with another example: profit improvement. There are four ways to achieve profit improvement: increase sales volume, increase price margin, reduce capital investments, or reduce costs.[5] Determining the amount of profit and when it must be received within the company involves the objective-setting strategy for directing the organization's mission. Let us assume that the organization needs to make a profit through an 18-percent reduction in costs while holding volume, price, and capital outlay constant. (See Figure 3.) This 18-percent reduction is broken down into smaller percentages and assigned to three categories: travel expense, material costs and waste rejects. Each of these categories represents a set of reduced cost results that must be met to achieve 18-percent reduction in costs. The objective for each category is formally written and represents a feeder-objective to all departments. The means and methods of attaining these feeder-objectives are the action plans within the departments. Each action plan contains a series of activities under a schedule, which, when implemented, will achieve the results specified in the feeder-objectives. The objective for the category of waste rejects is formally stated as "reduce ½ percent per month waste rejects for the next 12 months for all production departments." The objective for the category of material costs is formally stated as "reduce ½ percent per month material costs for the next 12 months for all purchasing departments and sections. The objective for the category of travel expense is formally stated as "reduce ½ percent per month travel expense for the next 12 months for all staff departments."

3. Use of Feeder-Objectives to Implement Strategy

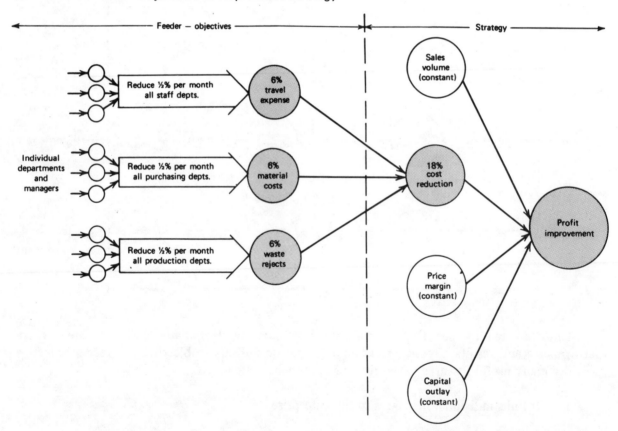

Once the feeder-objectives have been attained by individual managers and departments, the sum of all results should contribute to the overall organization's 18-percent cost reduction. Thus one can see that an individual production department that meets a feeder-objective of ½ percent per month is linked with the organization's 18-percent annual cost improvement. Since other individual departments or managers have the same cost commitment, they are said to be "interlocked" with each other in the same direction. The feeder-objective concept allows all departments to participate in a large-scale undertaking.

> The feeder-objective is the basic unit in a network of objectives. A network is a system of functionally connected segments and parts whose individual actions and interactions affect other segments, which, in turn, affect the system. Each separate segment is a link whose output is needed by other links in the system.

The organization chart is a network form. It captures the total management structure, displays the levels of authority, and identifies positions of incumbents. An organization that practices managing by objectives among all managerial levels can link each individual's feeder-objectives into a network of objectives. The network shows the interrelationships of objectives, subobjectives, and feeder-objectives in the various levels of a traditional organizational chart, as shown in Figure 4. The objective network can support formal and rigid lines of authority by connecting individual work plans and their contributions in a total flow system. This tends to promote a sense of teamwork which clarifies the organizational structure.

4. The Organization As an Objective Network

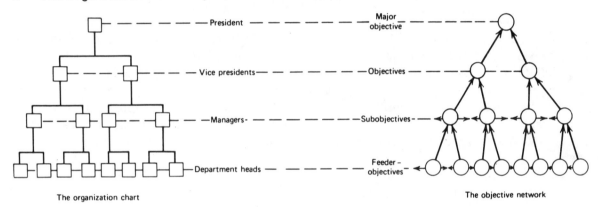

The organization chart   The objective network

The MBO strategist does not ignore the chain-reaction effects of feeder-objective in his strategy. He recognizes that as the performance of a feeder-objective increases, so should the performance of the entire flow process increase, assuming the feeder-objective is truly linked and interlocked with the expected output. If the contribution of the feeder-objective is not increased in quantity or time, it no longer feeds or contributes but is a constraint in the strategy. It will hold back and prevent the contributions of other feeder-objectives. For example, the production function must manufacture a product in terms of its output per unit cost. If inventories are reduced or increased without a view toward meeting the entire system's objectives, such as marketing, then output per unit cost goes up or down independent of the system of which it is a part. The production function controls output per unit cost but is unrelated to marketing. The production function is a constraint on marketing. On the other hand, if the per unit cost goes up or down as a part of an overall strategy of the system, the production and marketing functions are linked and both are resources for the system. The performance of the total system goes up as the performance of linked feeder-objectives goes up. Conversely, it will go down when the performance of the linked feeder-objectives goes down. The interactions among the feeder-objectives require phasing and juxtaposition to create a positive chain-reaction effect. Simply pushing the cost per unit down with lowered inventories may be wrong in terms of stockout frequency which disrupts and has a negative effect on the marketing function. The MBO strategist develops his overall strategy as a "best fit" among the various parts that will make it work. The feeder-objective concept is

● *Integrative.* It exists solely for the purpose of uniting feeder-objectives to form a "locked effort" toward an ultimate end.

- *Interdisciplinary.* It cuts across established functional boundaries and routines.

- *Preemptive.* The good of the system preempts the good of any one of the feeder-objectives.

All this discourages managers from trying to enhance their own personal performance at the expense of the overall system. Because the feeder-objective approach is concerned with level interactions among managers, it thus provides a basis for building a framework. Several system elements are important in building this framework: the number of feeder-objectives in an organization; the size and scope of each feeder-objective; the critical nature of the feeder-objective; and the input-output relationships among management levels and functions. An increased number of management levels and functions within an organization will increase the complexity and variation among the feeder-objectives. This, in turn, creates a greater need for synthesis or connection among the many units. An organization that truly practices managing by objectives as a total management effort will assure the connection and interlocking among its many feeder-objectives in various levels.

◄ SUMMARY ►

This chapter has attempted to provide a perspective from which to view the material that follows. Thus it has been little more than an outline establishing the conceptual framework of the methodology of managing by objectives. The chapter defines managing by objectives, describes four principles of operations, and demonstrates how managing by objectives is a systems approach to planning and procuring results for an organization. The chapter explains how a management system emerges whereby individual managers can link their individual plans to those of the firm. The concept of feeder-objectives is introduced and defined as the interrelations in a system.

1. Alfred P. Sloan, Jr., *My Years with General Motors.* MacFadden-Bartell, New York, 1965, pp. 46-47; 53-55.

2. C. Northcote Parkinson, *Parkinson's Law,* Houghton Mifflin, New York, 1967, pp. 2-8

3. Dan Voich, Jr., and Daniel A. Wren, *Principles of Management-Resources and Systems,* Ronald Press, New York, 1968, pp. 21-29

4. James L. Riggs, *Economic Decision Models,* McGraw-Hill Book Company, New York, 1968, pp. 7-13.

5. Phil Carroll, *Profit Control,* McGraw-Hill Book Company, New York, 1962, pp. 10-16.

Chapter 1 Review ——————————————————————

$\mathcal{VV}$ Doublecheck

Answer briefly.

1. What is the basic strategy of managing by objectives?

    _____

    _____

    _____

    _____

    _____

2. What are the four fundamental principles of managing by objectives?

    _____

    _____

    _____

    _____

    _____

3. Describe the following MBO phases.

    a. Isolating the Objective

        _____

        _____

        _____

        _____

    b. Validating the Objective

        _____

        _____

        _____

        _____

c.   Controlling and Reporting the Status of the Objective

_____

_____

_____

_____

_____

4. What is a schedule? Why is it useful in managing by objectives?

_____

_____

_____

_____

5. What does it mean to say that an effective MBO manager forms an overview of the system?

_____

_____

_____

_____

6. What are feeder-objectives and what are their advantages?

_____

_____

_____

_____

● Doublecheck Answers

1. The basic strategy of managing by objectives is to create a consistent structure of objectives for the entire management organization. This set of objectives provides focus in achieving overall goals and can motivate individual managers to commit themselves to accomplishing the specific desired results in the specified period of time. Subsequently, those stated objectives become the basis for performing a periodic evaluation of performance.

2. The four fundamental principles of management by objectives which flow directly from the MBO elements of objectives, time strategy, total management, and individual motivation are as follows:

    a. Unity of managerial action is more likely to occur where there is pursuit of a common objective.

    b. The greater the focus and concentration on results one wants to achieve on a time scale, the greater the likelihood of achieving them.

    c. The greater the participation in setting meaningful work with an accountability for results, the greater the motivation for completing it.

    d. Progress can only be measured in terms of what one is trying to make progress toward.

3. *Isolating the objectives* involves an examination of the organization, how it is constituted, and the desires and goals of its many parts. This phase is complete when a list of attractive and needed potential objectives has been developed.

    Validating the objectives is done by transforming the formal statement of objectives developed in the second phase into a statement of commitment. This requires that each objective be examined in detail in order to identify inconsistencies and the feasibility of accomplishing the objective.

    The final phase, *controlling and reporting the status of an objective*, is based on the principle that progress can only be measured in terms of what one is trying to make progress toward. Through use of feedback (measurement of past progress) and feed forward (measurement of expected future progress), the management team obtains an idea of their present position in relation to where they are going. This phase is completed when a status of work schedule, reporting progress toward an established target, has been developed.

4. The schedule is a list of details that must be accomplished to complete a large-scale mission. All of the planned details are timed for start and finish in order to coordinate the interrelationship of these details with the clock and the calendar. Schedules are particularly useful in managing by objectives since the schedule uses time as a reliable pace setter in identifying the sequence of tasks that must be performed, thus providing a basis for comparison over time.

5. In MBO systems, the manager designs and organizes all the elements so as to guide, integrate, and control all resources toward some objective. Managers take unrelated resources, disorganized facilities, and unused skills to build a framework for accomplishing a mission. When this is done effectively, it provides the manager with an overview of the entire system.

6. Feeder-objectives are closely related to the tactical-strategic interrelationship that coordinates action plans of a section, department, or manager. When completed by an individual manager or department, these feeder-objectives feed into the overall organizational plan and act as a source of supply to the entire strategy. Thus they help to coordinate and communicate the efforts of the various subparts of the organization.

Key Concepts

- *Problem Solving With MBO.* In addition to guiding the development of a set of measurable objectives for the organization, MBO also provides concepts and techniques that are particularly helpful in solving management problems. Understanding these techniques and aspects of MBO not only enhances the effective use of the entire philosophy but also enables the solution of specific problems common to organizations today.

- *Progressive Performance Improvement.* An integral part of the concept of MBO is that continual improvement in an organization's performance is both required and possible to achieve. Many of the rules and techniques developed in this chapter are aimed at establishing procedures in the organization that will ensure progressive performance improvement over time. These improvements involve both cost reductions as well as increases in efficiency and productivity.

[handwritten margin note: MBO does: 1. SET MEASURABLE OBJECTIVES FOR THE ORGANIZATION 2. PROVIDES CONCEPTS AND TECHNIQUES TO HELP SOLVE MGMT PROBLEMS.]

Learning Objectives

After you have completed this chapter, you should be able to

- Define seven current and typical management problems.

- Explain the impact of these problems upon organizations.

- Describe several practical MBO approaches to resolving these problems.

THE CHANGING ENVIRONMENT

The period in which we are now living has been called the age of cyberculture, the postindustrial age, and the age of automation. It is a time of unprecedented and continuing change. It is a time in which an organization must address itself to a changing environment in order to grasp the conditions that may prevail during the period for which objectives are set and to establish appropriate methods for reaching them. Unfortunately, many organizations become so involved in day-to-day operations that there is a tendency to forget undercurrents that cause drifts in undesirable or unknown directions. These undercurrents, at first, consist of trends in the consumer market, technological innovations, social redirections, and changing competitive profiles. Later, they emerge in the organization to produce critical management problems such as scarcity of competent managers, low employee morale, and obsolete or unnecessary products or services.

The purpose of this chapter is to define some typical management problems and challenges and then to explain how concepts fundamental to managing by objectives can help to solve these problems, thus demonstrating why managing by objectives is relevant in today's environment and what it can do for the individual manager and company.

GROWING DILUTION OF EFFORT

Changes in business are unpredictable. Products, services, and methods often become obsolete before they reach the final stage of planning. Innovations force a faster pace in business growth, resulting in greater complexities, cross purposes, multiplicity of goals, and a variety of possible directions. We now have hundreds of thousands of people devoting their full time to making obsolete our present products, services, and methods of doing business. They are reaching out for new products and services. Not only are more new ideas generated each year, but they are also applied sooner. A single change triggers several changes, forming a chain reaction. Management attempts to keep pace with this tempo and complexity by stretching wider and wider its scope of activities. Managers compress within hours or days the work that formerly took weeks or months. A manager must give time and attention to more and more items over a wider spectrum of activities. Consequently he can easily end up by doing many things and doing none of them well.

Business, generally, is evolving and developing into patterns new and different from those of the past. The current technical and social revolutions have made the manager's job formidable. He finds himself faced with many variables that he must sort and act upon. These variables are found in job content, human relationships and effort, the company and its relationship with stockholders, labor relations, government controls, and the requirements of the business community. Such variables have complicated the task of the manager. He expends prodigious amounts of energy, time, and money to operate legally and competently as these variables make demands on him.

The practice of managing by objectives helps a manager to face this spectrum of demands and to proceed to sort, select, and concentrate on the critical few. It forces a manager to deploy his limited resources where they count most. It also forces him to focus upon those variables that the enterprise needs for survival and growth. The practice identifies and separates the many trivial and insignificant variables. This separation is called the *Pareto effect*, named after the Italian economist Vilfredo Pareto. The Pareto concept states that it is uneconomical to devote the same amount of time and attention to the inconsequential that one devotes to the critical.[1] The Pareto principle translated to management functions directs concentration to the few critical tasks which should receive the most skillful treatment, because such functions produce the most good to the organization. Managing by objectives requires in its practice the assignment of priorities and weights to those objectives most important to the organization. From a list of a manager's potential accomplishments, the critical few are separated from the trivial many.

The manager recognizes that out of the total spectrum of objectives possible, he must commit himself to the critical few that most benefit the organization. These few are not always obvious but are often found to involve a key customer, a star salesmen, the production foreman, receiving and maintaining good services, meeting schedules, and keeping costs at rock bottom. The trivia are not always obvious, either, but they frequently appear in such areas as small customer orders, community involvement, career development, drop-in visitors, lengthy telephone calls, and the nuts and bolts of inventory. One method for sorting these two categories, based on the Pareto principle, is called the *MBO Rule for Focus*.

MBO Rule for Focus

1. List all the demands.

2. Arrange the list in order of importance.

3. Select the top 20 percent as the critical few.

4. Identify the remaining 80 percent as the trivial many.

5. Spend most of your effort on the critical few.

The 20/80 percent MBO Rule for Focus has shown, on the average, that 80 percent of the results in a situation can be attributed to 20 percent of the possible causes. The 20/80 percent breakdown has been derived and popularized by H. Ford Dickie of the General Electric Company and designated as *ABC analysis*.[2] Dickie used this analysis to divide inventory into classes according to dollar usage. The A class, upon which attention is concentrated, includes high-value items whose dollar volume typically accounts for 75 to 80 percent of the quantity volume. The proportions are reversed in passing from the A class to other, less important, classes. (In a later chapter, the Situation Action Model will provide an addition method for separating classes in order of importance.)

Thus objectives can be set giving top priority to vital considerations, leaving matters of lesser importance to be dealt with later. The MBO Rule for Focus helps reverse the trend toward dilution of effort and satisfies completely one of the basic principles of managing by objectives.

> The greater the focus and concentration on the results one wants to achieve on a time scale, the greater the likelihood of achieving them.

NEGLECTING OPPORTUNITIES AS A RESULT OF CRISIS MANAGEMENT

Making key decisions is enormously difficult. Risks are an essential part of planning and getting the work out. Every company seems to run into a certain number of troubles and complications that might be interpreted as crises. The term *crisis*, however, suggests major problems of the kind, for instance, that could lead to bankruptcy or organizational failure. Many managers consider any sudden difficulty a crisis. It is not. The problem a manager faces at any one time is merely a materialization of symptoms. The crisis itself has been long in the making, usually the result of months or years of delay in facing up to problems once and for all. It is the nature of crisis that it seldom arises from a single cause but from a variety of causes, one central and the others contributory. For example, one may be financial and the others nonfinancial.

The crisis can be regarded as a problem situation. If a crisis has been long in the making, it follows that problems have long been standing without solution. The following principle underscores the growth of a crisis:

> A crisis is in the making when the rate of problem generation is equal to or greater than the rate of problem solution.

The trend toward generating more problems than a company is able to solve sets in motion the crisis situation that moves the enterprise toward liquidation and bankruptcy. This trend toward problem generation saps and drains the energy and time of managers. It involves the manager so fully that he has little time to consider alternatives or opportunities. Crisis management may even be defined as total involvement in problems of the past, leaving little or no time to look into the opportunities offered by the future. Pursuing a reasonable number of opportunities is almost by definition the entrepreneurial task. What then is the reason for most companies' failure to pursue a reasonable number of these opportunities? The answers are many and varied; among them are unwillingness to take risks, insufficient personnel, and lack of competence. Probably the major reason, however, is preoccupation with recurring problems: preoccupation, that is, with a crisis situation where the rate of problem generation exceeds the rate of problem solution and where, consequently, the company never catches up.

An examination of so-called permanency of problem solutions reveals that problems reappear even though they seem to have been solved many times before. A manager begins to feel that he is not getting anywhere, that he is caught in a rat race where he must make too many decisions too rapidly. Consequently, problems are solved partially, incompletely, or temporarily, only to have the original problems reappear later. When a manager devotes most of all of his time to these problems, he is, in effect, caught in the circuit of the past and ignores and neglects the opportunities of the future. Since problem solving is resolving a conflict or overcoming a barrier in the past, the manager who devotes most or all of this time to these problems has become a "historian."

Many problems are not merely complex but are in reality complexes, that is, groups of problems referred to under one general name for the sake of convenience. A large problem is often settled by solving the smaller ones of which it is composed. For instance, an acute problem of high operating costs can be solved only by controlling the small, myriad strains on the budget of the entire operation. Recognition of problems is not always easy, because the problems are part of the situation which generated them.

Managing by objectives requires a manager, through the objective-setting process, to solve problems in a system of expectations. It changes the manager's orientation so that he looks toward the future instead of toward the past. Instead of devoting full time to solving crisis types of problems, the manager searches and identifies opportunities that will lead the company in new directions. He must still solve problems but he solves them with a view to shaping the future. Problem solving that shapes the future requires that defining new opportunities become an essential ingredient in the objective-setting process. Objectives that are not opportunistic are objectives that maintain the status quo and perpetuate the existing structure. Time and energy should not be wasted in solving problems for which there are no solutions or that are trivial to the needs of the enterprise.

One method of assisting an organization or a manager to keep future oriented is to follow the *MBO Rule for Future Action.*

MBO Rule for Future Action

1. List all the responsibilities required of a manager (job description).

2. Arrange the list into two categories:

   a. Responsibilities requiring job review time for past performance.

   b. Responsibilities requiring action on current or future results.

3. a. For higher management, reduce time spent for category 2a, not to exceed 20 percent of available time. Allow time for category 2b to reach 80 percent of available time.

   b. For middle management, reduce time spent for category 2a, not to exceed 80 percent of available time. Allow time for category 2b to reach 20 percent of available time.

   c. For lower management, reduce time spent for category 2a, not to exceed 80 percent of available time. Allow time for category 2b to reach 20 percent of available time.

4. For higher, middle, and lower management, delegate excesses in category 2a to subordinates.

The percentage breakdown of the MBO Rule for Future Action has been derived from studies made by Ralph E. Lewis on the percentage of time spent on future planning at the various echelons of a company.[3] The MBO Rule for Focus also supports this method.

$\mathscr{V}$Checkpoint: MBO Rules for Focus and Future Action ─────────────────

Indicate true (T) or false (F).

1. Under the MBO Rule for Future Action, no higher-, middle-, or lower-level manager should spend more than 20 percent of his time on problems relating to past performance. ─────

2. An MBO manager directs himself toward the future rather than toward the past. ─────

3. Recognition of problems is not always easy, because the problems are part of the system which generated them. ─────

4. If it is to grasp the conditions that may prevail during the period for which objectives are set, an organization must address itself to a changing environment. ─────

5. Under the MBO Rule for Focus, 80 percent of identified demands should be regarded as critical. ─────

6. The first step in both the MBO Rule for Focus and Rule for Future Action is to list all the potential problems. ─────

7. The second step is to decide which problems will take 20 percent of your time. ─────

8. According to the Pareto concept, the same amount of time should be spent on all problems. ─────

9. The critical-few objectives on which an MBO manager should focus are always obvious. ─────

10. The MBO Rule for Future Action is a means of minimizing the need for crisis management. ─────

─────────────────

• Checkpoint Answers

1. F   2. T   3. T   4. T   5. F   6. T   7. F   8. F   9. F   10. T

UNCOORDINATED PLANNING WITHIN MANAGERIAL LEVELS

The purpose of all organization is to unify effort, that is, to coordinate. The employment of more than one person toward a given end involves specialization and division of labor. Organization assures that these specialties and divisions work smoothly, that there is unity of effort. Coordination is the orderly arrangement of human effort toward unity of action in the pursuit of a common objective. In spite of its advantages, the division of labor, both horizontal and vertical, has some basic limitations. What this division does is to specify what activities must be performed and who will perform them. This might seem easy enough. For example, four men are rowing across a bay. The labor is divided so that John steers, Harry bails out the boat, Tony pulls on the right oar, and Jim pulls on the left oar. At first glance, this may seem to be all there is to it. But there is more to rowing across the bay than bailing, steering, and rowing. First, toward what point on the land are they headed? Second, how long should it take? Third, are they performing all the activities in unison? Additionally, each may have quite different personal goals for wanting to cross. Their decision to join forces was a decision to form an organization. The organizational objective is to get the boat across the bay even though each private goal is different.

> What makes any organization work is that individual actions contribute to an overall accomplishment even though each person has an individual goal. The more difficult it is for members of the organization to perceive this relationship, the more difficult coordination becomes.

As in the boating example, it might seem easy to determine the division of labor in an organization. The marketing manager sells to customers, the production manager produces the product, and the quality control manager assures quality. But is it so easy? Are these individuals working in unison? Do they have the same direction, the same objectives, and the same time pace?

Historically, highly specialized activities of both individuals and groups have been assembled into functions, each function depending on the others and all operating in closest coordination. Thus we have the engineering function, the research function, the marketing function, the purchasing function, the production control function, and other similar groupings. The experiences of many companies are yielding evidence that functional formation, which has dominated industrial corporations for some time, is outmoded. The common occupational background of employees does provide an effective bond, encouraging coordination and cooperation within the function, but there is serious question as to whether any such bond exists between and among the functions. It is a natural tendency for functional organizations to emphasize their separate functional elements at the expense of the whole organization. Frequently, functional units treat their objectives and pursuits as primary, considering secondary the goals and objectives of the enterprise as a whole. The engineer makes a decision to complete a design. This decision affects production in terms of difficulty and cost, which, in turn, affects the salesmen, who must find customers to buy the product. The specialist, more often than not, is not part of a team. His record shows experience in which he has always set his own goals, planned his own work, and fixed his own schedule. Assimilation of the specialist into the organization is frequently difficult and a common sense of purpose is not easily arrived at. Under functional organization, efforts to integrate across the functions to meet organizational needs are not always made. Theoretically, this task is the general manager's responsibility. However, the capability and skill necessary for coordinating is not readily found in these managers. To add to the difficulty, organizations of the functional type do not as a rule develop competent general managers, since each manager develops through his functional specialization.

These concerns raise some important questions about the usefulness of the functional form of organization.

- How many companies are truly unified in effort and well coordinated in desired directions?

- Is Parkinson's law of work elasticity[4] operating within managerial levels without the company's knowledge?

- Does each manager accomplish work to meet his personal goals at the expense of the company's objectives?

- Do companies allow their managers to wheel and deal with relative abandon?

How much waste is there in company time, energy, and money when the direction, scope, and contribution of individual managers from top to bottom are not coordinated? It is tragic to see how the untiring efforts of many competent managers are diffused in different directions. It is equally tragic to note the result of their combined efforts for the enterprise. Managers are like vectors[5] with objectives (O) and drives (D). The vector resolution of several managers can produce a result for the enterprise smaller than any individual manager's contribution, as illustrated in Figure 1.

More often than not, the result of a scattered-force system is less than the result of any individual manager. Since work and activities are elastic (according to Parkinson), each manager will pace himself not only to meet his own time requirements but to give a "fit" necessary to satisfy his own personal commitments and needs. The "empire builders" will take directions most opportunistic for themselves rather than for the organization. How to bring about coordination among the functions and between the hierarchy levels is probably the most important single issue in organizational efficiency.

1. Scattered Managerial Efforts Yield Small Results for Enterprise

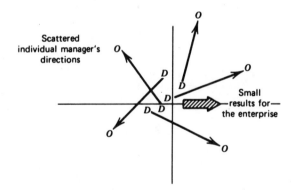

Managing by objectives requires interlocking action between people and departments. This combines functions and allows them to flow in a prescribed direction. The very nature of the interlock will make it seem that functions are being duplicated, but they are not. They are joined together with feeder-objectives to yield unison of action. One method of bringing about a unifying structure is to make use of joint feeder-objectives. This technique is explained in the *MBO Rule for Interlocking Functions.*

MBO Rule for Interlocking Functions

1. List all the feeder-objectives desired by a functional manager.

2. Separate from the list those that can be completed only as joint efforts with other functions or departments. These are called *joint feeder-objectives.*

3. Negotiate and gain agreement to combine resources and effort toward achieving these joint feeder-objectives.

4. Assure that all managers on different levels of the hierarchy have a reasonable number of two- or three-way joint commitments.

Two-way feeder-objectives combine the efforts of two departments or managers toward a single commitment, whereas three-way feeder-objectives combine the efforts of three departments or managers. Some examples of two-way feeder-objectives are to reduce machine downtime 50 percent by machine shop and maintenance department; to reduce average handling time of customer statements 10 percent by billing department and mail room; to increase merchandise turnover in store from 4 to 6 percent within the current fiscal year by sales and inventory control. Some examples of three-way feeder-objectives are to achieve a product line mix in which 80 percent of sales is made by no more than 20 percent of R & D customers by marketing, engineering, and finance; to reduce frequency of lost time injuries from 21 to 6 per million manhours within six months of instituting a new safety program by production, maintenance, and safety.

Managing by objectives encourages extrafunctional understanding. The MBO Rule for Interlocking Functions provides a method whereby managers can combine their efforts in a single direction. This encourages coordination and interlocking among the diverse functions and levels. The feeder-objective concept takes private and personal needs of the manager into consideration but in a context of a management system. The concept of joint feeder-objectives results in a greater alignment among the various managers, yielding more efficient results for the enterprise, as suggested in Figure 2. It fosters the attitude that all members of a company are mutually dependent, that no one individual can go charging out to wherever his empire building impulses lead him.

2. Joint Feeder-Objectives Coordinate Planning Within Managerial Levels

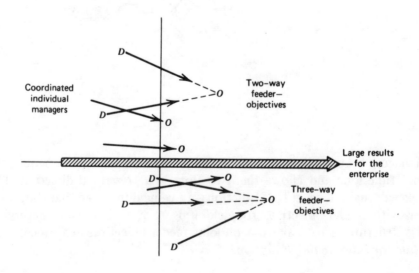

CONSTANT INCREASE OF COSTS

Today, increase of costs is the rule rather than the exception. When revenues remain steady or decline while costs escalate, profits are diminished. Overcompetition or even wasteful competition has created tight markets in which price margins are very narrow. It is not unusual for companies to become desperate to salvage what they can for a respectable profit year. These companies have not paid close attention to keeping operating costs at rock-bottom levels and thus find themselves on the brink of disaster. News of cost cutting may indicate several conditions: the failure of a good many long-range plans, the existence of both profitable and unprofitable departments within the same company, the lack of a consistent cost-control program throughout the company, or simply cost mismanagement. The inescapable fact is that cost control is not a matter of choice for any company. It is part of the profit performance expected from managers. The degree of profit making is, in the short or long run, directly dependent upon the extent to which a firm has developed a cost-managed system.

Cost control is a significant function of management. Ill-considered cost cutting and last ditch slashing are moves by panicked management. This panic may take the form of a special and centralized group whose only purpose is to conduct cost-reduction programs. As cost cutters, they are given license to prune where necessary. Usually they take drastic one-shot measures such as laying off workers, reducing overhead, consolidating operations, reducing wastes, eliminating advertising, cutting out training and development, reducing inventory, and curtailing public relations. These sudden one-shot cost-cutting moves may cause irreparable damage to company systems, functions, customers, personnel, and morale. For example, the insistence on substituting cheaper materials for more expensive ones may lose valuable long-time customers, which reduces sales volume but leaves the cost margin still high. The elimination of advertising and promotional programs may damage beyond repair the sales potential for short- and long-range needs. Hasty layoffs of staff personnel may mean that heavier demands in time and effort are made on line personnel, resulting in a slow-up or drop in productivity. When cost-cutting action is sudden and not well thought out, it may actually generate more costs and result in long-term damage.

> Cost control must be considered as a way of life. It is not something a special group sets out to accomplish quite apart from in-plant activities. It is the heart and core of managing and, therefore, cannot be separated from managing.

Cost control must be carefully established, thoughtfully applied, and continuously followed up as part of the on-going, day-to-day work of each employee. Although it may be regarded as a program, it involves all groups, both management and employees. Costs are usually thought of in terms of facts, figures, and accountants, but primarily they are a matter of people working and performing efficiently. Every move an employee makes has an effect, no matter how indirect, on cost performance in his group or department. In this respect, the supervisor is in the ideal spot to keep costs under control. Under the stress of getting out the work, a supervisor often finds it difficult to plan and emphasize how costs will be the basis of his efficiency, but it must be part and parcel of his job.

Cost control begins with the recognition of the need for cost control. It is not enough simply to tell people they must reduce costs. They must understand and accept for themselves why and how costs fit into the overall picture, as well as into their individual jobs. Job security, job benefits, and job satisfaction must relate to costs and demonstrate a clear connection between causes and effects. Employees must believe in and understand this connection. This recognition may be the biggest stumbling block to making cost control a way of economic life.

Cost control requires the active participation of every employee in the enterprise. If costs are to be attacked at all, they must be attacked on all fronts by all personnel. The total cost picture is what counts. Many cost control programs have failed because only a certain percentage of the organization was involved. A prevalent attitude of department heads is, "I'm already down to the bone; it's the other department that needs to cut."

Managing by objectives is an approach that not only plans on a certain amount of work being accomplished at the end of a given period of time, but also builds into the plan the constraints and the limitations necessary to achieve the goal. Cost control is natural in managing by objectives, since it provides a vehicle in which the need for cost improvement is identified. Additionally, participation, implementation, and control are phased and interlocked among personnel throughout the management system. The focus capability of managing by objectives can give the cost improvement effort a precision and direction not normally found with other managerial strategies. In addition, cost targets can be formalized and coordinated in progressive steps: avoidance, reduction, and control. Cost avoidance is the elimination of a cost item anticipated and budgeted but not expended. Cost-control standards are guidelines set up according to average or best costs incurred in the past. They form the basis on which actual costs may be compared. Cost reduction is the deliberate attempt to work below the cost levels expected and allowed by the standards.

One method for giving the cost improvement effort successive stages of effectiveness is to follow the *MBO Rule for Progressive Cost Improvement.*

MBO Rule for Progressive Cost Improvement

1.   List cost improvement possibilities.

2.   Separate from the list those that have high cost requirements.

3.   Apply the three-step progressive rule to each cost item:

     a.   *Avoid* the costs where possible.

     b.   *Reduce* the costs from standards where and when possible.

     c.   *Control* the costs to standards where avoidance and reduction are not possible.

4.   Write cost improvement requirements into a formalized statement of a feeder-objective.

Here is an illustration of step 4: It is not "cut costs 10 percent next year with machine shop operations." Rather, it is "turn out 20,000 units of X 36 with no greater than 5 percent rejects while dropping unit costs from $2.50 to $2.25." The cost cutting pattern is built into the work plan itself. The manager controls and reduces costs as he carries out the technical and functional responsibilities of his job. The MBO Rule for Progressive Cost Improvement provides a method to cope systematically with steadily rising costs.

Fill in the blanks with the correct answers.

1. _____ is the orderly arrangement of human effort toward unity of action in the pursuit of a common objective.

2. _____ organizations are not the best kind of organizations to produce good general managers, because under such systems each manager develops through, and is basically limited to, his specialization.

3. Under a _____ system, "empire builders" will take directions most opportunistic for themselves rather than for the organization.

4. To achieve _____ , managers of more than one department combine their resources and efforts toward a single commitment.

5. According to the MBO Rule for Progressive Cost Improvement, selected cost improvement possibilities that cannot be avoided or reduced should be _____ .

Indicate true (T) or false (F).

6. Under the MBO Rule for Interlocking Functions, it does not matter if some managers are without joint commitments. _____

7. The feeder-objective concept takes private and personal needs of the managers into consideration, but in the context of the management system. _____

8. The MBO Rule for Progressive Cost Improvement suggests that cost control be accomplished by a special group that is set apart from in-plant activities. _____

9. Because employee performance has an effect on cost performance, the supervisor is in an ideal spot to keep costs under control. _____

10. Under the MBO Rule for Interlocking Functions, organization functions are duplicated. _____

● Checkpoint Answers

1. coordination   2. functional   3. scattered-force   4. joint feeder-objectives   5. controlled   6. F   7. T
8. F   9. T   10. F

TENDENCY TO TOLERATE MEDIOCRITY

The first characteristic of a good manager is the high value he places on performance, especially his own. The manager who sets his goals low or who tolerates indifferent performance in others is one who practices mediocrity. Mediocrity contaminates and spreads. If it is tolerated in one subordinate, it will eventually infect all. The mediocre employee is not one who does unacceptable work; he is the employee who does barely acceptable work: enough to justify his employment but not enough for him to be called highly productive. He has an extra 20 to 30 percent productive performance he could deliver if he were motivated. The supervisor who tolerates mediocrity in subordinates develops an equal tendency to tolerate it in himself. When the supervisor does not urge the subordinate to reach for higher levels of performance, it insidiously influences him not to stretch for higher levels of performance either.

All organizations tolerate mediocrity. It is a question of how much and where. The precious competitive edge that all companies seek to find and hold on to has often been regarded in terms of site, facilities, services, and market position. These are part of it, but competitive edge is not a static phenomenon. It is the "stretch" in performance that the enterprise continually makes. With the stretch, improved services, better timing, and unique marketing position result. It is the stretch in the performance of the entire enterprise that is, fundamentally, the competitive edge all organizations seek and need. Additionally, this total stretch is the summation of the individual stretches of the employees.

Three reasons are suggested for this tolerance of mediocrity:

- The shortage of qualified personnel

- The practice of seniority within union ranks

- The difficulty of evaluating employee performance

Shortage of Qualified Personnel ►

Probably the greatest reason for tolerating mediocrity is the shortage of qualified personnel within the ranks. There are many employees who need to be upgraded and developed. Time and money are not available for this effort. They are accepted on the job because the labor market may not offer anyone more qualified. Sometimes a manager is stuck with a mediocre subordinate in his ranks because potential employees from the labor market are below mediocre. Naturally he prefers the mediocre employee to the alternative.

Practice of Seniority Within Union Ranks ►

Seniority confers on its possessor a relative claim to available work or other benefits flowing from the organization. The collective bargaining agreement is a balancing mechanism among the interests of various groups of workers. Seniority grants preferential treatment to long-service employees almost at the expense of short-service employees. In times of business distress or organizational changes, the seniority rights of long-service employees provide protection against the company's attempt to weed out those causing problems. As long as an employee with seniority does barely acceptable work, he is protected from the weeding-out process.

Difficulty of Evaluating Employee Performance ►

Traditionally, performance appraisals center on the descriptor approach. A listing of descriptors such as quantity of work, quality of work, and ability to cooperate are itemized on one side of the appraisal. On the other side is a scale for measuring the degree of performance in each of these areas. The emphasis in this approach is on measuring effort and activities rather than results delivered. Most supervisors dislike these procedures, since they are forced to defend themselves in a confrontation with the employee appraised. Their defense is often weak, since they have used subjective impressions as the basis of the evaluation. These subjective factors are difficult to define, let alone measure and prove. To avoid this type of confrontation, supervisors tend to give acceptable or high ratings even when they know the employee has serious deficiencies. In other words, they practice mediocrity. Add to this difficulty the tendency of supervisors to give high ratings for actual performance when they really are looking at potential performance. They say, "I know he hasn't done the job quite as well as it must be done, but I know he can do it." But potential performance should not be confused with actual performance. The former is capacity and ability to do work, the latter is actual measurable work completion on the job. The former is a prediction and projection of likelihood, the latter is a matter of fact.

> A prime requirement of managing by objectives is identifying in advance the results to be accomplished on the job. These results must be clearly defined as attainable, yet they must also provide a challenge, a stretch in performance.

In the objective-setting process, there is a meeting of the minds between a supervisor and his subordinates on what this stretch entails and how to go about accomplishing it. The subordinate knows what is expected of him. He has agreed to work to attain this end. A period is assigned for measurement of these stretches to see how well employees are doing. Failure to reach expected goals reflects on the individual, the supervisor, or both. It is the results that evaluate the individual. The supervisor is no longer in the difficult position of appraising a subordinate on highly subjective factors. Mediocre performance can be readily identified and corrective action taken.

Management should actively seek ways and means to release the potential stored within human beings. It is a false notion that if one works at maximum potential, he will be prevented from going further. As one works to his maximum potential, that potential increases steadily. The old adage is true: Give the busy man the job to do and he gets it done. Why? The more he does, the more he is capable of doing, and the more he is capable of doing, the more he does. One begets the other. Conversely, the less he does, the less he is capable of doing, and the less he is capable of doing, the less he does. Performance and potential are interrelated and inseparable. Each is a determinant of the other. When performance is increased, potential is unfolded. When performance is decreased, potential is stored.

One method to use in releasing this potential and breaking the trend toward mediocrity is the *MBO Rule for Stretching Performance.*

MBO Rule for Stretching Performance

1. Identify employee potential.

    a. Make a list of performance responsibilities required of an employee.

    b. Allow employee to select those of great interest to him.

    c. Allow employee to add responsibilities he wants and needs.

    d. Consolidate list and organize as feeder-objectives according to priority of interest. Keep the list short.

2. Unfold employee potential.

    a. Build a 5 to 15 percent performance stretch within each feeder-objective that is of high interest to the employee.

    b. Make each performance stretch realistic, letting there be a high probability of success.

    c. Select objectives for employees that are new (opportunistic) and traditional (problem solving).

3. Utilize employee potential.

    a. After a successful initial 5 to 15 percent reach, a series of 5 to 15 percent stretches should follow in the same performance area.

    b. Allow individual to reach highest job growth possible.

    c. Plan a series of performance stretches in allied areas.

The practioner of managing by objectives has four basic elements he can use to set a 5 to 15 percent performance stretch. These elements are: decrease time to complete a job, decrease resources needed, increase quality of the performance, and increase quantity or output.

- Decrease time
  Research Engineer
  Contribute feasible marketing ideas at the rate of one per quarter.

  Stretch Performance to:
  Contribute feasible marketing ideas at the rate of one per month.

- Decrease resources
  Salesman
  Follow up on new inquiries while holding sales expense to 5 percent of total sales.

  Stretch Performance to:
  Follow up on new inquiries while reducing sales expense to 3 percent of total sales.

- Increase quality
  Welder
  Perform welding operations using acetylene equipment on 1½-inch flat steels with 7 percent weld rejects.

  Stretch Performance to:
  Perform welding operations using acetylene equipment on 1½-inch flat steels with 5 percent weld rejects.

- Increase quantity
  Truck Driver
  Operate three motor trucks: 1½-ton cargo, 5-ton dump, tractor trailer.

  Stretch Performance to:
  Operate five motor trucks: 1½-ton cargo, 5-ton dump, tractor trailer, ¾-ton utility, 10-ton cargo.

GROWING DISPARITY BETWEEN EMPLOYER AND EMPLOYEE GOALS

Most of the techniques of motivating workers have been dominated by what is loosely called the human relations movement. This movement searches for the reasons workers behave as they do and postulates how management should treat them to get greater productivity. It recognizes the plain truth that, for most people, work is no fun. The emphasis in this movement is on the individual, and jobs are designed to meet his needs. This approach has given us greater insight into motivating workers, showing us how to get an employee more excited about his work and indicating the factors that influence job satisfaction and morale. But a problem remains even after motivation has been instilled.

How is motivation to be sustained and raised to higher levels?

How can one recharge, replenish, and regenerate the drive once the highly satisfying original work has been completed?

Does a manager re-evaluate changing needs of workers and reorganize to meet these needs?

What about the thousands of work assignments that cannot yield employee satisfaction yet must be done?

As automation and mechanization of work procedures continue, the number of jobs that are dull and unsatisfying, yet necessary, is increasing. The trend toward automation carries with it a trend toward monotony, routine, repetition, and a low level of skill requirements. As these factors continue to grow, the job of instilling and sustaining motivation becomes even more crucial and difficult. Management is taking a hard look at traditional job designs and methods improvement in order to consider job content and automation in the light of human needs. The components of motivation, such as pride in work, job meaningfulness, identification with the product and the company, are given careful attention.

The strategy of managing by objectives, when properly used, recognizes that "sense of achievement" must be planned into the work and projected on a time scale.[6] Jobs, both satisfying and dissatisfying, can be laid out in such a natural way that plateaus or time periods exist to relieve the sense of dissatisfaction. These plateaus can be planned with a view toward replenishing and recharging a declining motivation. They allow an individual to see and to experience the set of results he has achieved, thus reinforcing his motivation for achieving the next set of results. Also, these plateaus can be used for appraisal periods, informal discussions of work completion, time-off periods, or natural leveling points in the work progression itself. However, in order for the sense of achievement component to have an effect, the work must be challenging or interesting. Simplification of jobs practically eliminates any interest and challenge. The sense of achievement component of motivation will work only when there is a combination: challenging work and a plateau from which the employee can see how he is progressing. In addition, the employee must somehow be made to feel that personal needs are taken care of. This is based on a simple truth, as described by Myers: "Ideally every employee should be able to think of himself as an entrepreneur, not working for a company, but working for himself within a company."[7] Employees work primarily for themselves and only secondarily for their employer. Their wages and personal needs do not usually fall within the framework of company needs. An employee goes to work for a company with a set of expectancies that may or may not coincide with the set of expectancies the company has for this employee. The wider the disparity between these two sets of expectancies, the more difficult the motivation. Since it is natural for employees to want variety, novelty, and change, we can expect this disparity not only to exist but to fluctuate within both wide and narrow limits. As between two vectors[8] that represent directions and expectancies of the employee and the employer, an angle of disparity (d) exists.

3. Motivational Intensity Caused by Employer-Employee Disparity

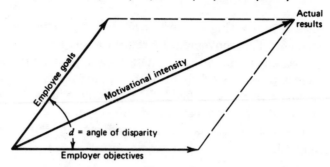

The actual result for the company depends on two forces: employee drives toward goals and employer drives toward objectives. Motivational intensity increases when the angle of disparity between these two forces becomes small.

The question is not whether a goal disparity exists between employee and employer, but rather how wide, how varied, and how amenable to change this disparity is. The goals of employees are continuously changing as a result of influences outside the enterprise. Take, for example, education. Surveys have consistently shown that the more education a worker acquires, the less satisfied he is with factory work and the less satisfied he is with work that was previously satisfying to him. As a result, he readjusts his expectancies, which, in turn, increases the angle of disparity. Similarly, the employer is continuously reassessing and reevaluating his own expectancies. Surveys have shown that the disparity angle becomes wider and motivational intensity becomes weaker when employee expectancies are disregarded and employer objectives are ignored.

4. Motivational Intensity Changes With Employer-Employee Disparity

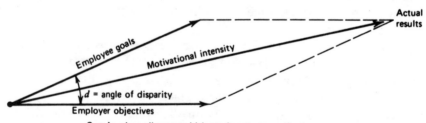

Case I: close alignment; high results; strong motivation

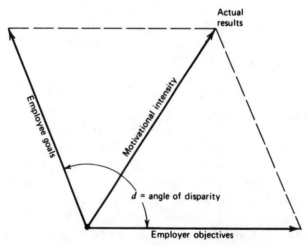

Case II: wide alignment; moderate results; moderate motivation

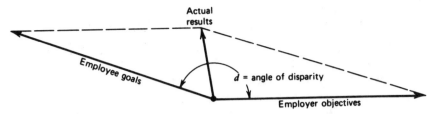

Case III: very wide alignment; poor results; weak motivation

Managing by objectives recognizes that perfect alignment between company expectancies and employee expectancies is virtually unattainable. If it should be attained at any point, it will last only briefly. The changing nature of both parties' needs makes coincidence of the vectors a highly improbable event. The objective setting process, however, attempts to explore and assess the breadth of the differences. The supervisor tries to measure this difference when he sits down with his subordinate and asks: "What are your personal goals?" "What do you expect from your job?" "Why did you come to work for this company?" Answers to these questions give the supervisor an idea of the breadth of the disparity and what must be done to bring about a closer alignment. The supervisor must realize that the disparity can change and take several positions, as illustrated in Figure 4.

Each position of the vectors will yield a different motivational intensity toward actual results. The supervisor should strive to move both vectors or states of expectancies to a closer alignment, as indicated in case I. Motivational intensity becomes stronger as disparity becomes smaller. The employee is accomplishing his own personal goals while at the same time meeting the employer's objectives. Conversely, motivational intensity becomes weaker as disparity increases, as indicated in case III. The employee is attempting to meet his own expectancies but is in disalignment with his employer. It is when objectives of both employer and employees are brought into alignment in content and time phase that greater contributions are made to the enterprise. Motivational intensity is high when both the employee and the employer win. The objective setting process measures this angle of disparity and attempts to bring about an alignment.

One method for aligning employee and employer interests is called the *MBO Rule for Aligning Divergent Objectives*. It is based on the third principle of managing by objectives cited in Chapter 1. This principle is the following: *The greater the participation in setting meaningful work with an accountability for a result, the greater the motivation for completing it.*

MBO Rule for Aligning Divergent Objectives

1. Supervisor makes a list of requirements needed by the organization.

2. Employee makes a list of personal goals and job interests.

3. Supervisor and employee together select items from both lists that require similar actions and parallel activities to achieve.

4. A feeder-objective is established by both supervisor and employee based on matched items.

5. Unmatched items are dealt with by the supervisor as unilateral requirements of the organization.

If supervisor and employee are not able to match any items on their lists, there is serious doubt whether the employee is properly placed. This indicates that the employee's motivation will be a continuing problem. The MBO Rule for Aligning Divergent Objectives is a form of participative management. It allows members of a group to take an active part in influencing and contributing to decisions. Organizations in the past, because of their formal structure, tended to be autocratic in nature. Those in authority complied with the rigid requirements of the structure, thus discouraging employees from contributing toward decisions that might affect them. The practice of participative management recognizes the following truth: Employees find great satisfaction and need fulfillment when they actively participate in plans and activities that affect them. The extent to which widespread participation should be allowed in a company depends on the definition of the situation and the styles of management. Organizations operating under union constraints may find it difficult to put this principle into practice to its fullest extent, although the collective bargaining contract can be regarded as "legalized participative management." Many factors or prior commitments may not allow this participation. Nonetheless, whether or not employees can participate, the involvement and participation of total management is an absolute must in the practice of managing by objectives. If a management system is to be created within an organization and if each member of management is to make a contribution to this system, then each member of management must be involved.

> Participation and involvement by individual members of the management staff does not mean separate decisions on what to do. It means that management members share the opportunity to make a decision that affects all of them.

An agreement will tend to narrow any disparity among management personnel. This narrowed disparity creates a greater alignment within the hierarchy for organizational teamwork and coordination. The MBO Rules for Aligning Divergent Objectives and for Interlocking Functions provide practical approaches for achieving this teamwork and coordination. Involvement and participation by total management form a vital part of the objective-setting procedure.

Complete these lists.

1. Three reasons for the tolerance of mediocrity are:

   The shortage of qualified personnel

   _____

   _____

2. The three steps to the MBO Rule for Stretching Performance are:

   1. _____

   2. Unfold employee potential

   3. _____

3. The four different elements an MBO manager can use to stretch performance are:

   _____

   _____

   Increase quality

   _____

4. The five steps to the MBO Rule for Aligning Divergent Objectives are:

   1. Supervisor makes a list of _____

      _____

   2. Employee makes a list of _____

   3. Supervisor and employee together select items from both lists that require similar actions and parallel activities to achieve.

   4. A _____ is established by both supervisor and employee based on matched items.

   5. _____ are dealt with by the supervisor as unilateral requirements of the organization.

   ─────────────────────────

   ● Checklist Answers

   1. the practice of seniority, the difficulty of evaluating employees
   2. (1) identify employee potential (3) utilize employee potential
   3. decrease time, decrease resources, increase quantity
   4. (1) requirements needed by the organization (2) personal goals and job interests (4) feeder-objective (5) unmatched items

IMBALANCED ORGANIZATIONS

An organization is a structure of resource utilization designed to meet objectives. Ideally, organizing should begin as soon as objectives are set and a logical framework for assembling and grouping resources is established. The purpose of establishing an organization is to enable the resources to work more effectively as units. Unity of command is based on the idea that no one can do an effective job if he is subject to conflicting directives. Hence the organization structure defines reporting relationships, duties, and authority. A system of authority emerges, giving some idea of the decision-makers acting in the enterprise. The organization chart becomes a representation of the organization. It indicates:

- How the work is broken down into various functions and products

- How people in the company are to work together

- What job positions there are and the names of individuals assigned to execute the duties of each position

- How relationships among levels of authority and channels of communications flow

The concept of division of labor is exploited, since an operation can be made more efficient by dividing the work. Functions and specialists are assigned in such a way that proficiencies and efficiencies are maximized in the course of time. The vertical and horizontal channels of the chart are considered formal since they are legitimate ways through which directives and reports flow. This formality provides links by which connection and coordination are effected. The organization chart becomes an important tool for management of the enterprise.

The principal deficiency of the organization chart is its inability to show the dynamic nature of work completion by individuals who vary in their drives, pressures, and activities. In viewing the organization, there is a tendency to consider it as a static and quiescent structure, rather like a photograph in which people, objects, and the environment are captured and frozen. This is a misleading conception; the organization is more like a motion picture: dynamic and changing. People vary in their roles; objects and equipment change; and the environment is continually altered.

5.   Decision-Makers Are Stress Forces in the Organization

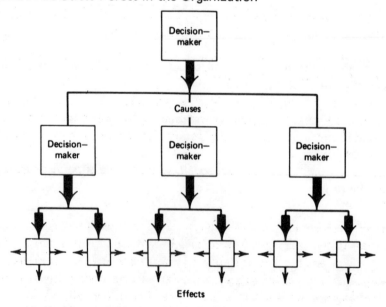

If one views the system of authority in an organization as dynamic, each decision-making manager acts as a force applied downward, as illustrated in Figure 5. The collective forces of the decision-makers tend to stress the organization at the point of application, causing fluctuations, imbalances, and disunities. The strength of the force or decision varies from manager to manager and results in horizontal as well as vertical stresses in the entire organization. It is this dynamic nature of the organization that makes unity of action in a focused direction difficult. How to get individuals to perform the right action at the right time is the key to the "quantum jump" in results for the enterprise. Over a period of time the stresses exerted by the stronger decision-makers lead to their acquisition of many functions and responsibilities, resulting in an imbalanced organization.

Traditionally, coordination has been attained by either the directed method or the voluntary method. In the directed method, the individual is told what to do and when to do it. A master plan is evolved by a central authority and tasks are linked to this authority on a time-phased basis. Formal procedures and policies are written up and coordinated work is attained through these procedures. Often the individual finds himself responding to numerous unrelated one-man acts of control.

In contrast to the directed method, in which the individual is told what to do, is the voluntary method. Here the individual is allowed to see the need to coordinate; he waits until he can take the action to effect it. This approach sets the stage for the exercise of authority and power. It becomes a power base for those who will use it. It is no wonder that, in those companies that practice this approach, highly motivated individuals use their newly acquired power base to impose their personal needs and wishes on the corporate life. Competition for power is characteristic in voluntary, permissive organizations. Under these conditions, the organization tends to cluster around the power usurper. This results in fragmenting the managerial functions and processes, such as planning and control, which are normally structured in the functional forms of organization. Although this approach may appear useful for finding the leaders of the organization, it poses many problems.

Limitations of the Voluntary Method

- The decision-maker is not aware of all the factors outside of his domain that might affect his particular situation. Besides, he has a relatively great need for independence and will ignore outside factors unless he needs them to attain his ends.

- Coordination becomes a chance event. Voluntary interlocking and dovetailing occur infrequently.

- A sense of timing is lost. A manager may plan and drive in a very desirable direction, pulling and pushing his group with him, but he is lost in his own personal schedule, ignoring how his efforts affect other groups.

A manager must look forward to his objective, but he must also relate his own time point to those of other managers by looking sideward and backward to gain a sense of phasing, cycling, and moving as part of an entity. The inability to coordinate with other managers on a timetable basis leads to disruptions and results in greater power-playing among the structural units. Instead of a dynamically changing, well-balanced structure that allows all managers to influence the organization, a static, imbalanced organization is created.

6. Imbalanced Organization Results From Uncoordinated Managerial Dominance

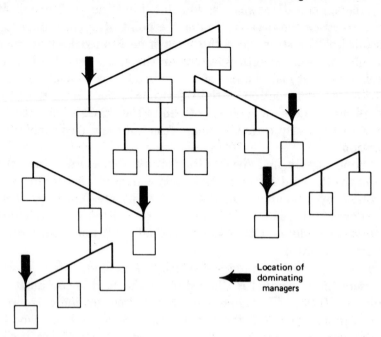

Location of
dominating
managers

Managing by objectives, in practice, is a combination of the voluntary and directed methods of organizational coordination. It is voluntary in that managers are expected to initiate and reach out for opportunities. It is directed in that managers once committed to an objective must interlock and dovetail in a timetable with other managers. It is voluntary in that managers are allowed to express personal drives and needs in goals and day-to-day work. It is directed in that managers obey the reality principle. They strive within the boundaries of the overall system they themselves helped formulate. It is voluntary in that managers can exercise power and authority through a set of expected results. It is directed in that the power exercised is not the result of impulse but part of a system of activities designed to reach a set of objectives. Power is generated or attenuated on the basis of the type and significance of the results rather than on the dominating nature of the manager's personality.

A method of eliminating a tendency toward imbalance within an organization is to follow the *MBO Rule for Balancing Organizations.*

MBO Rule for Balancing Organizations

1. Each manager makes a list of the major functional responsibilities of his position and of the subordinates reporting to him. He identifies them by brief titles and makes a list of minor responsibilities.

2. Manager rewrites each major responsibility as a feeder-objective, being guided by the MBO Rules for Focus, Future Action, and Aligning Divergent Objectives. All minor responsibilities should be combined under one low-priority feeder-objective.

3. Manager uses the organization chart to get a good balance or spread as follows:

    a. Keeps the number of feeder-objectives for all managers about equal.

    b. Includes at least three joint feeder-objectives for each managerial position.

c. Keeps the number of subordinates reporting to each manager approximately equal.

d. Holds the number of organizational levels under each managerial position about equal.

Managers with more responsibilities than they can handle tend to be overwhelmed for lack of time. With lack of time, coordination and interlocking are not likely to occur. The MBO manager acquires a systems style of defining a set of expectancies for the future but gets together with other managers to build an overall system for the company, using their personal commitments as building blocks. He will not be rebuked for taking control and dominating in pursuit of an objective; the organization expects this because of prior involvement, agreement, and commitment. Rules, and restraints on behavior are bound up in the commitments made through the objective-setting processes. The MBO Rule for Balancing Organizations serves as a vertical and lateral integrator among the various groups.

◄ SUMMARY ►

This chapter defines some typical management problems and then explains how concepts fundamental to managing by objectives can help to solve them. To assist the manager in dealing with the ever-increasing spectrum of demands that face him, managing by objectives offers him a rule for sorting and selecting the most critical demands, on which he should concentrate his attention. To help himself keep future oriented, the manager can apply the MBO Rule for Future Action. There is a rule to help him coordinate his planning, and a rule to help him avoid, reduce, and control his costs. There is a rule to help him motivate employees, and a rule to help him be sure that those employees and their employers are working in the same direction. This chapter also offers a rule by which the MBO manager can combine voluntary and directed management methods, in order to achieve organizational coordination.

1. J. M. Juran, "Universals in Management Planning and Controlling." *The Management Review,* November 1954.

2. H. Ford Dickie, "Hard-Nosed Inventory Management," in Donald G. Hall (ed.), *The Manufacturing Man and His Job,* American Management Association, New York, 1966, pp. 238-254.

3. Ralph E. Lewis, *Planning and Control for Profit,* Harper and Row Publishers, New York 1970, pp. 3-8.

4. C. Northcote Parkinson, *Parkinson's Law,* Houghton Mifflin, New York, 1967, pp. 2-8.

5. The illustration of vectors with sense, direction, and magnitude has been adapted from a well-known principle of physics and was previously used by Weber and Karnes as effective leadership, a resolution between Service and Profit, *Industrial Leadership,* Chilton Co., New York, 1959, pp. 10-19.

6. David C. McClelland, *The Achieving Society,* Nostrand Co., Inc., New York, 1961, pp. 20-24.

7. M. Scott Myers, *Every Employee a Manager,* McGraw-Hill Book Company, New York, 1970, p. 46.

8. See note 5 on the use of vectors.

Chapter 2 Review

✓✓ Doublecheck

Answer briefly.

1. How might the MBO Rule for Focus help a manager deal with the increasing rate of innovations and the faster pace in business growth?

_____

_____

_____

_____

2. How does the MBO Rule for Future Action help a manager compensate for the limitations of crisis management?

_____

_____

_____

_____

3. How does the MBO Rule for Interlocking Functions assist the manager in coordinating planning within managerial levels?

_____

_____

_____

4. How does the MBO Rule for Progressive Cost Improvement work?

_____

_____

_____

_____

5. Why do organizations tend to accept mediocrity?

_____

_____

_____

_____

6. How does the MBO Rule for Stretching Performance suggest employee potential be developed?

_____

_____

_____

_____

7. What is the purpose of the MBO Rule for Aligning Divergent Objectives? How, briefly, does it suggest this purpose be achieved?

_____

_____

_____

_____

8. What are the limitations of the purely voluntary method of organization?

_____

_____

_____

_____

9. What are the three steps of the MBO Rule for Balancing Organizations?

_____

_____

_____

_____

- **Doublecheck Answers**

1. The MBO Rule for Focus is based on the principle that the greater the focus and concentration on the results one wants to achieve on a time scale, the greater the likelihood of achieving them. By following the steps involved in the application of this rule, the manager can better identify those innovations that are important and that relate to the achievement of growth objectives. This allows the bulk of the manager's efforts to be devoted to the demands on his time that represent the most critical 20%.

2. The MBO Rule for Future Action is aimed at concentrating an appropriate amount of the manager's time on those tasks involving the future as compared with review of past performance. Since a crisis is in the making when the rate of problem generation is equal to or greater than the rate of problem solution, focus on future action enables the manager to solve potential problems before they become major and require much more time for a solution than is the case in early stages.

3. The MBO Rule for Interlocking Functions involves listing feeder-objectives in two categories: those that can be completed only as a joint effort with other functions or departments and those that do not require joint effort. In making such a list, the manager is able to concentrate on those areas that require negotiating and gaining agreement to combine resources and effort among departments toward achieving joint objectives. If all managers on different levels of the organization have a reasonable number of two-way or three-way joint commitments, it helps to ensure effective coordination of planning.

4. The basic premise for progressive cost improvement is that cost control must be considered as a way of life. It is not something a special group sets out to accomplish quite apart from in-plant activity. It is the heart and core of managing and therefore cannot be separated from managing. The MBO Rule for Progressive Cost Improvement involves application of a three-step procedure to cost improvement possibilities. These three steps are

   a. Avoid the cost where possible.

   b. Reduce the cost from standard where and when possible.

   c. Control a cost to standard where avoidance and reduction are not possible.

5. Organizations tend to develop and accept mediocrity for three main reasons.

   a. A shortage of qualified personnel

   b. The practice of seniority within union ranks

   c. The difficulty of evaluating employee performance

6. The MBO Rule for Stretching Performance involves a three-step procedure for developing employee potential.

   a. Identifying employee potential

   b. Unfolding that potential by building in a 5%-15% performance stretch on objectives of high interest to the employee

   c. Utilizing employee potential through an ongoing series of performance stretches

7. The purpose of the MBO Rule for Aligning Divergent Objectives is to continually match employee objectives with employer objectives. The basis for achieving this alignment of objectives involves greater participation in setting meaningful work with an accountability for results. This leads to greater motivation for completing that work. Open discussions between the supervisor and the employee regarding organization objectives and employee objectives and tying those to the MBO network is the key to achieving this purpose.

8. There are three main limitations of the purely voluntary method of organization.

   a. The decision maker is not aware of all the factors outside of his domain that might affect his particular situation.

   b. Coordination becomes a chance event.

   c. A sense of timing is lost.

9. In order to eliminate the tendency toward imbalance within an organization, the MBO Rule for Balancing Organizations follows a three-step procedure.

   a. Each manager lists the major functional responsibilities of his position and of subordinates reporting to him.

   b. The manager rewrites each subordinate's major responsibility as a feeder-objective, following the MBO guidelines and placing all minor responsibilities under a single low-priority objective.

   c. The manager uses the organization chart to get a good balance or spread of feeder-objectives and joint feeder-objectives among subordinates and each manager.

Since becoming president of Valley Litho in late 1974, things had not gone as expected for Earl Sasser. Upon his initial appointment as president, he had developed a series of plans for expanding the business, increasing its profitability, and strengthening its competitive position. Unfortunately, he had found during the past 12 months that there were a number of problem areas at the company that were blocking achievement of these objectives. In hopes of avoiding another very frustrating year, Earl wanted to spend several days away from the office with some of his key people in order to determine what kinds of changes should be made in the future that would enable the company to achieve its objectives and goals.

The Valley Litho firm was engaged in commercial printing of a high quality nature for both corporate accounts and advertising agencies. (The latter group acted as designers for various companies who did not have their own full-time art staff or marketing group.) Much of Valley Litho's work was of the annual report type with the balance being specialized full-color brochures and limited subscription magazine work. The company had been in business since the late 1940s and had been managed by two brothers until 1974. At that time one of the brothers passed away and the other decided to seek early retirement. Knowing the excellent quality reputation of the firm, Earl was most interested to learn that they were looking for a president and that he might fit those qualifications. After several discussions with the general manager and the other stockholders, he decided to accept the position of president with the understanding that it would be for three years at which time his performance and the performance of the company would be reviewed by both parties.

Earl's first step as president had been to assess the existing capabilities of the firm. He found those to be excellent, but in his view they were underutilized. He had found that productivity had been declining gradually in recent years and that while the employees were very capable in their trades, they were not overly zealous in their output during working hours. He had also found that production schedules were handled rather loosely and that considerable excess equipment seemed to be on hand. Thus, as an immediate step he felt that he could increase the sales of the organization without a corresponding increase in the workforce or equipment capacity, and thereby substantially improve the profitability of Valley Litho.

When he initially tried to increase sales, he found the sales force very set in its ways and while they were perfectly willing to make new calls, they had very limited success from those. When he went out on calls with these salesmen, he found that they did not aggressively sell the company and its services and that they were reluctant to promise and commit themselves to meeting customer timetables and demands. Thus, while he found that most of their potential customers felt that Valley Litho offered excellent quality at reasonable prices, those potential customers were reluctant to take a job away from one of Valley's competitors and give it to Valley simply because they felt Valley had nothing special to offer either in the way of price or better delivery.

In response to Earl's assessment of the marketing opportunities, he decided that it made sense for the firm to aggressively seek new business by selectively cutting prices for the most attractive potential customers and promising delivery in somewhat less than the normal three-week period. As he began to do this and work with the salesmen, he found that they were indeed able to obtain new business. However, he then found that since production was used to working on a three-week cycle that it was extremely difficult, even with available excess capacity, to produce the product on time without substantial mistakes or his looking over workers' shoulders on a day-to-day basis. The result was that the increased level of sales simply required more time on his part in supervising each production step if commitments made to customers in obtaining those sales were to be honored.

Finally, he found that the productivity of the workers had declined substantially with the increased volume. It appeared that they were spending too much time going from one job to another rather than completing each job and thus eliminating duplicate set-up times. It also appeared that the scheduling and production planning systems did not adequately control the production in each of the nine departments of the plant and thus jobs were often late which, upon checking, were found to have been sitting idle for several days in between departments.

In light of the many problems facing the company and the fact that even with increased sales in 1975, profitability was likely to be down from the previous year. Earl was most anxious to alter his own style of management and various policies in the organization to prevent a repeat of this performance in the coming year.

Assignment

Analyze the Valley Litho situation in terms of the common problems facing organizations today. How can management by objectives be used by Earl Sasser in overcoming these problems and in designing his own approach to guiding the company in the future?

- Valley Litho

Earl's initial plan involved increasing both sales and profitability and strengthening the company's competitive position. He recognized the existing strengths as capable employees and a good reputation for the firm in the marketplace but thought that existing facilities were underutilized due to excess equipment and a gradually declining productivity level. During the past year, Earl has tried to get the sales force to acquire new business through the promise of shorter delivery times. Unfortunately, production has gotten worse in that productivity has further declined, the stakes have increased, and deliveries have not been met.

In applying some of the concepts of MBO, it can be seen that each of the following problems has contributed to Earl's frustration in the present situation.

- A lack of focus for the organization.

- Earl's changes have caused new problems and the rate of problem solving has not been high enough to keep the organization on a continual path of improvement.

- Earl is the only one really committed to the present path of development.

- Production is not committed or really involved in supporting the new efforts.

- Cost control and other kinds of production control seem to be lacking.

In summary, it would appear that Earl is doing most of the work and that the main problem is that the organization has gotten out of balance because sales have been pushed beyond the area where production can handle them. The organization needs to rethink its goals and plans and then to tie together the entire efforts of the various groups in the organization to meet those. MBO can be particularly valuable in this respect, supplying guidance in developing a structure of objectives that will relate each of the parts of the organization in their effort to accomplish selected goals. This should help to balance the efforts in production with the efforts in sales, allowing the firm to consistently make progress toward its objectives.

II. ISOLATING AND SETTING OBJECTIVES

SELECTED READINGS

3. Isolating Objectives

Brincklose, William D., *Managerial Operations Research,* McGraw-Hill Book Co., New York, 1969.

Ferber, Robert, *Market Research,* McGraw-Hill Book Co., New York, 1949.

Forecasting Sales, Studies in Business Policy No. 106, New York, 1964. National Industrial Conference Board.

Gardner, John W., *Excellence: Can We Be Equal and Excellent Too?* Harper and Row, New York, 1961.

Heidingsfield, Myron S., and Frank H. Eby, Jr., *Marketing and Business Research,* Holt, Rinehart and Winston, New York, 1963.

Hodnet, Edward, *The Art of Problem Solving,* Harper and Row, New York, 1955.

McConkey, Dale P., *Planning Next Year's Profits,* American Management Association, New York, 1968.

Merger Policy in the Smaller Firm, Studies in Business No. 10, New York, 1969. National Industrial Conference Board.

Miles, Lawrence D., *Techniques of Value Analysis and Engineering,* McGraw-Hill Book Co., New York, 1961.

O'Dell, William F., *The Marketing Decision,* American Management Association, New York, 1968.

Osborn, Alex F., *Applied Imagination,* Scribner's and Sons, New York, 1953.

Riggs, James L., *Economic Decision Models,* McGraw-Hill Book Co., New York, 1968.

Riggs, James L., *Production Systems: Planning, Analysis and Control,* John Wiley and Sons, Inc., New York, 1970.

Smith, Richard A., *Corporations in Crisis,* Doubleday and Co., New York, 1963.

4. Setting Objectives

Anderson, Clifton A., "Performance Rating," *Industrial Engineering Handbook,* McGraw-Hill Book Co., New York, 1963.

Barnes, R. M., *Motion and Time Study,* John Wiley & Sons Inc., New York, 1968.

Emory, William and Niland Powell, *Making Management Decisions,* Houghton Mifflin Co., New York, 1968.

Ferguson, George A., *Statistical Analysis in Psychology and Education,* McGraw-Hill Book Co., New York, 1959.

Landekich, Stephen, "Budgeting," in H. B. Maynard (ed.), *Handbook of Business Administration,* McGraw-Hill Book Co., New York, 1967.

Miller, Ernest C., *Objectives and Standards,* American Management Association, New York, 1966.

Nunnally, J. C., *Educational Measurement and Evaluation,* McGraw-Hill Book Co., New York, 1964.

Odiorne, George S., *Management by Objectives,* Pitman Publishing Co., New York, 1965.

II. ISOLATING AND SETTING OBJECTIVES

3. ISOLATING OBJECTIVES

Key Concepts

- *Capacity Decision.* As a manager plans future goals and objectives designed to improve organizational performance, he often becomes involved in capacity decisions. Adoption of a set of improvements involves relating desired results to the resources and capabilities of the organization. The organization's capacity (resources and capabilities) in such areas as technology, production, manpower, capital, marketing, management, and information processing are all significant in this regard.

- *Improvement Forecasting.* In the first phase of MBO, isolating objectives, improvement forecasting is of vital importance. The improvement forecasts become the basis from which MBO selects alternatives for creating a management system. Using a combination of both numerical and non-numerical forecasting techniques, the MBO manager engages in long-range, short-range, and immediate-range forecasting — trying to achieve the greatest immediate return that is consistent with the organization's long-term interests.

- *Situation Action Method.* The situation action forecasting model offers one way of isolating objectives and forecasting improvement. It consists of the four sequential steps of collecting effects from a situational analysis, determining causes of situational effects, finding eliminators of (alternatives to) causes in the situation, and choosing the best eliminator (alternative).

Learning Objectives

After you have completed this chapter, you should be able to

- Explain the importance of applying the concept of improvements to isolating objectives.

- Decide whether a desired effect can best be achieved through long-range, short-range, or immediate-range improvement forecasts.

- Describe various numerical and non-numerical methods of improvement forecasting.

- Describe several management models for improvement forecasting.

LOOKING AHEAD FOR IMPROVEMENTS

Understanding the Need for Objectives ►

Organizations tend to get so preoccupied with the present and past that they leave their future directions ill defined. In contrast to this, managing by objectives is basically concerned with the future. MBO strategy allows managers to search out and plan a certain set of objectives — to make a future commitment for their organization. This commitment includes people, money, facilities, time, and resources. The value of this commitment is high because the stakes are high. Thus, finding an objective cannot be left to caprice.

A knowledge of the past and the present is desirable since it provides a perspective for decisions. These decisions should be sequential: they should, in other words, be a series of related steps or problem-solving adjustments intended to bring an organization from achievements today toward an anticipated set of achievements tomorrow.

The concept of formulating objectives is inherent in any decision-making process. Sometimes the objective sought in a decision is implied rather than explicitly stated or formulized. A series of these implied decisions, in addition to solving their immediate concerns, can and does provide explicit impact on the entire operation. This is, however, without forethought or planning.

> The failure of managerial decision-making to set formally and deliberately explicit objectives represents a great deficiency in the art of managing.

The first goal for any organization looking for directions lies in the mission of improvement—improvement from the standpoint of the interest and needs of the organization. The mission of improvement is the foundation for the practice of managing by objectives. It means looking into the future in an attempt to visualize changes that, once adopted, will better the existing situation. This search for opportunities and alternatives is part of the manager's job.

Traditionally the manager seeks improvement to

- Increase the organization's share of opportunities available

- Develop new products and services

- Lead other organizations in the technology or professions

- Reach a needed level of operational services

- Increase volume of sales, customers, clients, or prospects

- Provide a needed return on investment

- Reduce waste and costs

- Improve the quality of products or services

- Strengthen the organizational image

- Improve morale in the work force

A decision to adopt a set of improvements formalized into objectives must be a result of analysis and evaluation based upon the organization's needs. It begins by forecasting how an organization can make use of this future situation.

Translating Capacity Into Results ►

The manager's look ahead often involves a capacity decision. To adopt a set of improvements is to relate desired end results to the resources and capabilities of the organization. It is also to plan to improve existing capacity. A capacity definition may be one or several of the following:

- *Technological Capacity.* Technological skills and know-how for the conception, design, production, and use of products and services

- *Production Capacity.* Facilities and equipment types and layout for flexible manufacturing designed for changing markets

- *Manpower Capacity.* Type and availability of employee skills and degree of employee willingness to work under a variety of conditions

- *Capital Capacity.* Cash position, budgets, assets, and ability to raise capital to support competitive projects engaged in by most companies

- *Marketing Capacity.* Markets created and maintained through promotion, service, and distribution

- *Management Capacity.* Effective in-house application of the managerial processes of planning, organizing, and controlling resources on all organizational levels of the enterprise

- *Information-Processing Capacity.* Data generation, storage, and retrieval within a timetable for effective communication and decision-making

An organization must appraise and define "what it is" as it addresses itself to "what it can be." Objectives set and reached can be viewed as new capacity that does much or little for the existing business. In some cases, this added capacity may even dilute an existing capability.

The future direction of an organization or department may be thought of as the future direction of existing capacity. Initially, for example, airlines defined their business as the airline industry. Later in their development, they considered themselves to be in the transportation business. Today, many airlines are redefining their operations as the recreational business, since new capacity "chunks" such as hotels, car rentals and resorts have been added to their initial capability. The MBO practitioner should outline, describe, interpret, and set forth the capacities that exist within an organization as he proceeds formally to find new objectives or to add new capacities.

> Improvement forecasts are the vital element in isolating and setting objectives for an organization. The MBO strategy uses these forecasts as a basis from which to collect alternatives for creating a management system.

Creativity, intuition, and rationality form the basis for making these forecasts. As one faces the future, one faces complexity, obscurity, and confusion. In spite of this, an objective must be found and a commitment must be made; improvement forecasts provide the method. These can be classified in many ways. One classification is by time period; that is, long range, short range, and immediate. These categories are interrelated. Collecting alternatives from each of these categories to form the basis for setting objectives requires a systems view from future segments of time, as illustrated in Figure 1. The shaded areas show the course of what started out a long-range forecast and ended up a rejected notion.

1. Collecting Alternatives From Future Segments of Time

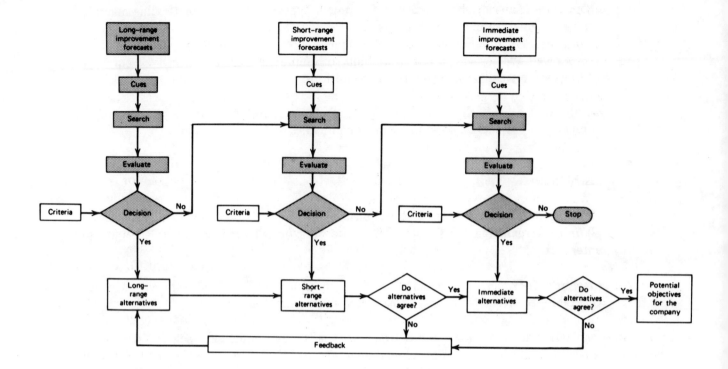

Forecasting Long-Range Improvement ▸

Long-range improvement is usually concerned with the fundamental issue of any organization anywhere — self-preservation. What changes in the organization are necessary? Looking ahead — 3 years, 5 years, 10 years, 15 years—what should the organization be like? To find the answers, economic, social, and political trends and indicators must be considered and interpreted, since the long view must take into account technological changes, competitive position, new product developments, capital expansion, and new equipment acquisitions. The head of a department—engineering or quality control, for example—must bear in mind the state of the art of his function, the direction it is taking, new skills that are emerging, and the effects of obsolescence. He must look for changes that will improve his effectiveness in the total system.

Long-range improvement decisions are usually trade-offs against immediate and short-range gains. The manager must weigh carefully the acquisition of value on the short-range basis versus value over the long-range. For example, reducing inventory by cutting down production may reduce costs in the short run if full production capacity is not a factor. Reduced inventories, however, reduce the advantage for ready shipments and quick services to customers in the long run.

Long-range improvements must be measurable in terms of the consequences to the organization as a whole. In order for a long-range improvement to be adopted, its anticipated effects must be clearly recognized and understood. Long-range improvement forecasts provide guidelines by which management can evaluate its own performance. These forecasts force management to think about present-day problem solving in the context of long-range survivability. The chronological scope of a forecast should be governed by the objectives sought. The 5-year forecast has traditionally been a useful rule. But the 5-year forecast may be too long or too short for the purpose intended and the information available. A useful way to determine the length of the forecast is to follow the *MBO Guideline for Long-Range Forecasting:*

MBO Guideline for Long-Range Forecasting

Select and decide on long-term improvements within the time period that valid and useful information is available.

An organization that embarks on a 5-year plan when information is available for only a 3-year forecast is pursuing a course based on guesswork and hope.
To fit the time period to the information available is to provide management with confidence in regard to its long-range course of action.

Forecasting Short-Range Improvement ►

Long-range improvement forecasts deal largely with the organization as a whole for a future period of time. Questions must be raised concerning the consequences of these long-range forecasts in the short run and for the individual departments and functions of the organization. Short-range improvement forecasts deal with smaller changes, shorter time periods, and consistent delivery of results. A long-range improvement may be to increase the share of the market from 23 to 30 percent. A short-range improvement may be to prevent profit fluctuations from dipping below 12 percent after taxes. Or a long-range improvement may be to make a technological breakthrough in metallurgical conductivity. A short-range improvement may be to maintain a consistent sales volume of prepackaged electrical conductors with the same customers. Uncertainty, risks, and unknowns for the short range are not so great as for the long range. Therefore, critical changes needed in the organization should be considered short-range rather than long-range goals. The chronological scope of short-range forecasts should be governed by two considerations: the availability of useful and valid information, and the importance of achieving an improvement within a desired period of time.

The 1- to 2-year period for short-range forecasts traditionally has been a useful rule. On the other hand, this may be either too long or too short for short-range needs. A useful way to determine the length of the forecast is to follow the *MBO Guideline for Short-Range Forecasting:*

MBO Guideline for Short-Range Forecasting

Select and decide on short-range improvements within the time period in which consistent and critical results must be achieved by the organization and in which valid information is available.

An organization that embarks on a 2-year cost-improvement program based on 2-year breakeven cost data of newly installed capital equipment is pursuing a course of action within a time interval and based on valid information.

Forecasting Immediate Improvement ►

The immediate forecast deals with urgent problems covering periods of 3 to 12 months. It involves looking ahead and setting up performance standards that can guide a manager, department, or company to a specific improvement within a very short period of time. For example, in financial budgeting, forecasts set up standards by which management can judge its own performance independent of factors not under its control. Immediate improvement forecasts can range from accepting a production run to quoting price on a single order, or from submitting acceptable contract proposals to reducing weld rejects in a welding shop.

To be sure, immediate improvements have short- to long-range implications. Lower price quotations in contract proposals may be an immediate objective. The consequences of the contract award can be far reaching, however. The reduction of weld rejects may have an immediate effect on the quality acceptance of a product by a customer. The long-range effect may be to change the company's percentage of the market. Improvements, whether long range, short range, or immediate, interact with each other in their effects. Yet value accrued within the specified time period must remain the major criterion for adopting an improvement measure. A useful way to determine the length of the period for an immediate forecast is to follow the *MBO Guideline for Immediate-Range Forecasting:*

MBO Guideline for Immediate-Range Forecasting

Select and decide on immediate-range improvements within the time period in which realistic performance standards can be set up for solving critical organizational problems.

Commitments on either a long-term, a short-term, or an immediate basis have effects on balance, speed and progress in certain directions. Conflicts among the alternatives offered by the three time spans will always emerge. The manager must resolve these conflicts on the basis of organization need. The decision to adopt a future set of improvements always leaves some regret or uncertainty as to whether the conflict resolution is optimal. But the decision to pursue an objective does not stop the search for additional improvements. In many ways, this is a concept of progressive looking ahead. The adoption of an objective to be accomplished in any one period should be the best selection for value from many alternatives offered by the three time spans. *Balance of value*, a term used in this regard, is defined as greatest return for effort from actions taken during a current year consistent with an organization's long-term interest. No action should be taken to divert an expected gain from a future year to a smaller gain for the current year. Similarly, no action should be taken to divert an immediate gain for the current year to a smaller gain from a future year. This rule for balance of values requires a progressive view toward making commitments. Some organizations get into difficulties not from inherent flaws in the practices of decentralization, centralization, or diversification, but rather from the inability to find the balance of value among these three time ranges.

The quality of an objective is very much influenced by the changes and needs brought about by time. An MBO manager assesses the impact these changes and needs will have on his objective program with progressive evaluation after each period. His continued improvement forecast gives him an inventory of alternatives from which he can make progressive changes.

Indicate true (T) or false (F).

1. Because it is neither rational nor scientific, intuition plays no part in improvement forecasting. _____

2. Long-range improvement decisions are frequently trade-offs against immediate and short-range gains. _____

3. A failure of managerial decision-making to set formally and deliberately explicit objectives represents a great deficiency in the art of managing. _____

4. Planning improvements means planning improvements in existing capacity. _____

5. Added capacity is always improved capacity. _____

6. Improvement forecasts are the vital element in isolating and setting objectives for an organization. _____

Fill in the correct answer.

7. Self-preservation is the primary aim of _____ improvement forecasts.

8. Immediate improvement forecasts deal with urgent problems covering periods of

   _____ or less.

9. _____ is defined as greatest return for effort from actions taken during a current year consistent with an organization's long-range interest.

10. A good MBO manager assesses the impact that anticipated changes will have on his objective

    program by making a _____ after each period.

──────────────

● Checkpoint Answers

1. F   2. T   3. T   4. T   5. F   6. T   7. long-range   8. one year   9. balance of value
10. progressive evaluation

THREE NON-NUMERICAL FORECASTING METHODS

The principal aim of improvement forecasts is to provide a reliable estimate of future conditions on the basis of which objectives may be set. A good forecast is a set of realistic expectations. These expectations are essential to MBO practice. Obviously, the methods to be used to determine these expectations are influenced by a number of factors. These include:

- Background in and understanding of the field

- Number and type of assumptions to be made

- Amount and validity of available information

- Available time and facilities

- Ability to sense the factors controlling market demand

- Skill in interpreting qualitative and quantitative trends that cross, run parallel to, or diverge from each other

Improvement forecasts are never precise. At best, they provide a structure of expectations without much detail. The skillful forecaster always forecasts the market before attempting to forecast his own organization's role in the market. The progressive forecasting concept, discussed earlier, provides a way of both validating the expected structure of the market and providing pertinent details for a manager's own organization. The MBO practitioner will use as many aids as possible to help him determine future structure. The more intimately acquainted the practitioner becomes with the field, the more valuable his forecast will be.

There are a number of methods — both non-numerical and numerical — available to the forecaster. Most organizations take a multiple-method approach, adopting those techniques most useful for predicting the type of improvement desired. This multiple-method approach appears rational, because the objectives of forecasting tend to expand from solving the problems of a specific department to dealing with a broad range of future concerns, as suggested in the following forecast ranges:

- *Extensively broad:* Economic, political, and social indicators

- *Very broad:* General business conditions

- *Broad:* Specific industry movements

- *Narrow:* Products, services, and consumer needs

- *Very narrow:* Individual organization directions

- *Specifically narrow:* Needed specific future improvements

Those organizations that elect to rely on a single method to find their improvements usually experience clear forecasting results. This is often, however, an oversimplification. The multiple-method approach offers a more realistic and reassuring series of checks and balances.

This section describes three non-numerical methods of improvement forecasting. They are: the consensus method, the problem-area method, and the maximize opportunity method.[1]

The Consensus Method ►

The consensus method relies on opinions held by a group, committee, or conference concerning the future. It is a highly subjective approach and relies on both the experience and the intuition of the participants. Each individual contributes his opinion as to the improvements he deems necessary during some future time. He makes this contribution on the basis of problem trends he has observed or experienced. These data must be acknowledged to be biased and individualistic. But when several such individuals are brought together, the consensus approach combines and averages the contributions of each participant. Each contribution is a single estimate. The estimates are compared to find those that have high consensus. The coordination of the various estimates can help in deciding whether a single direction can be agreed to by the participants.

Obviously, the participants in the consensus method must be carefully selected for this activity, since each represents a resource for the improvement forecast. Participants may be assembled as homogeneous or heterogeneous groups. Homogeneous groups might consist entirely of executives, engineers, salesmen, foremen, or planners. Heterogeneous groups might consist of members from each of the homogeneous groups within or outside the organization. The selection and assignment of individuals to groups for consensus improvement forecasting will be governed by the nature of the forecast and the areas of improvement deemed critical.

> The pooling of experience and judgment, the ease and simplicity of the contribution, and the involvement and participation of individuals who may ultimately set the objectives help to provide a motivational climate in which objectives can be most easily reached. The disadvantages of the approach — reliance on opinions, lack of objective data, and non-numeric averaging — must be weighed against these valuable advantages.

The Problem-Areas Method ►

The problem-areas method starts with the identification of areas in which problems recur and are difficult to solve. This approach is critically needed in organizations practicing crisis management. Improvement forecasting using this involves an analysis of the types of problems, histories of these problems, problem trends, and probabilistic occurences. Future solutions are searched for in order to eliminate these problem trends once and for all. This approach is also a grass-roots approach, since it involves examining the opinions, data, reactions, and reports in the areas where problems are generated. Probable improvements are solicited from those who are part of the problems, as well as from those who merely relate to the problems. The employment of outside consultants may also be most useful.

Problem definition is important before the search for improvements can begin. This involves an historical analysis of the problem to see what the record has been. Variables and constraints in terms of personnel, methods, equipment, facilities, and resources are identified for cause-effect relationships. It does not make sense for any objective-setting program to plan future improvements without addressing itself to current problems.

The Maximize Opportunity Method ►

A careful study of existing and potential customers for information on expected consumption, purchases, and needs is another useful method for making improvement forecasts.

User-expectation surveys provide data and profiles from which opportunities for developing new products, new services, and other improvements can be identified.

The maximum opportunity approach focuses upon opportunities that are innovative for the organization. It searches outside the organization for improvements that would make the best use of internal resources. The improvement forecast is, in effect, an attempt to maximize resources by scanning possible applications outside the organization. In this respect, markets are not necessarily existing and ready to be exploited. Often, markets are created by merger, one organization devoting its underutilized resources to the unexpected applications for consumer use offered by the other organization. This is one reason that organizations pursue programs of acquisitions and mergers. True, it is often to supplement internal growth and complement existing activities, but in many cases it is a substitute for internal growth. Acquisitions are seen as quick means of spreading existing overhead, buying skillful management and technical know-how, and expanding through acquiring capital equipment and facilities.

Improvement opportunities can be identified by any member of the organization's management. Making the future happen requires ideas — improvement ideas. The maximize opportunity method is a deliberate effort to organize brainstorming for innovative ideas. This is not to suggest that the MBO practitioner need be a creative genius like Edison, Sloan, or DuPont. Improvement ideas can range from breakthroughs that cause the organization to progress by leaps, to minor innovations that advance the organization by increments. Improvement forecasts, using the maximize opportunity approach, are made according to the following steps:

1. *Identify the totality of customer needs in a market.* This is accomplished through user-surveys, mail questionnaires, interviews, and telephone checks.

2. *Find customer needs that company can serve.* This is accomplished by removing from the totality of customer needs the needs that cannot be served.

3. *Link capabilities of company to needs that can be served.* Resources of the firm are identified and matched to needs that can be served. This matching takes into consideration the magnitude and timing of both customer needs and company resources.

4. *List constraints and limitations on matched needs.* This step involves identifying competitors, governmental constraints, community demands, and political influences.

5. *Arrange according to maximum opportunity the list of matched capabilities and customer needs.* Several criteria are used to find maximum opportunity. These are profits, return on investment, utilization of capacity, market penetration, company image, and product leverage.

6. *Formulate maximum opportunities as company objectives.* This is accomplished through the formal process of setting objectives.

- *Quick Quiz: Three Non-numerical Forecasting Methods*

Draw a line to connect each item on the left with the correct non-numerical forecasting method on the right.

1. Conducts user-expectation surveys

2. Emphasizes historical analysis to see what the record has been

3. Relies on a group's opinion about the future

4. Critically needed in organizations practicing crisis management

5. Studies existing and potential customers for information on expected consumption, purchases, and needs

Maximize Opportunity
Method

Problem-Areas
Method

Consensus
Method

THE SITUATION ACTION FORECASTING METHOD

The situation action model, which offers another way of isolating objectives and forecasting improvements, contains four sequential steps:

1. Collecting effects from a situational analysis

2. Determining causes of situational effects

3. Finding eliminators of (alternatives to) causes in the situation

4. Choosing the best eliminator (alternative)

As in navigation, plotting a course requires locating two positions — where one is and where one is heading. Once existing resources, commitments, and capabilities are known, an objective can be set and a course of action plotted. By following the steps of the situation action method in sequence, the MBO manager has a useful and practical tool for isolating objectives for his organization.

1. Collecting Effects From a Situational Analysis ►

A situational analysis is a deliberate method of raising questions and collecting data about what the organization's immediate situation is and how it arrived there. It is an analysis of significant trends and changes occurring within the organization and a forecast of where the organization is heading as a result of these conditions. This approach discourages picking objectives out of thin air and relates objective setting to the needs of the enterprise. The

---

- Quick Quz Answers   1. Maximize Opportunity Method   2. Problem-Areas Method   3. Consensus Method
4. Problem-Areas Method   5. Maximize Opportunity Method

collection and analysis of information will disclose a series of facts, both strengths and weaknesses, relating to services and product requirements. It will also provide information as to the organization's resources and capability of delivering these services and products.

A number of methods can be useful in uncovering symptoms of problems in a situation — conducting audits, collecting statistical data, holding conferences, making purposeful observations, analyzing reports, and interviewing individuals are among these. However, asking questions is the heart and core of diagnosis. There is no easy system for formulating questions, but the seven basic guidelines have always been useful: Who? When? Where? Which? What? How? and Why? Organized questions are valuable as a starting point, because they can penetrate the problem and provide information that enables the questioner to examine different facets of the problem.

To stimulate thinking and to help a manager get a good grip on situational effects, the following questions can be posed. Space is provided so that you may make notes on these questions in terms of problems facing your own organization.

Worksheet: Situational Analysis

A. Problem analysis

1. What is the potential product obsolescence and length of product life?

   _____

   _____

2. What directives, policies, positions, and organizational conditions are impeding growth and performance improvement?

   _____

   _____

3. What problems can be expected within 3 months? 6 months? 12 months?

   _____

   _____

4. What changes can be made in job requirements to enlarge responsibilities and currency?

   _____

   _____

5. What are the barriers that have prevented the organization from reducing cost and being more efficient?

   _____

   _____

B. Opportunity analysis

1. Where is the highest probable rate of growth for each product or service?

_____

_____

2. Where are the possible technological breakthroughs and what are the effects on present facilities and equipment?

_____

_____

3. Where is the greatest number of potential customers for volume sales with emerging new technologies?

_____

_____

4. Where have product or service values closely aligned with customer needs?

_____

_____

5. Where are the unique advantages over competitors' products that could be expanded?

_____

_____

C. Personnel analysis

1. Who are the marginal or submarginal personnel who are draining the resources of the organization?

_____

_____

2. Who are those impeding improvement and what can be done to help them better their performance?

_____

_____

3. Who are the individuals who have ideas but have not been able to implement them?

    _____

    _____

4. Who are the individuals who would double their performance if they were shifted to a new set of challenges?

    _____

    _____

5. Who are the individuals who are too big for their small jobs or too small for their big jobs?

    _____

    _____

D. Schedule analysis

    1. When can existing commitments be moved up for completion?

        _____

        _____

    2. When can a new schedule be adopted for implementing a new idea?

        _____

        _____

    3. When can additional manpower be added to complete commitments earlier?

        _____

        _____

    4. When can cost targets be given to personnel to meet commitments?

        _____

        _____

    5. When can changes be included to reduce rejects and defects?

        _____

        _____

E. Methods Analysis

1. How can the sequence of work assignments be altered or regrouped to reduce costs and improve schedule?

_____

_____

2. How can the layout be revised for improved coordination and shortening distances?

_____

_____

3. How can a rearrangement improve morale, satisfaction, and results?

_____

_____

4. How can a suboperation be modified, changed, or redesigned to incorporate the functions of other suboperations?

_____

_____

5. How can a major operation be improved by eliminating or modifying a suboperation?

_____

_____

The questions in the preceding worksheet can help the manager to identify the needs and deficiencies of the enterprise. They are particularly useful in discovering effects or symptoms of a situational problem. The following is a partial list of these effects:

Excessive backlog	High rates of shipping returns
Schedule slippage	Ineffective advertising
Excessive pollution	Shrinking economy
Loss of key customers	Negative attitudes
High accident rates	Strikes
High waste and spoilage	Insufficient space
Excessive repairs	Poor timing
Interdepartmental disputes	Poor methods and procedures
Rivalries	Mismatched job and employee
Individual resistance	Unacceptable products
Low sales growth	Too much quality
High corrective work	Insufficient lead time
Low inventory	High wage rates
High overhead	Seasonal influences
Excessive turnover	Wrong materials

Loose quality control	Lack of job skills
High costs	Not enough controls
High machine downtime	Insufficient records
High material-handling costs	Low motivation
Production delays	No preventive planning
High absenteeism	Inadequate safety practices
Insufficient dividends	Poor organization
High pilferage	Inadequate standards
High rejected rates	Dominant personalities
Low profits	Weather conditions
High grievance rate	Old or faulty equipment
Sales volume off	Lack of needed information
Low morale	Bad layout
Continuous errors	Insufficient inspection
Rumors	Lack of coordination
Poor public image	No shipping schedules
Overtime deterioration	Insufficient communications
Imbalanced organization	

2. Determining Causes of Situational Effects ►

Once there has been an examination of effects pertinent to the organization's immediate situation, a search can be made for causes. There are desirable as well as undesirable cause-effect relationships. Those causes producing undesirable effects represent areas in which improvements can be proposed for reduction or elimination. Those causes producing desirable effects represent areas in which improvements can be proposed for continued growth. A greater understanding of cause-effect relationships can provide additional insight into situational analysis. The following are some principles designed to provide a better understanding of these relationships.

Principle I. A single cause can generate an ever-widening chain of primary effects. These primary effects become causes of secondary effects.

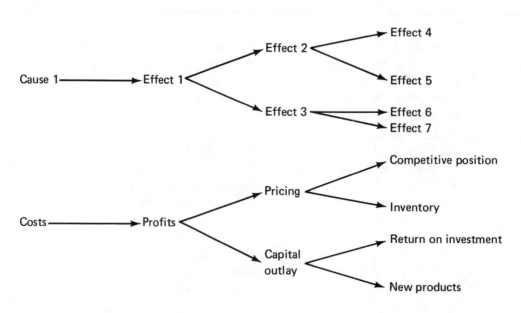

Principle II. A cause-effect relationship can be interchanged when directed toward a new objective or new situation.

Principle III. When there are multiple causes producing multiple effects, cause-effect relationships can be selected and directed toward an objective.

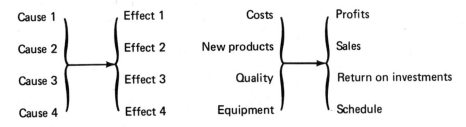

Principle IV. A cause constraint occurs when causes hold back the completion of a desired effect.

The enormous importance of cause-effect relationships in objective-setting processes and to the ultimate commitments of the organization makes their analysis worthwhile. Every time a person says, "What would happen if we tried . . . ?" he is thinking and forecasting from cause to effect. And every time he asks, "Why did this happen?" he is thinking and analyzing from effect to cause.

3. Finding Eliminators of (Alternatives to) Situational Causes ►

An understanding of cause-effect relationships according to the preceding principles can give insights into identifying causes. Finding eliminators of — or alternatives to — these causes should not be a hit-or-miss affair. Rather, it should result from a careful search for the specific action that will eliminate the undesirable cause or strengthen the desirable one. A methodology can be applied to this search for causal variables and their effects.

Such a methodology should in part be based on an understanding of the idea that a multiplicity of causes implies a multiplicity of eliminators and, in turn, a multiplicity of alternatives. Thus, an MBO manager should develop an "alternative generator" by identification and analysis of causal variables. The more causes a manager can identify, the more alternatives he can make available. The more alternatives he has, the better the quality of his decision for a future commitment is likely to be. A good decision-maker always asks, "How many more alternatives are there?" In this question lies the difference between a fair decision-maker and a first-rate one. The superior decision-maker does not accept three or four possible alternatives easily, even when they are good.

Merely gathering a number of possible courses of action does not mean that the best course of action is among them.

> The manager not only searches for all the possible courses of action; he also develops a gradient among them to reveal those that are best. In addition, he recognizes that doing nothing is an alternative. He has a choice between maintaining the status quo or changing it.

When the consequences of doing nothing appear better than those of doing something, then the good manager chooses to leave well enough alone. He is also the judge of when he has a sufficient number of alternatives to make a decision. He knows whether to stop at three, four, or ten alternatives, basing his judgment on the importance of time. Often the search for the "best" alternative can be a waste of effort as well as time. Often the "better" one will suffice. One can easily fall into the trap of continually putting off making a decision on the hope that the best alternative is just beyond the horizon. This delay can be disastrous. The amount of time available should be the guide to how many alternatives can be considered.

There are a variety of practical ways of finding eliminators.[2] Question checklists and idea checklists, two such ways, are based on the assumption that lists of ideas or questions serve to stimulate further ideas and lead to new directions. Brainstorming, probably the most widely used technique, is based on the principle that suspension of judgment allows the mind to free wheel. It is assumed that an individual can come up with more alternatives when he does not have to evaluate and weigh each one.

Still another approach to the search for alternatives is *value analysis*.[3] This approach considers procedures, products, and problems as causes and tries to identify their primary, secondary, and tertiary effects. How, for example, does each part of the overall activity contribute to the basic function? Herein lies the value of generating alternatives, since any suggestions as to how to improve the function while maintaining cost and quality requirements also suggest other new ideas for consideration. A complicated situation may consist of several functions, each related to the others. The value analysis approach enables one to compare one function with another in terms of cost, quality, and time. This comparison results in a scale of value. Suggestions can be made on how to improve the value of these functions. Thus alternatives are generated within the function itself.

More personalized, creative techniques may also be used to generate alternatives for the objective decision process — even techniques that work well for one person but not for another. The situation action method has a logical structure, but it offers flexibility within this structure for each individual to pursue a method useful and meaningful to him as he isolates alternatives, or possible objectives.

4. Choosing the Best Eliminator (Alternative) ►

Painstaking effort and analysis have gone into the process up to this point. The challenge now is to evaluate the alternatives to find the best few. This means a decision must be made to weigh the alternatives in terms of value. One of the chief differences between an objective program that produces outstanding results and one that produces mediocre results lies in the utility or payoff weight that is assigned to the various alternatives. To determine which alternative has the greatest payoff, decision criteria, or *standards for action*, are needed. The weights that are assigned to each alternative on the basis of a standard for action are degrees of priority. A payoff or decision-making matrix can be a useful way to represent how the weights will be allocated to each standard of action. This kind of matrix is a grid on which the alternatives are placed with the standards — often in the form of numerical ranking procedures, probability assignments, or percentages — placed in an adjacent position. The step-by-step procedure for developing the best ranking from the decision matrix is as follows:

Step 1.   Select the standards for action that constitute greatest utility in the situation or problem at hand.

Step 2.   Using a numerical ranking sequence, weigh each alternative in order of utility for each columnar standard, 1 for greatest utility, 2 for next greatest, and so on.

Step 3.   Continue the process of ranking each of the alternatives by columns until all standards that have been selected are covered.

Step 4.   Add horizontally the cell values to arrive at the total score in the total score column.

Step 5.   Select the rank number in the total score column for the alternative that best meets all criteria.

Step 6.   If standards are to be given differences in value, rank the standards across in order of importance and multiply the cell value by this weight. Repeat steps 4 and 5. If standards are regarded as equal in importance, then ignore this last step.

This optimizing process is enhanced when a meaningful selection of standards has been made. The following is a checklist of standards for action that will help to determine the goals or objectives to be set.

☐ *Return on investment (ROI).* Increasing the rate or percentage of profit or interest returned to the enterprises as a result of undertaking an investment or capital commitment at some early period of time.

☐ *Sales volume.* Increasing the amount of disposed of or sold products, services, or merchandise in an existing or created market.

☐ *Cost benefit.* Maintaining minimal expense in the selection and deployment of resources, equipment, materials, methods, and manpower.

☐ *Schedule.* Meeting a predetermined time program that projects events, operations, arrivals, and departures. A sense of pace is structured and reached.

☐ *Feasibility.* Capable of being done or effected in a practical way.

☐ *Customer effects.* Avoiding situations that would retard patronage of an organization.

☐ *Competitive advantage.* Avoiding acts that will favor a rival organization that is engaged in selling goods and services in the same market.

☐ *Employee morale.* Creating a climate and mood conducive to willing and dependable performance.

☐ *Union unrest.* Avoiding actions disruptive to collective bargaining efforts.

☐ *Community image.* Avoiding acts which give the company an unpleasant appearance in the eyes of the community.

☐ *Legislative actions.* Avoiding illegal practices that may provoke legal action to retard or stop competition and growth.

☐ *Cash position.* Creating a favorable and necessary situation in which the turnover of capital follows a cycle from cash to assets to receivables and back to cash, in sufficient time for the organization's use.

☐ *Opportunities for improvement.* Exploiting uniquely timed situations for market growth expansion and diversification.

☐ *Quality requirements.* Avoiding acts aimed at reducing the ability of a product or service to satisfy its specified design.

☐ *Safety needs.* Avoiding activities that are unsafe and areas where safety standards are minimal.

☐ *Tax benefits.* Avoiding acts that exceed the statute of limitations and bring about tax increases.

			Standards to Decide*					
Effects (Symptoms)	Causes (Conditional Forces)	Eliminators (Improvement Alternatives)	Customer Effects	Sales Volume	Union Unrest	Feasibility	Total Rank Across	Best Alternative (Objectives To Be Completed)
Backlog excessive	Machine idleness and downtime high	Use preventive maintenance program	3	2	2	3	10	*Second objective:* set up preventive maintenance program
Schedule slippage	Unsequenced ordering of parts	PERT ordering of parts from vendors	2	1	5	1	9	*First objective:* PERT ordering of parts from vendors
High overhead	Excessive travel expense	Set up travel expense control	6	7	6	6	25	
Turnover excessive	Low motivation	Design jobs for job enrichment	5	5	4	5	19	
High grievance rate	Contract violations by supervision	Train supervisors in labor contract	7	6	1	4	18	
Loss of key customers	Product breakdown disrupts customers' operations	Improve design reliability	1	3	7	7	18	
Reject rates high	Careless errors among employees	Motivate and train employees	4	4	3	2	13	

*Rank order; probabilities; or percentages can be used for assessing alternatives against the decision standard within the column. Here the rank-order method is used.

The following worksheet can be used to focus upon the best alternatives to a situational problem facing your organization.

Worksheet: Situation Action Model

Situational Problem										
Effects (Symptoms)	Causes (Conditional Forces)	Eliminators (Improvement Alternatives)	Standards to Decide				Total Rank Across	Best Alternative (Objectives To Be Completed)

V Checkpoint: The Situation Action Forecasting Method ―――――――――――――

Fill in each box with a number 1 through 4 to indicate the correct sequence for the four steps of the situation action method.

1. Determining causes of situation effects ☐

2. Finding eliminators of causes in the situation ☐

3. Collecting effects from a situational analysis ☐

4. Choosing the best alternative ☐

Complete each statement by circling the correct letter.

5. Asking questions is a useful technique when

    a.   collecting effects from a situational analysis   c.   both choices

    b.   finding eliminators of (alternatives to) situational causes

6. Brainstorming is based on the assumption that

    a.   suspension of judgment allows the mind to free wheel

    b.   lists of ideas serve to stimulate further ideas

7. In seeking the best course of action, doing nothing is

    a.   a sure way to failure   b.   a valid alternative to consider

8. A numerical ranking sequence can be a useful device in

    a.   choosing the best alternative   b.   finding alternatives to causes

    c.   determining causes of situational effects

9. A cause-effect relationship

    a.   can be interchanged when directed toward a new objective

    b.   is always simple; there is always one cause for each effect

10. Poor public image

    a.   is a cause of problems   b.   is an effect of problems

    c.   could be either, depending on the problem you are considering

―――――――――――――

● Checkpoint Answers

1. 2   2. 3   3. 1   4. 4   5. c   6. a   7. b   8. a   9. a   10. c

FIVE NUMERICAL FORECASTING METHODS

With numerical forecasting methods,[4] movements within an organization or in the economy can be measured and projected with a reasonable degree of accuracy and objectivity. The quantification of the factors and relationships has a tendency to give a clarity and precision to the forecast. The projections can identify what variables will exist, the magnitude of the variables, and deviations from known directions. This can be most helpful for improvement forecasts, since the way that new directions and deviations from present conditions are shown will suggest new approaches and improvements an organization can adopt. This is so because numerical methods can be readily used as a basis for comparing improvement forecasts of one period with those of another period.

The objectivity offered by this approach permits verification by other forecasters, which tends to build validity of the forecast. And the relationships within an organization that are critical to its needs are not left to questionable intuitive judgment; the numerical description of these relationships makes it easier for management to check results. Of course, there are also many dangers in using numerical methods. They generally demand the skills of a specialist, since statistics, mathematics, and computers are the tools necessary for their use. Salesmen, production men, executives, and administrators may not possess these skills. Also, numbers tend to oversimplify and at best should be regarded as indicators. The numerical methods, in themselves, are based on assumptions that could fault the entire forecast in spite of its precision.

Only a partial description of numerical methods for improvement forecasting is given here. The methods described are graphical extrapolation, semiaverage method, method of moving-averages, trend method of least squares, and method of exponential smoothing.

Graphical Extrapolation ►

Graphical extrapolation is extending into future time the average line found by plotting past data patterns. The graphical scatter chart resulting from this plot shows both the individuality of each point and the general trend of all points, making it extremely useful in making improvement forecast decisions.

Step 1.   Plot past data pattern to a time series. (Operational costs in years 1950, 1955, 1960, 1965, 1970 were 20, 24, 23, 26, 25 thousands, respectively.)

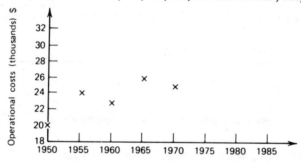

Step 2.   Draw a line through the data that represent a visual averaging process.

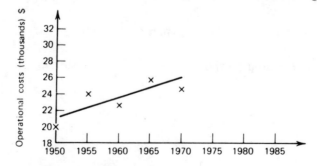

Step 3. Extend the drawn line to the period to be forecasted. (Operational costs for 1985 estimated at 31 thousand.)

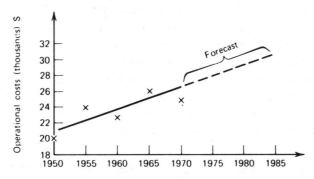

Semiaverage Method ►

Another simple numerical method that is not dependent upon an individual estimate is the semiaverage method. This makes use of the arithmetic mean ($\bar{x}$) for extending into future time a past data pattern.

Step 1. Split past data pattern of a time series into two equal parts. Compute totals (Σx) for each half. Divide totals by number of years in each semiperiod (N).

Year	Sales Volume (Millions $)	Semitotals	Semiaverage $\left(\bar{x} = \dfrac{\Sigma x}{N} \right)$
1953	10.0		
1954	10.5		
1955	11.2		
1956	12.0		
1957	13.4	→ 110.6	$\dfrac{110.6}{9} = 12.3$
1958	13.5		
1959	12.5		
1960	13.3		
1961	14.2		
1962	14.5		
1963	14.8		
1964	15.1		
1965	14.8		
1966	14.8	→ 137.9	$\dfrac{137.9}{9} = 15.3$
1967	15.2		
1968	16.0		
1969	16.1		
1970	16.6		

Step 2. Plot semiaverages and connect with a line.

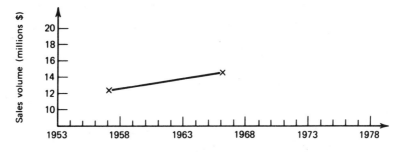

Step 3. Extend the drawn line to the period to be forecasted. (Sales volume for 1978 estimated at 18 million.)

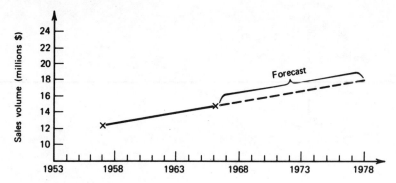

Method of Moving-Averages ►

In the moving-average method, the trend is obtained by smoothing out the fluctuations of the past data pattern by means of a moving-average. To obtain a 5-year moving-average, the first 5 years are added. Each succeeding total is computed by omitting the first year of the preceding period and including the year that follows the last year of the preceding period. The moving-average is computed by dividing each 5-year total by 5.

Step 1. Compute a series of moving totals by adding 5-year spans progressively (column 3).

Step 2. Compute an average for each total by dividing by 5 (column 4).

(1) Year	(2) Boxes Shipped (Number)	(3) 5-Year Moving Total	(4) 5-Year Moving-Average
1950	34	—	—
1951	62	—	—
1952	41	197	35.4
1953	22	207	41.4
1954	38	203	40.6
1955	44	207	41.4
1956	58	220	44.0
1957	45	252	50.4
1958	35	249	49.8
1959	70	276	53.2
1960	41	247	49.4
1961	55	274	54.8
1962	46	279	55.8
1963	62	306	61.2
1964	75	319	63.8
1965	68	331	66.2
1966	68	342	68.4
1967	58	343	68.6
1968	73	353	70.6
1969	76	—	—
1970	78	—	—

Step 3.   Plot the actual data and the 5-year moving-average (the trend).

Step 4.   Extend the trend line to the period to be forecasted. (Boxes shipped for 1980 is estimated at 100.)

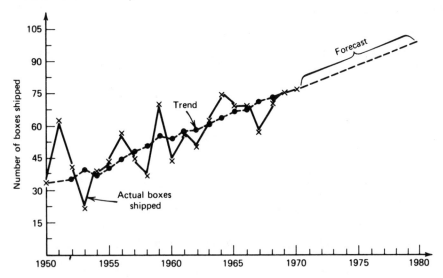

Trend Method of Least Squares ►

This method may be used to compute straight trend lines in a manner analogous to the three preceding methods. The main difference is that this approach uses a rigorous mathematical technique to determine the straight line. Estimates of trend are calculated in such a manner that the sum of squared deviations from actual data is at a minimum; hence the term *least squares*. It is based on the formula for a straight-line equation:

$$Y = a + bX$$

where

$$Y = \text{the variable undergoing a trend}$$
$$X = \text{the variable causing the trend}$$

Since X is the independent variable, estimates of long-time trend may be calculated as soon as the values of a and b have been determined. This is illustrated with the following example: The number of field districts that report equipment failures follows a data series. It is required to estimate the number of failures when 20 districts are reporting.

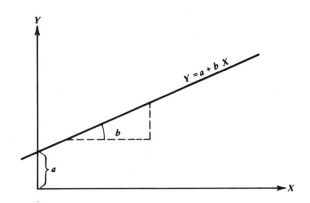

a = the value of *Y* when *X* is zero; height of the straight line above the horizontal axis.

b = the amount of change in *Y* that occurs with each change in *X*; the slope of the line.

N = total number of variables

Step 1.   Calculate values for *a* and *b*; failures = *a* + *b* (districts). This would generally be done using a standard computer routine. The results here would be:

$$a = .55$$

$$b = .64$$

Step 2.   Set up trend equation and calculate values for failure trend.

$$\text{Failures} = .55 + .64 \text{ (districts)}$$

Step 3.   Forecast using failure trend equation when 20 districts report.

$$\text{Failures} = .55 + .64 \,(20) = 13$$

Method of Exponential Smoothing ►

Any forecasting method attempts to smooth out fluctuations in a past data pattern. In exponential smoothing, the constant alpha (α) smooths the fluctuations by giving weight to the time period that appears significant. This method is based on the following exponential-smoothing forecast equation:

$$F_n = F_{n-1} + \alpha(Y_{n-1} - F_{n-1})$$

where

F_n =   forecast for next period

F_{n-1} =   forecast for previous period; can be calculated by a simple average of the most recent *N* observations. The moving-average can also be used.

Y_{n-1} =   actual value for latest period before forecast

α =   smoothing constant ($0 \leq \alpha \leq 1$)

$\alpha = 0.8$ when more weight given to recent values
$\alpha = 0.2$ when more weight given to past values

Exponential smoothing is a weighted-average method for allowing the forecaster to assign greater or lesser importance to an old forecast relative to current values. An example of this method is given with the following: The number of boxes shipped for the periods 1962, 1964, 1966, 1968, and 1970 is 44, 48, 56, 62, and 66 respectively. Estimate the number of boxes to be shipped in 1972.

Step 1. Determine forecast for previous period F_{n-1} by calculating a simple average between 1962 and 1968.

$$F_{1962\text{-}68} = \frac{\Sigma X}{N} = \frac{44 + 48 + 56 + 62}{4} = 52.5$$

Step 2. Establish actual value for the latest period before forecast (Y_{n-1}).

$$Y_{1970} = 66$$

Step 3. Decide on value for smoothing constant (α).

$$\alpha = 0.8 \text{ (heavy weight given to recent values)}$$

Step 4. Estimate the number of boxes to be shipped for 1972 with the exponential-smoothing forecast equation.

$$F_{1972} = F_{1962\text{-}68} + .8(Y_{1970} - F_{1962\text{-}68})$$
$$F_{1972} = 52.5 + .8(66 - 52.5)$$
$$F_{1972} = 63 \text{ boxes}$$

Fill in each blank with the correct answer.

1. _____ is the numerical forecasting method of extending into future time the average line found by plotting past data patterns.

Year	Boxes Shipped
1970	85
1971	64
1972	72
1973	79
1974	68
1975	65

2. In the chart at right, the 5-year moving average for 1972 is _____ .

3. The 5-year moving average for 1973 is _____ .

4. The two semiaverages for the data below are _____ and _____ .

Year	1964	1965	1966	1967	1968	1969	1970	1971	1972	1973	1974	1975
Sales (Million $)	4.3	4.7	5.1	5.2	4.9	4.8	5.4	5.5	5.8	5.2	4.7	4.6

5. _____ is a weighted-average method for allowing the forecaster to assign greater or lesser importance to an old forecast relative to current values.

• Checkpoint Answers

1. graphical extrapolation

2. $\dfrac{85 + 64 + 72 + 79 + 68}{5} = 73.6$

3. $\dfrac{64 + 72 + 79 + 68 + 65}{5} = 69.6$

4. $\dfrac{4.3 + 4.7 + 5.1 + 5.2 + 4.9 + 4.8}{6} = 4.8$ and $\dfrac{5.4 + 5.5 + 5.8 + 5.2 + 4.7 + 4.6}{6} = 5.2$

5. exponential smoothing

THREE MANAGEMENT FORECASTING MODELS

Management models are pictures of the situation that the manager manages. A model is a valid representation if it includes as much information as necessary for a particular purpose. It becomes an aid to seeing certain features of a system and to seeing the effects of the system when variables are forces of change. Models provide feedback to improve decisions, reduce uncertainty, identify conflicts, build confidence, and make predictions. It is this prediction function that is useful in improvement forecasting.

One limitation of the model is that it is oversimplified. The model has clearly defined boundaries, whereas the managerial situation is not so clearly separated from its environment. The model contains only a few variables and a few facts, whereas the managerial situation is a complex system of men, materials, money, machinery, and methods. The model, at best, is an attempted simulation of a situation. Through it, the manager wishes to test a decision or to see a certain cause-effect process.

A number of different types of models have been developed.[5] A brief discussion of three types follows.

Iconic or Physical Models ►

These are models that contain three-dimensional physical representations of a real situation. Physical models may be life-size, smaller, or larger. A scaled-model car is a miniature physical model of a real car. When several of these model cars are set on a street intersection designed to scale and are made to collide, a management model has been set up on the basis of which forecasts can be made as to possibilities for improving street design, setting up new traffic patterns, or both. A three-dimensional, scaled-down replica of a production system in which work flows as a result of equipment, people, machines, methods, and processes is a model of a managerial situation from which to judge the effects of changes in schedule, equipment locations, or work flow. A proposed layout is tested for improvements in the management model before making the real changes. Each part is constructed as a template and moved as a variable for distance, time, output, frequency, cost, and working conditions.

Graphic Models ►

Graphic models are two-dimensional graphic representations of a real situation. Usually they depict one aspect of the situation in such a way that it can be easily manipulated. Replacement-planning organization charts are graphic models. The divisions and the positions of the chart indicate the managerial situation. Transfers, promotions, retirements, and replacements by incumbents are the variables within the managerial situation that can be represented and moved around on the chart in order to find the best arrangement. In-flow process operations charts for production planning are graphic models demonstrating a situation needing change. On these charts the elements of operations, delays, storage, transportation, and inspection are manipulated to determine the effects of rearranging work to gain efficiency and increase motivation. Moving these variables provides insights into possible improvements over an existing situation. The breakeven chart is another graphic model. Fixed costs, variable costs, and total revenues are variables that can be moved in the chart in order to see how the breakeven point moves and what its effects on profits and losses are.

Network or Schematic Models ►

Network models deemphasize physical or visual relationships and stress connective input/output flow relationships. A network model provides an overview, showing the parts and the interactions among the parts. A systems flow results with network models. A computer program flow chart depicts the configuration that is necessary for data to flow and arrive at a set of computed results. A PERT network diagram (which we will discuss later) is a panorama of the events and activities necessary to complete a project. A method to change these events and activities is to manipulate time by either extending or contracting it.

◄ SUMMARY ►

Of the five MBO phases, the first is isolating objectives. The MBO manager should go about this phase in as explicit and thorough a manner as his resources permit. Vital to his effort is the application of various improvement forecasting techniques. It is MBO strategy to use these forecasts as a basis from which to collect alternatives for creating a management system.

Some of these forecasting techniques—like the consensus method, the problem-areas method, and the maximize opportunity method—are non-numerical. Others—including graphical extrapolation, the semiaverage method, the method of moving averages, the trend method of least squares, and the method of exponential smoothing—are numerical. There are also a number of management models for improvement forecasting. Iconic or physical models, graphic models, and network or schematic models are among these.

Most MBO managers take a multiple method approach, adopting those techniques that will be most useful for making the desired types of improvements. They engage in long-range, short-range, and immediate-range forecasting—trying to achieve the greatest immediate return that is consistent with their organization's long-term interests.

1. National Industrial Conference Board, *Forecasting Sales,* Studies in Business Policy No. 106, New York, 1964, pp. 12-62.

2. Alex F. Osborn, *Applied Imagination,* Scribner's and Sons, New York, 1953, pp. 227-243.

3. Lawrence D. Miles, *Techniques of Value Analysis and Engineering,* McGraw-Hill Book Co., New York, 1961, pp. 1-18.

4. Numerical methods for forecasting are presented in outline form. The reader is urged to consult with books such as the following for a more complete treatment.

   Steven C. Wheelwright and Spyros Makridakis, *Forecasting Methods for Management,* John Wiley and Sons, New York, 1973.

   Charles R. Relson, *Applied Time Series Analysis,* Holden-Day, San Francisco, 1973

5. James Riggs, *Economic Decision Models,* McGraw-Hill Book Co., New York, 1968, pp. 16-20.

Chapter 3 Review ─────────────────────────────

$V\!V$ Doublecheck

Answer briefly.

1. In what ways are explicitly stated objectives helpful?

   _____

   _____

   _____

   _____

   _____

2. Why are improvement forecasts necessary for the MBO manager?

   _____

   _____

   _____

   _____

   _____

3. What are the specific concerns of long-range, short-range, and immediate improvement forecasts?

   _____

   _____

   _____

   _____

   _____

4. Describe the consensus method of improvement forecasting.

   _____

   _____

   _____

   _____

5. Describe the problem-areas method of improvement forecasting.

_____

_____

_____

_____

_____

6. What are the four steps of the situation action method of improvement forecasting?

_____

_____

_____

_____

_____

7. What is value analysis?

_____

_____

_____

_____

8. What is the value of a decision matrix in choosing the best eliminator (alternative)?

_____

_____

_____

_____

9. Describe the method of moving averages.

_____

_____

_____

_____

10. What are management forecasting models and what purpose do they serve?

_____

_____

_____

_____

_____

11. Describe a graphic model of improvement forecasting.

_____

_____

_____

_____

_____

- Doublecheck Answers

1. Explicitly stated objectives enable the MBO manager to clearly relate his mission of improvement to that of the overall organization and to other departments. In addition, the explicitness provides a basis for evaluating progress. Without explicitly stated objectives, individual differences are never clearly identified and achieving the desired focus of effort becomes much more difficult.

2. Improvement forecasts become the basis from which the MBO manager selects alternatives for creating a management system. Since the philosophy of management by objectives involves setting objectives that stretch the organization's capabilities and that are in fact obtainable, good improvement forecasts are necessary in order to determine when such objectives have been developed. These forecasts also allow the organization to focus on those areas that can be attained and that represent the greatest value for the resources and capabilities extended.

3. Long-range improvement forecasts generally cover a time horizon of 5-15 years. Such forecasts deal with the fundamental issue of the organization's self preservation. This involves considering long-term trends for economic, social, and political indicators. The scope of short-range forecasts is governed by two considerations — the availability of useful and valid information and the importance of achieving an improvement within the desired period of time. Usually a 1 to 3-year period is covered by such forecasts. The immediate improvement forecast deals with urgent problems covering periods of three to twelve months. It involves setting up performance standards that can guide a manager, department, or organization to a specific improvement within a very short period of time.

4. The consensus method of improvement forecasting is a nonnumerical approach that relies on opinions held by a group, committee, or a conference concerning the future. It is based largely on the cumulative experience and intuition of the participants. The consensus approach combines and averages the contributions of each of these participants to find those that have a high consensus.

5. The problem areas method of improvement forecasting begins with the identification of areas in which problems recur and are difficult to solve. The types of problems facing the organization are analyzed in terms of their histories, their trends, and probabilistic occurrences. Future solutions are then identified in order to eliminate such problem trends once and for all.

6. The situation action forecasting model consists of four steps.
   a. Collecting effects from a situational analysis
   b. Determining causes of situational effects
   c. Finding eliminators of (alternative to) situational causes
   d. Choosing the best eliminator (alternative)

7. Value analysis is a useful approach in searching for alternatives. This approach considers procedures, products, and problems as causes and tries to identify their primary, secondary, and tertiary effects. An evaluation is made of how well the effects or functions are accomplished. On the basis of this, certain questions are asked about the value and nature of the causes. The value analysis approach enables the MBO manager to compare one function with another in terms of cost, quality, and time.

8. A payoff or decision matrix is a useful way to represent how the weights will be allocated to each standard of action in the final step of the situation action model. This approach is of

value in helping the manager to adequately compare alternatives and select the one most suited to that particular situation.

9. The method of moving averages is a numerical forecasting technique that smooths historical values in order to eliminate random fluctuation. This is done by computing an average of several past values and using that as the forecast or predicted value for the periods covered.

10. Three important classes of management forecasting models are

   a.   Iconic, or physical models
   b.   Graphic models
   c.   Network, or schematic models

These models are different ways of conceptualizing the manager's situation. They provide a representative but simplified picture of the situation that the manager manages. Such models facilitate testing of ideas and alternatives, serving much the same function as a scale model would for an engineer.

11. A graphic model of improvement forecasting is simply a graphic representation of a real situation. For example, a replacement planning organization chart would be a graphic model. Similarly, a breakeven chart or even a traditional organization chart is a graphic model. To make it an improvement forecasting model, it needs to represent the future at some specified period of time.

4. SETTING OBJECTIVES ————————————————————

Key Concepts

- *Characteristics of Good Objectives.* It is no simple task to develop a set of good objectives as part of the MBO process. Good objectives have certain characteristics regarding clarity, quantitative measures, motivational influence, selected focus, and performance stretch. These characteristics must be thoroughly understood by the MBO manager if objectives are to be defined and stated most effectively.

- *Performance Distribution.* The normal curve has been found in a wide range of empirical studies to represent the distribution of individual performance for a large number of individuals doing the same task. Based on the notion of the normal curve, it is possible to define a performance distribution. This is helpful in identifying individual managers and employees who fall into such categories as average, marginal, submarginal, and challenge. The aim of MBO is to continually shift the entire performance distribution upwards in order to achieve improved performance for the organization.

- *Continual Stresses.* Effective utilization of personnel means developing the latent potential of employees in a planned progression. Since objectives will be reviewed and updated on a regular basis, it is necessary in setting objectives to relate them to a planned and continual program that stretches individuals and the organization in their capabilities and skills.

Learning Objectives

After you have completed this chapter, you should be able to

- Formulate MBO objectives that are clear and, wherever possible, quantified.

- Limit the number of objectives to a critical few.

- Explain how objectives are selected for highest payoff.

- Explain how objectives are set for performance stretches.

- Describe six methods for interlocking objectives.

CLARITY IN MBO OBJECTIVES

To write a meaningful statement of objectives may seem a simple task. But evidence from many organizations reveals that it is not. They report that written objectives are more often fuzzy statements of commitments that eventually result in misunderstandings and misinterpretations. George Odiorne[1] observes this difficulty among many companies. Such statements of objectives are not explicit about the results to be accomplished, nor do they suggest a guide to action. Rather, they embody built-in comfort for those who wish to find a way to escape commitment.

The wording of statements of objectives is critical, since words carry different meanings for different people, depending on where or when they are used and who uses them. Words such as "total systems," "input," "indicator," "promotion," and "supervisor" pose such interpretive problems. And many other, more commonplace, words carry overlapping meanings and strong emotional connotations. One person, on the basis of his experience and education, may use these terms to mean something quite different from what his listener, on the basis of his own background, understands. The statement of objectives, since it is supposed to formalize the commitments of a number of people, should be formulated with such clarity that all those people understand what it is they are supposed to do and how they will know if they have done it. The statement must relate to those involved in terms of how they feel and what they think. To ignore this is to ignore the two-way communication that is necessary.

Being Specific ►

Inherent in certain generalities is a range of possibilities that no one can refute or reject, but that no one can pin down, either. Such generalities are called *motherhoods*. Motherhoods have a tendency to creep into statements of objectives because they sound good, are readily acceptable, and offer a comfortable distance and range. Managers also tend to use motherhoods either because they are uncertain about possible goals or because they lack the information necessary to pin down exactly what is required. Although motherhoods are an acceptable part of day-to-day management language, they should not be permitted in an MBO statement of objectives.

Sample Motherhoods

Improve managerial effectiveness	Streamline procedures
Achieve greatest efficiency	Achieve technological leadership
Increase profits	Complete planning for future requirements
Attain highest quality possible	Maintain good labor relations
Increase share of market	Cooperate in maintaining equipment
Continue existing management	Decrease delay time
Render better customer service	Increase sales volume
Improve delivery time	Communicate with other departments
Improve economic conditions	Provide more timely assistance
Complete study of new program	Develop cost awareness
Lower production costs	Maintain morale and attitudes

Quantifying Objectives ►

The more concrete the information an MBO manager can build into his objective statement, the more likely it is that he will be able to achieve a real meeting of minds among those involved. To refer again to the football analogy cited in Chapter 1, there is no ambiguity as to where the goal posts are located and in what direction the teams should travel. The field is marked so that each player can tell whether he is moving toward his objective or away from it. This precision brings clarity and meaning to football play. When management personnel do not know specifically where they are heading and how good a job they are doing, their results become divergent and their work inefficient.

These problems may be overcome by quantifying objectives. Quantification of motherhoods translates them to conditions that must exist when a job is well done. Therefore, to the greatest extent possible, objectives should be quantified.

Some Dimensions Useful in Quantifying

Time units	Phases
Frequency rates	Percentiles
Ratios	Quartiles
Index numbers	Deciles
Percentages or proportions	Mean deviations
Averages	Correlations
Number aggregates	Volume amounts
Degrees	Units of production

By including these dimensions within the objectives, the MBO manager indicates in precise, numerical terms the results that must be obtained. Furthermore, these dimensions can be broken down into subdivisions and projected on a time scale, providing points at which the status and progress toward achievement of the objective can be noted. For example, a 20 per cent cost reduction in office supplies within 4 months can be allocated at 5 per cent per month, and a progress chart can be developed to show present status and progress toward reaching this deadline.

Among the many advantages to quantifying objectives in the objective-setting process are:

- Quantified objectives define and clarify the elements of expected results better than any verbal description can hope to. They provide a better configuration of what is expected. "To improve morale" is a motherhood and a verbalized expectancy, but "to improve morale by reducing monthly grievance rate from 10 to 5" is a quantified objective and a specific target.

- Quantified objectives have a built-in measure of effectiveness. The process of measuring progress toward an end result is difficult, if not impossible, with qualitative statements. Using a measure to describe a future result also provides a way of measuring the current activities that will make it happen. Management can see the relationship among data, resources, and skills needed to deal with different situations.

- Quantified objectives can be enlarged or reduced for progressive performance stretches. This is hardly possible with verbal descriptions. An MBO manager can try to improve morale by reducing the grievance rate from 10 to 5 for the first year and then make a second-year effort to reduce the rate from 5 to 3. Reducing costs 10 per cent for the first year suggests a progressive reduction for subsequent years. Quantitative techniques give the statement an intrinsic manipulative value; that is, results can be manipulated as to both direction and the speed at which they are achieved.

- Quantified objectives help the MBO manager to figure out the specific means of bringing about desired results. To reduce the grievance rate from 10 to 5 implies the need for a sharper and better level of supervision. If training is necessary, how much will it cost? When can it be conducted? What will the program consist of? Implications of quantitative statements tend to make unknowns more knowable.

As suggested in the last chapter, there are also limitations to the quantification of objectives. Numbers are tricky. They may suggest a precision that does not exist, or they may oversimplify. Mathematics, statistics, and other quantifying techniques are not generally known by the average person. The liquidity ratio of current assets to current liabilities is an excellent quantified measure to use in an objective statement. It assumes, however, that everyone involved understands this measure, which often is not the case. Those who do not understand may regard the statement as impractical, or perhaps too theoretical. It may also be argued that quantification of human judgment is not entirely possible. One might say that the mechanical procedure offered by numbers is no substitute for an intuitive, experiential decision. Such intuitive decision-making should not be thrown out the window. Rather, it should be complemented by numerical methods.

These limitations are significant but do not outweigh the advantages and benefits offered by quantification. Insofar as it is possible, statements of objectives should be formulated carefully with built-in measures. You can use the following checklist to help ensure a clear formulation of objectives.

Is the Objective

☐ Defined in terms of results or conditions to be achieved rather than in terms of activities to be performed?

☐ Written so that it can be analyzed and reviewed from time to time?

☐ Limited in time so as to provide milestones of achievement?

☐ Written forcefully, starting out with such terms as *achieve, complete by,* and *replace,* which suggest results or performance stretches?

☐ Completed with an accountability assignment to a member of management?

☐ Formulated in the light of past experiences?

☐ Stated in positive terms, that is, in terms of what is to be done rather than in terms of what is to be avoided?

☐ Designed to cover a single end result and not a number of commitments?

☐ Communicated to managers involved when changed or modified?

☐ Designed to coincide work resources, facilities, and skills that are available?

☐ Planned to find the best fit among individuals and situations in deploying resources?

☐ Written to meet organizational improvement requirements, such as profits, opportunities, development of personnel, attainment of schedules, technical competency, and return on investment?

☐ Assigned a priority to foster a sense of importance and value in the organization?

☐ Documented to provide performance experience for future goal setting?

☐ Assigned a risk factor to indicate the level of confidence in completion?

☐ Written so as to be at least significant and perhaps critical to the individual as he carries out the responsibilities of his job?

☐ If possible, written in quantifiable terms that are easily measurable and hence, easily reportable?

☐ Designed as a commitment between the employee and his supervisor?

☐ Written to embody the basic ingredient of opportunity, which makes possible a leap forward in performance and results for the individual and the organization?

FOCUS IN MBO OBJECTIVES

How many objectives should an MBO manager set? What kinds of objectives should he be concerned with? Although different organizations vary considerably, their managers should limit their objectives, focusing on a few that are of most critical importance. Otherwise, the manager risks diluting his effort — spreading himself too thin. This is a common problem for beginning MBO managers.

> Review
> MBO Rule for Focus,
> page 26.

Limiting the Number of Objectives ►

There are several reasons why the number of objectives that should be pursued varies from organization to organization. First, the time period in which each organization seeks to reach its objectives varies. A chemical company may set objectives for its profit centers and major departments for 5 years; a restaurant chain may set the same kind of objectives but limit the time to 1 year. The time required to accomplish a given set of results will vary among organizations because the importance of their execution varies. Second, the nature of the job varies from organization to organization. Differences in product lines, types of markets, available resources, and organization size will cause corresponding differences in the number and type of responsibilities the chief executive, functional staff, managers, and supervisors must manage within their organizations. The president of a small organization that employs 500 has a job somewhat different from his counterpart whose organization employs 40,000. A company that deals in defense products has a different set of responsibilities from one that deals in nondefense products. Finally, the importance of achieving the objective will vary from organization to organization. Most organizations will agree that there are seven key result areas in which objectives should be specified. These areas are:

- Profitability and growth

- Market position and penetration

- Productivity

- Product leadership

- Employee morale, development, and attitudes

- Physical and financial resources

- Public responsibility

Few organizations will agree on the importance attached to each of the key areas within a given period of time. A pharmaceutical firm that has polluted a river for the past 10 years and is now concerned with possible litigation from the government and the community will place a greater emphasis on public responsibility within the next few years. A trucking firm that has experienced wildcat strikes and excessive labor grievances will give greater weight to improving employee attitudes, morale, and satisfaction. A small tool manufacturer that experienced a decline in defense contracts must give a great deal of attention to market position and product leadership. The number of objectives most suitable will be unique to each organization, because each differs in the type and number of improvements that must be made within a period of time. Each authority has his own definite idea about the number of objectives to be selected. Some have suggested that eight objectives for each of five major functions are appropriate.

Sample Objectives ►

The following lists contain objectives covering an entire organization, as well as objectives relating to the specific functions of finance, marketing, research and engineering, production, and personnel. Keeping the MBO Rule for Focus in mind, you may be able to use these lists as a guide in selecting the critical few objectives for your organization. Review each objective. Check off any that may apply to your situation. Then modify or complete the objective to fit your situation. You can use the comments section to explain in more detail.

Overall Organization

☐ Achieve a ___ per cent return on investment within ___ operating quarters.

☐ Reduce cost during the current operating year ___ per cent of approved budgets, prorated ___ per cent per quarter.

☐ Maintain current asset to current debt ratio not less than ___ for the next fiscal year.

☐ Achieve a net profit average at least ___ per cent of sales and ___ per cent of net worth.

☐ Increase market position for nondefense items from ___ per cent to ___ per cent; maintain market position for defense items at current levels.

☐ Achieve a product line mix in which ___ per cent of sales is made by no more than ___ per cent of R & D customers.

☐ Complete management controls reporting system of all operating divisions by _____ .

☐ Complete an operating and financial strategy statement for reaching objectives within ___ months for presentation to the board of directors.

☐ Obtain from research efforts two accepted improvements per month for 10 consecutive months to raise sales of product K ___ per cent.

☐ Reduce plant operating costs to $ ___ per 100 units produced by January 1.

☐ Develop technological capability to introduce two new products in market sector BB at end of 3-year profit plan.

☐ Reduce capital expenditures, class B, from $ _____ to $ _____ during the coming biennial.

● Comments

_____

_____

_____

_____

_____

Finance Objectives

☐ Reduce by ___ days the ___ -day time lag in preparation of division cost reduction reports using an agreed upon follow-through system.

☐ Achieve an average age of accounts receivable not to exceed ___ days.

☐ Restrict bad debt losses to less than ___ per cent of reporting nondefense sales.

☐ Improve margin by ___ per cent with same revenues but reduced costs of ___ per cent.

☐ Increase by ___ per cent the working cash required in each of ___ banks at the end of the year by holding inventory levels at 80 per cent capacity.

☐ Complete training of three replacements for key positions in accounting section by next June.

☐ Complete study and construct index of expense trends for all departments for the past 5 years and project anticipated expense of future at annual intervals. Set ___ per cent reduction targets from these projected expense trends.

☐ Collect ten suggested cost-reduction ideas per month from each of six operating managers.

☐ Complete write-up and acceptance of organization cost-reduction manual and distribute to all members of management within 2 months.

☐ Install ___ suggestion boxes in ___ locations to collect employee suggestions for cost reduction in their job procedures.

☐ Collect from ___ operating managers long distance telephone call analyses and recommendations for controls of number, type, and cost of calls.

☐ Reduce dollar value of cost of returned material credits from an average of $ ___ per month in the preceding year to $ ___ per month in the coming year.

☐ Reduce current debt to tangible net worth position to ___ per cent for proposed creditor portfolio.

☐ Reduce fixed assets to a level not to exceed ___ per cent of the tangible net worth in the next 2 years.

☐ Improve profits to payroll margin from ___ per cent to ___ per cent within the next four profit sharing quarters.

• Comments

_____

_____

_____

_____

Marketing Objectives

☐ Implement proposed system B for processing and expediting the filling of back orders at the rate of ten per month until 90 per cent of back orders are filled. Reinstate system A when back-order level is reached.

☐ Increase sales revenues of a new product ___ per cent within 12 months by concentrating existing expense levels of promotions in New England.

☐ Increase merchandise turnover in store from___to___within the current fiscal year.

☐ Hold sales expenses this coming year to ___per cent of total sales while increasing sales manpower ___ per cent.

☐ Secure 100 per cent distribution in markets D, E, and F of district 3.

☐ Convince three wholesalers to introduce new merchandising under a prearranged monthly schedule.

☐ Increase occupancy ratio in hotel rooms from a yearly mean of___to ___per cent while maintaining rate structure.

☐ Complete training program A for all district representatives to assure readiness for distributing product Y at the first of the year.

☐ Reduce average handling time of customer statements by ___per cent.

☐ Complete painting of ten trucks with new advertising campaign within 1 month.

☐ Complete___per cent follow-up calls of new inquiries within 3 days of initial inquiry.

☐ Reduce number of customer complaints on commercial business from___per cent to ___ per cent of orders billed. Dollars of settlement should not exceed___per cent of total commercial billing.

☐ Improve sales per employee to $___during the next 5-year profit plan.

☐ Achieve percentages of sales to consumer, industry, and government from ___, ___ , ___to ___, ___, ___, respectively.

☐ Complete a strategy statement within___ months for giving two new segments of the market brand X image to be introduced next season.

● Comments

_____

_____

_____

_____

_____

Research and Engineering Objectives

☐ Decrease research effort ratio of feasible marketing ideas to actual marketing products from____ to____within the coming fiscal year.

☐ Complete design and development of new prototype in____months within cost of $_____without farm-out work to vendors.

☐ Complete product design specification for product M within budgetary period.

☐ Supply three new products to marketing within the coming fiscal year, with forecasted sales not less than $_____.

☐ Get approval from three departments of production, plans for customer, costs, and schedule within 3 months.

☐ Complete PERT layout for contract B within the prebudgetary planning schedule.

☐ Complete value analysis job plan for three engineering sections during operating quarter.

☐ Increase diversification program with development and introduction of five new products within the small product line.

☐ Complete literature and patent search by end of year for five patentable ideas useful in entering new markets K, L, and M.

☐ Reduce research investment pay-out time from____to____years.

☐ Improve research know-how in section B by increasing Ph.D. hirings by____per cent.

☐ Reduce the R & D budget as per cent of net sales from____to____in the next 5-year profit plan while maintaining services and new product development.

☐ Maintain lead competitor's position in market with four new product introductions in the next 5-year profit plan.

● Comments

_____

_____

_____

_____

_____

_____

_____

Production Objectives

☐ Reduce frequency of lost time injuries from____to____per million man-hours within 6 months of installation of new safety awareness program.

☐ Maintain overtime hours at the level of____per cent of scheduled hours while completing emergency work program A.

☐ Reduce cost of pump and engine repairs from $_____to $_____per year per mechanic.

☐ Maintain a once-a-day contact with all subordinates at their work stations and hold a once-a-month work appraisal meeting in office with all subordinates.

☐ Complete construction of_____square feet,____-story approved addition to existing plan within cost of $_____by spring of next year.

☐ Master ten techniques in work simplification as related to machine-shop operations through a 6-month-by-month cost-reduction meeting for machine-shop supervisors.

☐ Reduce clerical labor costs in three departments by $_____with the installation of a data-processing system whose leasing and operational costs are not to exceed____per cent of the projected savings.

☐ Reduce weld rejects of Hy-80 steels from____per cent to____per cent of all plates in assembly S.

☐ Maintain total heat losses at____per cent of total heat transferred when changing from system A to system B.

☐ Deliver____units per day for less than $_____unit cost to shipping point B.

☐ Reduce inventory lead time from____weeks to____weeks while maintaining customer services.

☐ Reduce obsolete items and all adjustments to inventory to____per cent of commercial sales dollars.

☐ Complete master schedule of sales and inventories for fiscal year 19____to reduce stock-out frequency rate to____.

☐ Complete by next year a vendor rating system to maintain price, delivery, and reliability at or below an index established for the past 5-year record.

☐ Achieve for the machine shop a process layout by 19____ to reduce material-handling costs to____per cent of manufactured costs.

● Comments

_____

_____

_____

Personnel Objectives

☐ Select ____candidates in the third quartile from____trainees successfully completing supervisory training. These candidates to be temporarily appointed for 6 months at the new division.

☐ Reduce cost of recruiting each engineer from $____to $____while meeting requisition totals and dates.

☐ Complete preparations for labor negotiations by apprising all management personnel of needed contract changes; hold bimonthly meetings for discussions and conduct two simulated labor bargaining sessions to gain insights on strategy.

☐ At a cost not to exceed $_____ , conduct a sampling survey of the organization's hiring image in three adjacent labor markets.

☐ Complete for distribution at the end of a given month a 20-page, 10-topic industrial relations policy manual for newly hired employees.

☐ Decrease termination rate of clerical employees from____to____per cent.

☐ Increase outside correspondence answered from____to____per cent within 24 hours.

☐ Read 12 new books in management by the end of a year, at the rate of 1 per month.

☐ Complete course in statistics within the next semester with a grade of B or better.

☐ Set up and validate 5 standards of qualifications for new hourly employees.

☐ Complete within 3 months an attitude survey of labor-management relations among all employees, within cost of $_____.

☐ Reduce frequency of grievances by the end of the year from an annual average of____to____ .

☐ Complete planning, organization, and installation of an employee suggestion system at the start of next year's cost-reduction program.

☐ Complete training by December 19____ of ____ supervisors in 2-day seminars on managing by objectives.

☐ Reduce absenteeism record for next year from____ to____per cent.

• Comments

_____

_____

_____

_____

_____

Fill in each blank with true (T) or false (F).

1. In writing MBO objectives, a manager should consider the experience and education of those for whom the objective is intended. _____

2. To improve economic conditions is a good MBO objective because it permits a sensible range of interpretation. _____

3. The more concrete the information an MBO manager can build into his objective statement, the more likely it is that those involved will interpret it in a similar manner. _____

4. Quantified objectives define and clarify expected results better than any verbal description can hope to. _____

5. Quantified objectives may suggest a precision that does not exist. _____

6. All human judgments can be easily and accurately quantified. _____

7. The nature of the product should have no effect on the number and kind of MBO objectives a manufacturer sets. _____

8. If two departments set similar objectives, they should always set them for a similar time period. _____

9. The MBO manager should set only those objectives that are of most critical importance. _____

10. Public responsibility is one valid area in which an MBO manager should consider setting objectives. _____

───────────────────────────────

● Checkpoint Answers

1. T   2. F   3. T   4. T   5. T   6. F   7. F   8. F   9. T   10. T

COST IMPROVEMENT IN MBO OBJECTIVES

In practice, the improvement forecasts described in Chapter 3 are bound to yield several objectives with equal or nearly equal appeal. The MBO decision-maker is then faced with a situation in which he must select the objective or objectives that will give him

Review
MBO Rule for Progressive
Cost Improvement,
page 34.

the greatest return on his investments of time, money, and resources. Additionally, there may be long-standing objectives that he wishes to retain. For example, he may wish to maintain stable employment at a certain level, retain product leadership with percentage of the market, and reserve good labor relations. The MBO decision-maker is faced with a list of attractive goals from which he must select those critical few that will maximize his gain.

Calculating a Payoff Array ►

A useful guide for the MBO manager who wishes to select those objectives that will yield the greatest gain from a wide assortment of possibilities is to assign relative values and weights to these objectives. Through this method, he can get an idea of the whole picture, the pattern formed by all the possibilities together. This usually requires arranging the assortment of objectives and weighing them according to utility or payoff.[2] The *payoff array* is a list of objectives according to some expected value. It shows those objectives that have higher payoffs and those that have lower ones. Of course, payoff is relative; the value of anything depends upon its utility to the person who has it or wants it. Money is not an entirely objective measure of value, because the value of money will depend on its utility to whoever has it or wants it. For example, the importance of money will decrease in proportion to the amount already possessed or increase in proportion to the amount needed. So payoff values or weights may be assigned according to other criteria, as well. But the selection of cost improvement as a utility criterion is common, and it is the one that is illustrated in the table.

Assortment of Objectives	Cost Improvement (Dollars)	Probability of Occurrence (Percentage)	Expected Payoff (Dollars)
Objective 1	d_1	p_1	$d_1 p_1$
Objective 2	d_2	p_2	$d_2 p_2$
Objective 3	d_3	p_3	$d_3 p_3$
Objective 4	d_4	p_4	$d_4 p_4$
Objective 5	d_5	p_5	$d_5 p_5$
Objective k	d_k	p_k	$d_k p_k$

To make a choice among various possibilities involves an awareness of the probability of occurrence of each of those possibilities. This means risk. Risk is always present when deciding on some future event or some expected value. The higher the risk of failure, the lower the expected value; conversely, the lower the risk of failure, the higher the expected value, assuming equal dollars among all objectives.

> To find the expected payoff of a potential objective, multiply that objective by its probability of occurrence. To find the expected payoff of a cost improvement, the formula is:
>
> Cost
> Improvement X of Occurrence = Payoff
> (Dollars)
>
> Probability
> (Percentage)
>
> Expected
> Payoff
> (Dollars)

For example, an objective which contributes $20,000 in reduced costs with an 80 per cent probability of occurence has an expected payoff of $16,000.

$$\$20,000 \times .80 = \$16,000$$

In the same way, an objective which contributes $50,000 in reduced costs with a 20 per cent probability of occurrence has an expected payoff of $10,000. This procedure is continued until all of the objectives have an expected payoff. The MBO manager will then be able to tell at a glance at his payoff array which objective has the highest expected payoff.

Probabilities of occurrence should be assigned on the basis of past experience and historical data. Subjective assignments can be made in the absence of objective data, provided a validation procedure is followed. This may take the form of a test sample or group verification.

Finding a Rank-Order Correlation Coefficient ►

Once the payoff array has been calculated, the objectives should be reorganized in order of payoff. The objective with the highest expected payoff is assigned the rank of 1, and so on. Then, the use of a second criterion for the same assortment of objectives will yield a second list of expected payoff with a subsequent rank order of its assortment of objectives. For example, if "time of completion" is used as a criterion of utility, a second array of expected payoff can be calculated and arranged in rank-order ascending or descending payoff, similar to the array for expected payoff of cost improvement. At this point, the MBO practitioner may wish to investigate whether a correlation exists between the two ranks. If the correlation is high, it suggests that the high-ranking objectives on both arrays are strongly associated with both criteria. If the correlation is low, it suggests that the objectives have little or no association with both criteria. This aids the decision-makers in selecting the objectives that represent the vital few.

The rank-order correlation coefficient,[3] which is a measure of association between two utility criteria in a payoff array, is calculated as follows:

Step 1. Rank the objectives. Ten objectives, whose expected payoff is calculated according to the procedure explained in the last section, are ranked from 1 to 10 for each of two criteria: cost improvement and time necessary for completion. Those with highest payoff are assigned rank 1, and those with lowest payoff receive 10. This results in two separate ranks from 1 to 10.

Step 2. Calculate rank-order correlation. Using the rank-order correlation formula, calculate the rank-order correlation coefficient rho (ρ),

$$\rho = 1 - \frac{6 \, \Sigma \, d^2}{N(N^2 - 1)}$$

where N is the number of objectives that are ranked, d is the difference between the ranks, and Σd^2 is the summing of the differences squared.

Objectives	Ranks Cost Improvement	Time for Completion	Difference d	d^2
O_1	1	6	-5	25
O_2	2	3	-1	1
O_3	3	7	-4	16
O_4	4	2	2	4
O_5	5	1	4	16
O_6	6	8	-2	4
O_7	7	4	3	9
O_8	8	9	-1	1
O_9	9	5	4	16
O_{10}	10	10	0	0
Total			O	$\Sigma d^2 = 92$

$$\rho = 1 - \frac{6 \times 92}{10(100-1)} = .442$$

Step 3. Assess the correlation coefficient. The size or magnitude of the coefficient of correlation can be interpreted as the strength of association of a set of objectives with two different sets of expected payoff. A positive perfect correlation, $\rho = +1$, means perfect utility. A negative perfect correlation, $\rho = -1$, means perfect inverse utility. A zero correlation, $\rho = 0$, means no association between the ranks. Values between these limits may be interpreted as follows:

Size of ρ	Utility
.00 to .20	Little or no value
.20 to .40	Slight association
.40 to .60	Useful value
.60 to .80	Substantially useful
.80 to 1.00	Very high and definite value

Thus, the rank-order correlation procedure can be a useful guide for the MBO practitioner to measure the value of two sets of expected payoff arrays. In this problem, the coefficient .442 suggests that a useful association exists between the objective and the two criteria of cost and time.

Often a variety of criteria can be employed to search for expected payoff in many areas. The rank-order correlation coefficient can be an aid to finding which criteria are closely associated with each other. If this procedure is followed, the reader can see that an optimization occurs among several selected criteria.

PERFORMANCE STRETCH IN MBO OBJECTIVES

The MBO performance stretch must be designed to fit the latent potential within the individual rather than potential within a group. Each individual should be helped to find a challenge at his own particular level — a challenge neither too difficult nor too easy — and this challenge must be

Review MBO Rule for Performance Stretch, page 37.

related to the challenges accepted by others in the same group. That is, the level of challenge for an individual must be set as high as he can reach but must also fall within a range acceptable to the group. Group norms tend to give validity to the challenge level. They also tend to function as gauges for measuring individual performance. Although people differ widely in their ability to work and produce, an individual is always subject to the influences of the group in which he works. The group often strikes its own level of minimum or maximum acceptable performance. Such group effects on setting performance stretches within objectives need not be deleterious if it has been made clear that performance stretch is expected by all members of management.

Understanding the Normal Curve►

The normal curve has been a useful device for setting challenging objectives and for relating these challenges to a group. This curve, which is bell shaped, offers a method of distributing a large number of people according to the laws of probability. This is so because the normal curve occurs so frequently in practice that it makes sense to use it as a guide in defining such categories as *average region* and *marginal region* when setting objectives. The curve in Figure 1 suggests that 16 per cent of the members of any group will set and attain objectives in the challenge region, as far as group norms are concerned. Within the whole group, 84 per cent — all those above the marginal region — will achieve individual stretches of varying levels of difficulty.

1. Normal Curve — Estimated Percentage of Personnel That Will Perform at Various Levels of Difficulty.

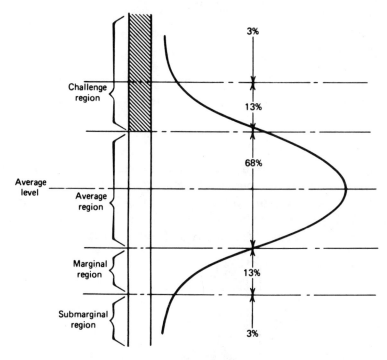

Applying the MBO Rule for Performance Distribution►

If the performance distribution of an entire group is known, the built-in performance stretch of each individual within the group can be more easily fit in. One way to find the performance distribution within a group is to follow the *MBO Rule for Performance Distribution Within a Group.*

MBO Rule for Performance Distribution Within a Group

1. Identify the best performer within a group. Validate this by comparing with other similar groups.

2. Identify the poorest performer within a group. Validate this by comparing with other similar groups.

3. Establish a midpoint performance level between the two.

4. Average performers of a group (68 per cent) will be clustered around the midpoint.

5. High performers of the group (16 per cent) will be above the midpoint.

6. Low performers of the group (16 per cent) will be below the midpoint.

Barnes and Anderson[5] provide a useful guide to establishing the performance level mentioned in step 3. According to them, the ratio of best operator to worst operator is 2 to 1. In other words, the capacity of the best operator is roughly twice that of the poorest. For example, a supervisor has fourteen electrical workers in his group. The best performer can wire 20 units per day. The poorest performer can wire 10 units per day. The supervisor can establish the performance distribution of his group as follows: ten workers will wire, on the average, 15 units per day; two workers will wire between 15 and 20 units; two workers will wire between 10 and 15 units. Thus the MBO Rule for Performance Distribution Within a Group provides a framework to assist in setting the challenge level of each individual as he relates to his group.

Planning Continual Stretches►

Effective utilization of personnel means developing the latent potential of employees in a planned progression. This means a continual and orderly development and release of the potential of employees.

This process of stretching continually for greater achievements has an effect on those of the lower levels of performance. There will always be a submarginal region, 3 per cent of the group shown in Figure 2, representing deadwood — people the organization cannot justify keeping on the payroll. These people are unable or perhaps unwilling to make the progressive performance stretch required by the organization. The process of stretching for improvement as a full-time job — month to month, year to year — will always uncover 3 per cent deadwood. This is because the performance of the entire organization is constantly shifting upward.

2. Weighing Objectives in a Payoff Array

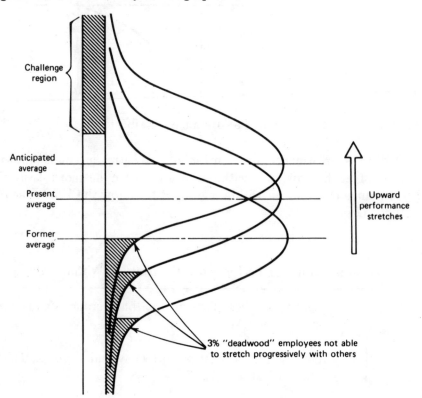

Challenge region

Anticipated average

Present average

Former average

Upward performance stretches

3% "deadwood" employees not able to stretch progressively with others

$\sqrt{}$Checkpoint: Setting Cost Improvement and Performance Stretch————————

Fill in each blank with the correct answer.

1. If the MBO manager must choose among objectives of nearly equal appeal, he should pick those objectives that will give him the greatest return on his investments of

    _____ , _____ , and _____ .

2. To find out which objectives will yield him the greatest gains, he should

    assign _____ values to each of them.

3. This usually requires arranging the objectives in a _____ and weighing them according to utility.

4. The formula for this is

    Cost   Probability   _____
    Improvement X of Occurrence $=$ _____
    (Dollars)   (Percentage)   _____

5. In the absence of objective data for the probability of occurrence, _____ assignments can be made.

6. The _____ is a measure of association between two criteria in a payoff array.

7. According to the normal curve, _____ per cent of any group will set and attain objectives in the challenge region.

8. The MBO performance stretch must be designed to fit the latent potential within

    the _____ , rather than the potential within the _____ .

9. In setting MBO objectives, the challenge to the individual must always fall within a range acceptable to the _____ .

10. The first two steps of the MBO Rule for Performance Distribution Within a Group are to identify the _____ and the _____ within a group.

11. Average performers constitute about _____ per cent of a group.

12. The output of the best performer is roughly _____ that of the poorest.

● Checkpoint Answers

1. time, money, resources   2. relative   3. payoff array   4. Expected Payoff (Dollars)   5. subjective
6. rank-order correlation coefficient   7. 16   8. individual, group   9. group   10. best performer, worst performer
11. 68   12. twice

INTERLOCKING OF MBO OBJECTIVES

To create an MBO system within an organization, a manager needs to develop an objective network in which all feeder-objectives are aligned and interlocked with each other. This alignment and interlocking must begin where the objective-setting process takes root. There appears to be a

<table>
<tr><td>Review
MBO Rule for
Interlocking Objectives,
page 32.</td></tr>
</table>

variety of entry points to the network process, and each organization must decide for itself which is the most feasible and practical. The following means of entry are used by many organizations:

- Profit plan approach

- Budgeting approach

- Top-down, bottom-up approach

- Common objective approach

- Appraisal by results approach

- Job descriptions approach

The search for organizational coordination is an intense one. To get unity of action among management levels, functions, and personnel is a formidable challenge. In this search, an organization will often use a combination of these approaches for interlocking objectives.

Profit Plan Approach ▶

A profit plan's basic objective is to target and reach a desirable return on investment. A management group must target a profit level and keep their operations pointed in that direction. This group never loses sight of their objective: to finish a period of time with a profit. In the past, profit plans were often nothing more than fiscal plans. Financial objectives were set, and operating plans were evolved by functional heads to describe how the financial objectives were to be reached. This traditional profit-planning approach has a basic flaw, however. It fails to provide a motivational vehicle through which all members of the staff can align and interlock with these objectives. In other words, it fails to develop a motivational approach to profits, which in an MBO system, should be a responsibility of all members of management. A profit plan could be an excellent vehicle for relating, involving, and committing personnel. Financial objectives should be a major part of the plan, but other objectives and targets from the major functions should be included.

> Each functional manager, rather than evolving an individualized "how to" operational plan, must develop a set of objectives that becomes a part of the organization's profit plan. Specific objectives are set up, aligned, and interlocked by such functions as marketing, engineering, manufacturing, research, quality control, industrial relations, and purchasing.

Budgetary Approach►

Under the MBO system, as under traditional systems, the accounting department has been a key area in initiating the objective-setting process through budgets and financial commitments. A budget is a plan for allocating and controlling resources to meet an expected schedule. Good MBO budgeting processes require participation and involvement by all groups responsible for the budget.

Comprehensive budgeting[6] is profit planning via the budgetary approach. It is an annual profit plan documented by several accounting statements that indicate expected profit position. Comprehensive budgeting is also called "drawing up a master budget." The sections or schedules included are the following:

- The budgeted income statement, which is a summary of income and expenses targeted within a coming period

- The budgeted balance sheet, which is the anticipated financial position of the organization on the closing date of the plan and in which assets, liabilities, and capital are projected for the period

- The supplementary budgets, such as capital budgets, overhead budgets, cash budgets, sales budgets, operating budgets, and long-range budgets, which are included as expected positions of the organization in a future period.

Thus the accounting sections of an organization, through budgeting performance analysis, can start the objective-setting process with appropriate schedules and participation.

Top-Down Bottom-Up System►

The president of any organization occupies a unique and important position. From his vantage point, he can oversee the entire operation as well as the parts of which it is composed. He is like the storyteller of Chapter 1, who sees both the whole elephant and its different parts. The president or general manager must make each of his subordinates understand that, although the subordinate's individual part description is correct, he cannot describe the entire operation correctly on the basis of it. The president or general manager is the one who has the overall view of operations and can judge how well they are going. The top-down system of initiating the objective-setting process requires that the president not only recognize the overall view but specify his own objective at the start of the problem solution. His position as president is symbolic. He initiates improvement in a common problem area and directs each succeeding level to provide subobjectives designed to meet the requirements of the preceding level. This process is continued until all levels are involved. Once the objective-setting process reaches the first-line supervisors, their objectives are passed up the line for coordination and approval.

The process is described as follows:

1. General manager A conducts a situation analysis with his B staff. This involvement eventually leads to long- and short-range objectives for the entire enterprise, in the areas of profit, return on investment, cost reduction, sales volume, and new products.

2. B conducts a situation analysis with his C staff using A's objectives as major targets to support. This involvement with B's staff eventually leads to long- or short-range subobjectives for the lower to middle levels in the areas of forecasting, organizing resources, controlling, and operating.

3. C conducts a situation analysis with his D staff using B's objectives as major targets. This involvement eventually leads to feeder-objectives for the lower levels in such areas as cost, schedules, personnel, production methods, and motivation.

4. D, on the last level, begins the validation process by assuring his immediate superior C that the work implied by C's objectives can be accomplished. C assures his immediate superior B that the work implied by B's objectives can be accomplished. B assures his immediate superior A that the work implied by A's objectives can be accomplished.

5. The assurance process, which builds confidence and reduces the risk of failure, requires dialogues and conferences in which the participating managers enter into give and take discussions and make tradeoffs, concessions, and adjustments. This process cannot be exclusively top-down or bottom-up; rather, it is top-down, bottom-up, and sideward as well. Managers at all levels have an opportunity to review and influence the content of the objective before its adoption.

> In practice, interlocking commitments to levels is far more difficult than implied here. The business of tradeoffs and concessions can become quite intense and disruptive. This is to be expected since coordinating and interlocking mean aligning individual drives and goals with overall goals of the organization.

Common Objective Approach►

The common objective approach to entering the objective-setting process requires that all managers set their objectives simultaneously and independently. A directive is issued to all managers to get together with their subordinates by a predetermined date and agree on a set of objectives for a future period. It is requested that these objectives be submitted to an individual who is designated the *objective coordinator*. His responsibility is to collect and categorize objectives acording to content, level, and functions. Common objectives, as well as related objectives, are identifed, clarified, and accepted by the submitting managers. Those objectives that do not contain common or related elements are either discarded or negotiated. There are interface areas where agreement is a must. For example, the selling of complex, technical products should not be split up between salesmen and engineers because both are responsible for developing and marketing new products that give consumer satisfaction. It is a senseless battle to find out who is accountable for poor sales of the new product.

The objective coordinator functions as a catalyst to assure that interfaces and common areas are brought together. Additionally, he sees that overlapping and divergent objectives are brought into a single direction through negotiation and tradeoffs. Those objectives that cannot be brought into a common alignment are discarded from the objective program. The objective coordinator makes sure that progress and results are maintained during the implementation phase. He resolves disputes and helps individuals fulfill their commitments.

Appraisal by Results Approach►

The appraisal by results approach has been widely adopted because it is useful in reviewing performance in stimulating motivation. It is generally spearheaded by the personnel department. There are several variations of this approach. The most prevalent variation is that in which the focus is on both a manager and an employee. The two begin the process by deciding jointly on ways performance can be improved. Jointly they develop short-term and long-term projects and ways in which performance can be measured. Plans for implementation are evolved and approved.

When the implementation period is completed, the employee evaluates what he has done and discusses it with the manager. The process is repeated for the next period with a set of new performance objectives for the individual. A comprehensive appraisal conference by superior and subordinate on results achieved forms the basis for setting new objectives for the next period. The process repeats itself through a cycle of performance review, objective setting, plan evolution, performance, performance appraisal, and setting of new objectives.

In another variation of this approach, the appraisal by results will be made through group participation. The manager will discuss with his entire group ways and means whereby performance can be improved. With his group, the manager develops a network of performance targets, each individual setting his own goals to reach those targets. This group process moves through the hierarchy so that eventually the entire organization is setting objectives for a coming period.

> The MBO appraisal by results approach focuses on improvement of employees' performance. It provides a means through which an employee can understand what is expected of him and how he should go about achieving it. Interlocking occurs in the objective-setting process through superior-subordinate or through superior-group relationships. A superior must set objectives jointly with his subordinates. He must also set objectives jointly with his boss. Thus interlocking occurs through people and throughout the levels of the organization.

Job Descriptions Approach►

The problems of interlocking and alignment in an organization are problems of relating the organizational role each manager plays. The organization chart shows what the basic divisions of work are and who reports to whom. It does not give details as to what each individual is expected to do. The *position description*, which is a first derivative of the organization chart, details the duties and tasks to be performed by the individual. Position descriptions are concerned with defining an individual's tasks rather than with detailing how these tasks are carried out. Traditionally, the position description has failed to describe how the individual's responsibilities and tasks relate to and interact with other members of the group and the organization. Traditionally, they have been written in such a way as to suggest complete independence from other positions. As a result, no common framework for relating and interlocking with other members of the group has been established.

Recently, however, position descriptions have come to be regarded as other than fixed statements of responsibilities. The new, dynamic view is that responsibilities change not only in terms of the requirements of the organization but also in terms of the relationships and roles of other individuals. Under this new approach to position descriptions, personal and functional relationships among superiors, peers, and subordinates are first identified through participation and group discussion. Positions, functions, and duties are related within an organization framework.

The objective-setting process begins with functional objectives at the higher levels of management. The process goes on through each subsequent level, defining and establishing relationships in position descriptions. The position descriptions are written flexibly to include:

• Objectives to be completed

• Performance standards necessary to reach objectives

• Duties required to meet both the standards and the objectives

Thus the new approach to position descriptions provides one method of interlocking and aligning various individuals in the organization.

◄SUMMARY►

There is a tendency among managers to regard the second phase of the MBO system — setting objectives — as simple. Actually, it is a demanding task. Not the least of the difficulties lies in formulating objectives that are clear and, if possible, quantified. If this is not done, employees may not really understand what they are expected to do and when it must be done. The MBO manager should also take care to set only a limited number of objectives; otherwise he may end up spreading himself too thin. Additionally, the MBO manager must know how to pick those objectives that have the highest potential payoff.

Besides these considerations, the MBO manager must consider the motivation of those who will carry out the objectives. He can do this by designing performance stretch into the objectives and by interlocking these objectives into a network.

1. George S. Odiorne, *Management by Objectives,* Pitman Publishing Co., New York, 1965, pp. 122–126.

2. William Emory and Niland Powell, *Making Management Decisions*, Houghton Mifflin Co., 1968, pp. 109 – 113.

3. George A. Ferguson, *Statistical Analysis in Psychology and Education*, McGraw-Hill Book Co., New York, 1959, pp. 179–183.

4. The normal probability distribution curve needs no justification here since it is a reasonable estimate of how human attributes are distributed in the population. If a large aggregate of performers were arranged along a baseline according to magnitude of performance, the vertical frequency scale would approximate the normal curve. For a thorough discussion of this see R.M. Barnes, *Motion and Time Study,* John Wiley, 1968, pp. 380–387; Clifton A. Anderson, "Performance Rating," *Industrial Engineering Handbook,* McGraw-Hill Book Co., New York, 1963, pp. 3–65; J.C. Nunnally, *Educational Measurement and Evaluation,* McGraw-Hill Book Co., New York, 1964, pp. 41–52.

5. R.M. Barnes and Clifton A. Anderson, *op. cit.* (see note 4).

6. Stephen Landekich, "Budgeting," in H. B. Maynard (ed.), *Handbook of Business Administration,* McGraw-Hill Book Co., New York, 1967, pp. 10–37.

Chapter 4 Review

✔✔ Doublecheck

Draw lines to match each description in the first column with the correct method for interlocking MBO objectives in the second column.

1. All managers set their objectives simultaneously and independently.

2. Useful in reviewing performance in stimulating motivation.

3. Makes use of an objective coordinator.

4. Makes use of a position description which details the tasks to be performed by the individual.

5. Requires that the president not only recognize the overall view, but specify his own objective at the start of the problem solution.

A. Profit Plan Approach

B. Budgeting Approach

C. Top-Down, Bottom-Up Approach

D. Common Objective Approach

E. Appraisal by Results Approach

F. Job Descriptions Approach

Answer briefly.

6. In setting MBO objectives, why should you avoid motherhoods?

_____

_____

_____

_____

_____

_____

7. Why should objectives be quantified wherever possible?

_____

_____

_____

_____

_____

_____

8. What are some of the factors that influence the number and kind of objectives an organization sets?

_____

_____

_____

_____

9. In very general terms, describe how an MBO manager, faced with a number of equally attractive objectives, might go about selecting those that will give him the greater return on his investments of time, money, and resources.

_____

_____

_____

_____

10. In what ways should an MBO objective be tailored to the individual? How must the objective be related to the group?

_____

_____

_____

_____

11. Describe the MBO Rule for Performance Distribution Within a Group.

_____

_____

_____

_____

12. Describe the following methods of interlocking objectives.

    a.   Top-down, bottom-up approach

_____

_____

_____

_____

_____

    b.   Common objective approach

_____

_____

_____

_____

_____

    c.   Appraisal by results approach

_____

_____

_____

_____

_____

1. D   2. E   3. D   4. F   5. C

6. Motherhoods have a tendency to creep into statements of objectives, because they sound good, are readily acceptable, and offer a comfortable distance and range. Motherhoods should be avoided because they mean different things to different people and lack specificity; they are too general to provide a basis for critically evaluating performance.

7. The more concrete the information an MBO manager can build into his objective statements, the more likely it is that he will be able to achieve a real meeting of minds among those involved. Quantified objectives define and clarify elements of expected results; they provide a built-in measure of effectiveness; they can be enlarged or reduced for progressive performance stretches; and they aid the MBO manager in identifying specific needs of bringing about desired results.

8. Some of the factors that influence the number and kind of objectives an organization sets are: the time period in which the organization seeks to reach its objectives, the current status of the organization, its existing environment and capacities, and the personalities of those involved.

9. The first step in evaluating a number of attractive objectives is to identify criteria that can be used to discriminate among them and on which the objectives can be ranked. In order to do these rankings, it is necessary to compute the expected payoff of each objective on each criteria. This involves multiplying the probability of achieving the objective times the payoff, if the objective is achieved. Once these rankings have been developed on each of the several criteria, the rank-order correlation can be computed to help determine which criteria are most closely related and consistent with what the organization is trying to achieve. Finally, judgment must be applied in determining which objectives are most important and most relevant to the MBO manager and his organization.

10. MBO objectives must be made in consideration of what the individual can accomplish in a specified period of time. They must also be aligned with the individual's personal objectives, in order to increase the chances of the organization's objectives being accomplished. Through interlocking objectives and through selecting personnel and assigning responsibilities in light of personal and organizational objectives, it is possible to more closely match the objectives of individuals and the organization.

11. The MBO Rule for Performance Distribution Within a Group has six steps:

    a. Identifying the best performer within the group

    b. Identifying the worst performer within the group

    c. Establishing a midpoint performance level between the best and the worst performance

    d. Identifying the average performers (68 per cent) clustered around the midpoint level

    e. Distinguishing high performers as the 16 per cent above the average group

    f. Identifying low performers as the 16 per cent below the average group

12. a. The top-down, bottom-up approach begins by starting at the top of the organization and specifying objectives that are then passed to the next lower level. After this is done down through the organization, feeder objectives for the lower levels in such areas as cost, schedule, personnel, production methods and motivation are developed. The process then moves back up through the higher levels of the organization, in order to validate the objectives and to ensure that commitment has been obtained for them.

    b. The common objective approach to entering the objective setting process requires that all managers set their objectives simultaneously and independently. The objectives are then brought together by an objective coordinator and common objectives are identified, clarified, and accepted by the various MBO managers. Those objectives that do not contain common or related elements are either discarded or subjected to negotiation to reach agreement on a common set of objectives.

    c. The MBO appraisal by results approach focuses on improvement of employees' performance. The process begins by the manager and the employee deciding jointly on ways performance can be improved. Working together, they develop short-term and long-term projects and ways in which performance can be measured over time. Plans for implementation are then developed and approved. When the implementation period is completed, the employee sits down with the manager and discusses what has been accomplished.

ALPHA CONCRETE PRODUCTS, INCORPORATED

Early in 1976, Mr. Rick Woodbury, President and General Manager of Alpha Concrete Products was contemplating how he might use the long-range forecasts of company sales that had recently been prepared by a local consulting firm. He was particularly concerned about relating those to the company's plan and setting up performance measures and budgets that would allow them to do even better than had been projected. As shown below, the consulting firm had not only provided a sales forecast for each of the next five years but had also supplied a confidence interval within which they were 90% certain that the actual sales would fall.

ALPHA Sales Forecasts with Confidence Intervals*

Year	Sales Forecast	Confidence Interval (90%)
1976	13,580,000	12,200,000 - 14,860,000
1977	14,364,000	13,084,000 - 15,644,000
1978	15,232,000	13,900,000 - 16,530,000
1979	15,993,000	14,687,000 - 17,300,000
1980	16,854,000	15,537,000 - 18,171,600

*Based on regression analysis

Obviously, Rick was anxious to be near the high end of that interval for each year. In addition, Rick was anxious to improve the firm's profitability, and he had collected historical data for the most recent five years relating to the company's income statement. This data is presented below in terms of the percentage breakdown of expenses and profit items for each year.

ALPHA's Historical Cost Structure*

	1970	1971	1972	1973	1974	1975
Net Sales	100.0	100.0	100.0	100.0	100.0	100.0
Cost of Sales	66.1	66.1	65.5	66.2	62.7	65.5
Gross Profit	33.9	33.9	34.5	33.8	37.3	34.5
Selling, G & A	24.8	28.0	22.3	23.1	20.9	20.8
Operating Profit	9.1	5.9	12.2	10.7	16.5	11.7
Interest Expense	2.3	2.8	2.3	2.4	1.8	2.2
Pretax Income	7.1	4.6	9.2	7.9	15.3	13.0
Income Taxes	3.4	2.3	4.6	3.7	7.3	5.8
Net Income	3.7	2.3	4.6	4.2	8.0	7.2

*Costs as a per cent of sales.

Alpha was in the business of manufacturing concrete pipe and reinforced concrete boxes used in highway, utility, and farm construction. The company maintained three production facilities — one each in Utah, Colorado, and Idaho. Sales were handled through the company's own distributors located throughout the Intermountain area. Approximately two thirds of the company sales had gone to the major Intermountain public utilities in recent years, with the balance going to mostly agricultural construction in the Idaho region and to about an equal mix of highway and agricultural construction in other regions. In 1975, total annual sales came 60 per cent from Utah, 22 per cent from Idaho, and 18 per cent from Colorado.

While the company generally submitted bids on all the major projects in its marketing area, it was awarded only about 30 per cent of those contracts. In aggregate, such major contracts accounted for over 80 per cent of its volume. The company had noticed in the past that the total volume of bid requests was growing at a modest rate each year. However, the fraction of bid requests from each of the major market segments — utilities, highways, and agricultural — varied substantially from year to year.

In the previous two years, Alpha Concrete Products had used as a basis for its forecasting and preparation of long-range plans the following set of objectives.

1. To increase the company's share of the existing market for its products

2. To increase the volume of sales, customers, clients, and prospects

3. To increase the profitability of the company

4. To increase the company's return on investment

5. To strengthen the company's strategy and long-run market position.

6. To continue to develop a capable and satisfied workforce.

Assignment

What is your reaction to the company objectives as they have been stated in the past? How should Rick isolate and establish objectives for his company? Develop a set of specific objectives relating to overall corporate performance that would be satisfactory in this situation. Develop a specific subset of objectives for the sales and marketing area based on the information about this case and relate them to your corporate objectives.

- Alpha Concrete Products, Incorporated

The company objectives as they have been stated in the past are clearly of the motherhood variety. It is impossible for the company to measure its performance against those objectives in any consistent and useful manner. What is needed is to quantify the objectives in such a way that it will be possible to measure performance after the fact so that they can be used as guides in allocating a company's efforts.

One of the ways in which Rick might isolate and establish objectives for his company would be to take the objectives as they are now stated and then use the results of the consultant's report to quantify them as well as using inputs from other members of the management team as to what is feasible and could serve as an effective goal. For example, the first objective (increasing the company's share of the existing market) could be broken into two separate objectives. One would state the annual increase in number of bids prepared by the company (that is, an increase in the number of jobs that the company is actually a competitor for) and the other would be an increase in the percentage of those jobs that the firm actually obtained. That percentage is now 30 per cent and thus it might be gradually increased year by year. It probably does not make much sense to specify for a single year how much business is going to come from each segment that the company serves since this varies widely on a year-to-year basis.

Besides increasing market share, the company should state specific quantifiable objectives in terms of the volume of sales to be accomplished, the number of customers, and the number of perspective customers and clients. In regard to the volume of sales, the results of the consultant's forecast might be used as a good base. For example, knowing that the expected sales level in 1976 is $13.58 million, the company might choose as its goal a sales level of $14.86 million. This goal would clearly place the company at the top end of the consultant's estimate and yet is one that the consultant thought was attainable even without a special effort in that regard. Obviously, setting such specific objectives must be tempered by management's own judgment.

The other general objectives as now stated would also need to be quantified. This would involve looking at what has been accomplished in the past (for example, the profitability level over the past several years and the return on investment rate) and then selecting and getting commitment to improvements over time that can be quantified and easily measured. For example, one of the things that might be done would be to take the historical cost-structure data for 1970-1975 and develop a composite cost structure that can be used as part of the set of objectives in planning and decision making. For example, the cost of sales has varied from 66.2 per cent of net sales to 62.7 per cent. Initially, the company might set as its goal reducing the cost of sales in 1976 to 65 per cent. As such performance measures get quantified and as the company has experience in determining what affects the actual outcome, the objectives can then be increased so that they continue to stretch the organization and yet remain within the reach of the company.

The types of specific marketing objectives that Rick might develop are similar to those shown in Chapter 4 under Sample Marketing Objective. These should be made explicit and should cover all aspects of the marketing operation. Thus there should be specific objectives related to the number of active customer accounts, the volume of sales, the sales by territory, the cost of obtaining those sales, the number of salesmen, the revenue per salesman, the percentage of the customer's work being done by Alpha, the number of customer complaints, and budgets for promotion and advertising. In addition, very specific objectives can be set for each salesman and for some of the staff support people working in the marketing area.

III. VALIDATING AND IMPLEMENTING OBJECTIVES

III VALIDATING AND IMPLEMENTING OBJECTIVES

SELECTED READINGS

5. Validating Objectives

Carroll, Phil, *Profit Control,* McGraw-Hill Book Co., New York, 1962.

Hanson, Kemit O., and George J. Brabb, *Managerial Statistics,* Prentice-Hall, Englewood Cliffs, New Jersey, 1961.

Magee, John F., "Decision Trees for Decision Making," *Harvard Business Review,* July-August 1964.

Miller, Robert W., *Schedule, Cost and Profit Control with PERT,* McGraw-Hill Book Co., New York, 1963.

Moder, Joseph J., and Cecil R. Phillips, *Project Management with CPM and PERT,* Reinhold, New York, 1964.

Virts, John R., and Richard W. Garrett, "Weighing Risks in Capacity Expansion," *Harvard Business Review,* May-June 1970.

Walker, M. R., and J. S. Sayer, "Project Planning and Scheduling," *Report 6959,* E. I. duPont de Nemours and Co., Inc., Wilmington, Delaware, March 1959.

Wiest, Jerome D., "Heuristic Programs for Decision Making," *Harvard Business Review,* September-October 1966.

6. Implementing Objectives

Abelson, Herbert I., *Persuasion,* Springer, New York, 1959.

Bellows, Roger, *Creative Leadership,* Prentice-Hall, Englewood Cliffs, New Jersey, 1959.

Bittel, Lester R., *Management by Exception,* McGraw-Hill Book Co., New York, 1964.

Clark, Charles H., *Brainstorming,* Doubleday, New York, 1958.

Ford, Robert M., *Motivation through the Work Itself,* American Management Association, 1969.

Gullerman, S. W., *Management by Motivation,* American Management Association, New York, 1968.

Herzberg, Frederick, B. Mausner, and B. B. Snyderman, *The Motivation To Work,* John Wiley & Sons, Inc., New York, 1965.

Herzberg, Frederick, "One More Time: How Do You Motivate Employees?" *Harvard Business Review,* January-February 1968.

Herzberg, Frederick, William J. Paul and Keith B. Robertson, "Job Encrichment Pays Off," *Harvard Business Review,* March-April 1969.

Kellogg, Marion S., *Closing the Performance Gap,* American Management Association, New York, 1967.

Maslow, Abraham H., *Motivation and Personality,* Harper and Brothers, New York, 1954.

McGregor, D., *Human Side of Enterprise,* McGraw-Hill Book Co., New York, 1960.

Nadler, Gerald, *Work Simplification,* McGraw-Hill Book Co., New York, 1957.

Niebel, Benjamin W., *Motion and Time Study,* Richard D. Irwin, Homewood, Ill., 1967.

Vroom, V. H., *Work and Motivation,* John Wiley & Sons, Inc., New York, 1964.

III. VALIDATING AND IMPLEMENTING OBJECTIVES

5. VALIDATING OBJECTIVES

Key Concepts

- *Decision Tree Analysis.* This technique will provide the graphical and computational approach for relating the various uncertain events and alternative decisions to a specific area in which objectives are being established. Thus it allows examination of the risks surrounding accomplishment of objectives and the establishment of performance measures that adequately consider the management situation over time.

- *Program Evaluation and Review Technique (PERT).* The PERT approach was initially designed to help in identifying and relating the many steps involved in complex projects. Since the accomplishment of organizational objectives is very similar in nature to, for example, a major construction project (in terms of the need for each to coordinate tasks and time phase those effectively), PERT is a very useful technique in validating objectives.

- *Work Breakdown Matrix.* This technique for validating objectives starts with the objective to be validated and relates all elements of the work to the organization's resources and activities in achieving those objectives. The matrix simply relates the various elements in a form that helps clarify for the MBO manager the sequence of tasks to be completed in achieving those objectives.

- *Simulation.* The concept of simulation is one of testing management judgments and assessments about the future before the fact. Such testing usually involves either a conceptual or a graphical model and facilitates the MBO manager's investigation of contingencies and uncertainties and helps avoid costly mistakes due to unforeseen difficulties.

Learning Objectives

After you have completed this chapter, you should be able to

- Understand how decision trees may be used to validate MBO objectives.

- Understand how work breakdown structures may be used to validate MBO objectives.

- Explain the value of Program Evaluation and Review Technique in validating objectives.

- Describe the importance of manipulating and reviewing models in the process of validating objectives.

DECISION TREES

To set objectives, management must confront the uncertain future and make decisions about it, which means dealing with risk. The risk lies in estimating the likelihood that an event will occur. Finding meaningful objectives and formalizing them into written statements is at best a process that leads to tentative commitments — commitments in which the degree of risk is not yet clarified. The MBO manager is wise to validate these tentative commitments. The validation procedure will indicate which objectives are most likely to be reached.

Decision-tree analysis[1] is one method of validation. The decision-tree schematic reduces abstract thinking to a visual pattern of cause and effect that extends from a starting point through a series of logical possibilities. A decision tree, which is also known as a probability tree, is a shorthand notation for the likelihood of each event in a chain of events occurring when certain decisions are made.

1. A Decision Tree

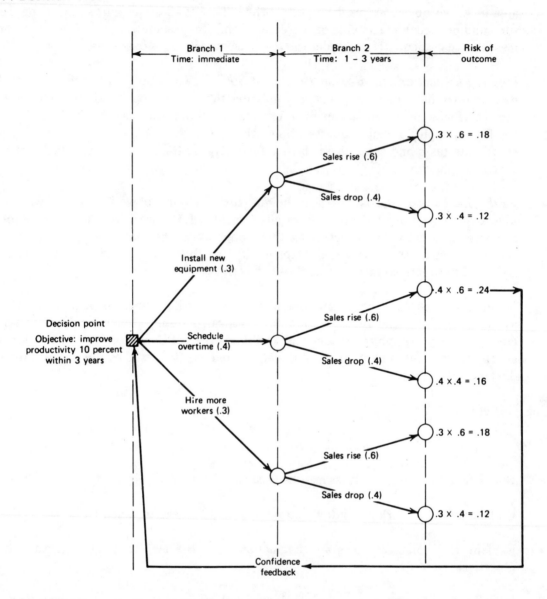

The tree is made up of a series of nodes and branches. At the first node on the left, the manager is faced with setting an objective for productivity improvement. He has three choices: install new equipment, schedule overtime, or hire more workers. Each branch of the tree represents an alternative course of action or an alternative decision. At the end of each branch or alternative course is another node representing a chance event — whether sales will rise or drop. Each subsequent alternative course to the right represents an alternative outcome of this chance event. Probability assignments are made with each branch. This probability can be stated in values of a scale running from 0 (absolute impossibility) through 1.0 (absolute certainty), or in percentages ranging from 0 per cent (absolute impossibility) through 100 per cent (absolute certainty). Thus if we assign the probability $P = 0.5$ to some event E, such as reaching the largest share of the market, this means we think the event has a 50 per cent chance of actually occurring.

A probability assignment is an expression of the level of confidence and risk. High probabilities mean high confidence and low risk. Low probabilities mean low confidence and high risk. There are two ways in which probability assignments can be made:

- Probability assignments can be made on the basis of verifiable data from the past. The weight given to past data is based on statistical extrapolations, correlations of related series, or other reliable survey information.

- Probability assignments can be made on the basis of subjective judgment — that is, personal opinion supported by experience with similar types of situations. A better decision can be made on this basis than would be possible if each outcome were arbitrarily given an equal probability.

The use of a decision tree allows an MBO manager to go through a trial run of likely events. A simulated feedback is obtained to check and recheck the original decision. The objective in Figure 1 is to improve productivity 10 per cent in 3 years. The decision tree graphically and simply shows the alternatives possible after the decision is made to pursue this objective. The risk factor of 0.24 reveals the highest feedback confidence; thus, out of all the alternatives, a sales rise has the greatest chance of occurring as a result of scheduled overtime.

In this way, the network branching of a decision tree can help an MBO manager clarify potential changes and problems. It allows him to foresee a variety of effects by deliberately imposing faults and critical conditions on his model. The advantages and disadvantages can be analyzed in a payoff table for such criteria as present or future profits. This validation procedure can frequently lead to restatement of the objective or selection of a new one.

The possibility of building a new production facility may be structured into an objective and a decision tree may be developed to see outcomes of main, secondary, and tertiary branches, as illustrated in Figure 2. Examining the factors involved in site determination, transportation

2. Decision Tree for a New Production Facility

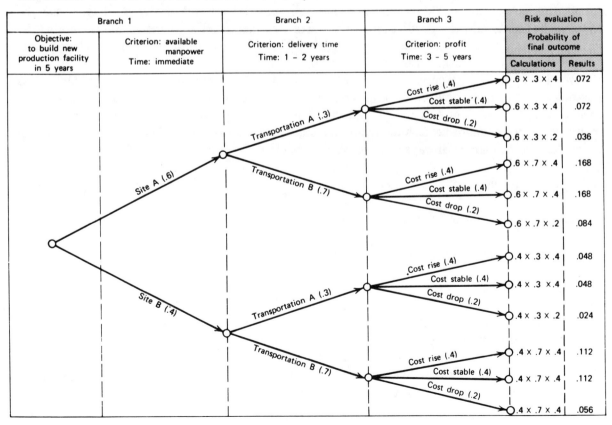

systems, and development costs for future time spans helps in determining the likelihood of profits. Feedback of risk factors strengthens or diminishes the decision to build a new production facility and may give some insight to other possible objectives to pursue.

> The basic point of a decision tree is the assessment of probable outcomes of a decision to pursue an objective. The investigation gives valuable information as to the validity and appropriateness of the objective, while also considering the risk involved.

WORK BREAKDOWN STRUCTURES

Work breakdown structure is probably the most important single planning tool for linking objectives with resources and activities in a framework in which other planning activities can be correlated. The work breakdown structure concept[2] is a logical separation into related levels and functions of the total work required to do a job or reach an objective.

> In using the concept of work breakdown as a validation procedure, the MBO manager starts with the objectives to be validated and relates all elements of the breakdown structure to these objectives.

He begins the breakdown by identifying the total effort required at the top management level to support the objectives. The second level contains work that must be completed to support the first level. The third level contains more detail and a finer division of the work necessary to support the second level. This work breakdown continues until the last level of work that can be delegated is identified. The subdivisions of the work at each level are verified by examining the whole, to be sure that it equals the sum of its parts. The subdivisions under a particular item must define completely all considerations making up that item.

Work breakdown structure can be used to validate an organization's profit objective, as illustrated in Figure 3. The profit objective to be reached in that figure is an increase in net earnings by 20 per cent within 24 months. The work necessary to reach this objective is organized in a pyramidlike fashion from the highest to lowest level. This particular example shows the four fundamental ways to improve profits in any organization, namely,

1. Improvement of sales volume

2. Improvement of price margin

3. Reduction of capital investment

4. Reduction of costs[3]

The subdivisions of the profit objective are work areas for sales volume, pricing, capital investment, and cost reduction. Further subdivisions of the total work show the requirements for meeting these four fundamental work elements. More subdivisions are made until an ultimate level is reached; these final subdivisions are referred to as *end items.* An end item is the smallest division of work that can be delegated to a functional department or supervisor.

3. Work Breakdown Structure as a Validating Tool

Level 1

Objective: increase net earnings 20% within 24 months

Profit plan

Level 2

Cost-reduction plan — Capital investment plan — Pricing-policy plan — Sales volume plan

Level 3

Labor unit costs — Expenses — Equipment utilization — Downtime — Credit position — Marginal items — New products — Sales strategies

Level 4

Waste — Handling — Supplies — Overhead — Layout — Inventory levels — Preventitive maintenance — Training — New suppliers — Quality indices — Diversity — Marginal services — Sales forecasts — Promotion — Incentives — Services

The work breakdown structure provides a perspective from which all the work, including the smallest functions and responsibilities, can be seen easily. Only three levels of breakdown are illustrated in Figure 3, but the reader can see that several additional levels can be added to depict in finer detail the work necessary to complete upper-level tasks. For example, *layout* — meaning layout for work flow — under capital investment can be further divided into process flow, operational activities, material flow, and motion economy.

The MBO manager's ability to develop a work breakdown structure depends on his use of good judgment after he reviews all information and requirements necessary to reach an objective. He may need to make several preliminary trials before he can come up with a structure in which all major tasks are tied together. Once he has the structure, he has defined the substance of work required to reach an objective. Herein is the key to validating objectives, and it can be enunciated in the following principle: The greater the accuracy of work breakdown definition, the greater the likelihood that the actions necessary to complete objectives will be understood.

> If the work is understood, readily identified, and easily achievable, the confidence in reaching objectives is high. If the work is hazy, highly uncertain, and not easily achievable, the confidence in reaching objectives is low. A range exists between these two extremes. The MBO manager proceeds to instill a level of confidence in those who will attempt to implement his objectives.

By preparing a work breakdown structure so that it can be read from left to right (rather than from top to bottom) and by displaying end items in a matrix, the MBO manager can provide himself with additional clarification and understanding for completing a set of objectives. Such a work breakdown structure, with end items at one end and responsibility assignments at the other, is illustrated in Figure 4.

WP in the work breakdown matrix stands for "work package." The total number of work packages represents the total work necessary to achieve an objective. A work package is a work unit to be completed. It consists of several related items: an end item, an accountability assignment, a time to complete the package, a work description or a method to implement the package, a cost estimate, and a probability factor. The following is a brief description of each.

- *End Items.* These are the smallest divisions of work that can be assigned. They are the action links between how the work is broken down in the overall picture and how the functional areas of the organization are tied to this picture. End items relate the purpose of a contribution and make it clear to all involved in the matrix how each individual contribution is related to the whole. Another name for end items is "feeder-objectives." As brought out in earlier chapters, they are the roots from which a network system of objectives is developed.

- *Accountability assignments.* Accountability assignments, either individual or departmental, are of prime importance in organizing and implementing work. They are the obligations to accomplish end items on the basis of established performance standards. It is important to define the tasks that need to be done. But, if the tasks are to be achieved, it is also vital that the individual or individuals who are to perform each task be clearly designated. Clear-cut assignments of responsibilities transform the plan from a statement of intent to a statement of commitment to action.

- *Work descriptions.* These are descriptive statements of the methods that will be utilized in completing the work package. The individual or departments assigned the responsibility for completing an end item must develop the methodology, facilities, and resources and assure that they are available and can be deployed.

4. Work Breakdown Matrix With Work Packages

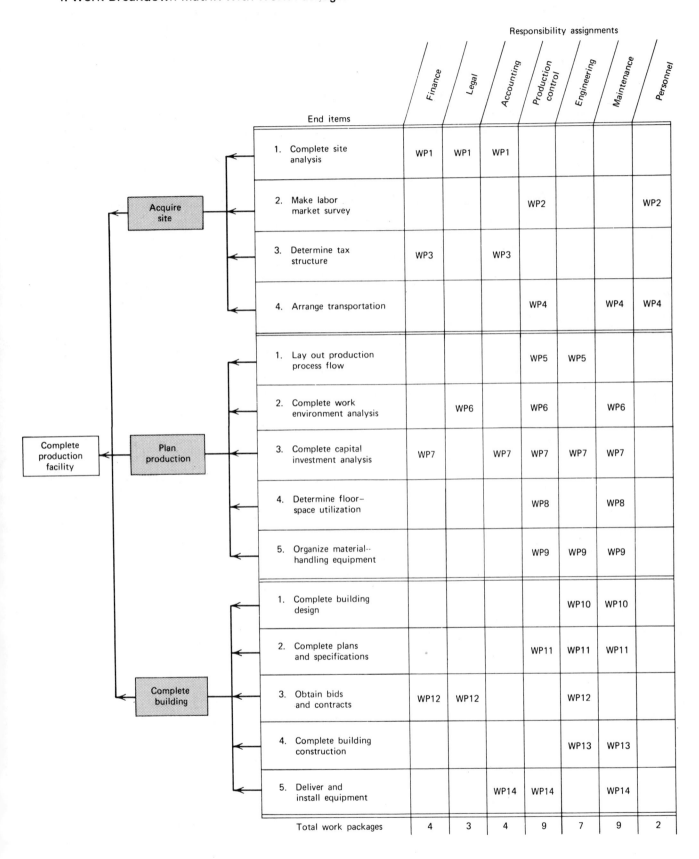

Responsibility assignments

End items	Finance	Legal	Accounting	Production control	Engineering	Maintenance	Personnel
Acquire site							
1. Complete site analysis	WP1	WP1	WP1				
2. Make labor market survey				WP2			WP2
3. Determine tax structure	WP3		WP3				
4. Arrange transportation				WP4		WP4	WP4
Plan production							
1. Lay out production process flow				WP5	WP5		
2. Complete work environment analysis		WP6		WP6		WP6	
3. Complete capital investment analysis	WP7		WP7	WP7	WP7	WP7	
4. Determine floor-space utilization				WP8		WP8	
5. Organize material-handling equipment				WP9	WP9	WP9	
Complete building							
1. Complete building design					WP10	WP10	
2. Complete plans and specifications				WP11	WP11	WP11	
3. Obtain bids and contracts	WP12	WP12			WP12		
4. Complete building construction					WP13	WP13	
5. Deliver and install equipment			WP14	WP14		WP14	
Total work packages	4	3	4	9	7	9	2

Work breakdown structure: Complete production facility → Acquire site, Plan production, Complete building.

- *Time allotments.* Each cell of the work breakdown matrix contains not only a work description, but also a specification as to the amount of time that will be necessary to complete the individual work package. The total time to complete all the work necessary to reach a specified objective is the sum of the time allotments needed to complete each work package.

- *Cost estimates.* Each responsible individual or department assigned to complete an end item must estimate the costs that will be incurred. Reliable and realistic cost estimates of each package, when totaled, can give a close idea of the total cost of implementing an objective. This has a high value for transforming tentative objectives to validated commitments.

- *Probability assignments.* Cells of the work breakdown matrix also contain probability, or risk, assignments. These were described under "Decision Trees."

√Checkpoint: Decision Trees and Work Breakdown Structures ─────────────

Fill in the correct answers.

A (1)_____ is a shorthand notation for the likelihood of occurrence of each event in a chain of events. It is made up of a series of nodes and branches.

(2)_____ are made with each branch. These assignments can be stated in a scale of numerical values running from 0, which represents (3)_____ , to 1, which represents (4)_____ .

A (5)_____ is a logical separation, into related levels and functions, of the total work required to reach an objective. In using this concept, the MBO manager begins by identifying the total effort required at the (6)_____. The final subdivisions in this system are called (7)_____.

Indicate true (T) or false (F).

8. Probability assignments can be made on the basis of subjective judgments._____

9. The validation procedure can lead to restatement of the objective or selection of a new one.
   _____

10. The more accurate and complete the work breakdown, the greater the likelihood that the actions necessary to complete the objective will be understood.

Draw lines to connect each component of a work package with its definition.

11. End items

12. Work descriptions

13. Accountability assignments

14. Probability assignments

15. Time allotments

A. Obligations to establish end items

B. Risk assignments

C. The smallest divisions of work that can be assigned

D. Specifications of time needed to complete a work package

E. Statements of the methods that will be utilized in completing the work package

─────────────────────────

PROGRAM EVALUATION AND REVIEW TECHNIQUE

Program Evaluation and Review Technique (PERT)[4] has been used to deal with a wide range of planning and control problems of a nonrepetitive nature. As such, it lends itself easily to validating objectives, because setting and reaching for results is a nonrepetitive activity. PERT permits a manager to "play the clock" in such a way that a job is accomplished in the shortest period of time with well-organized resources and activities. It is a special application of network analysis for estimating and controlling the time required for activities and work packages about which little information from past experience is available.

Work packages, as described in the discussion of work breakdown structure, can be interconnected to form a network of objectives. Such a network traces the development of all the work necessary to reach final objectives. The network gives an overview from start to finish, clearly indicating the steps that must be taken before the end objective is reached. It shows why some events must follow others; why some cannot be done immediately; and why the total operation takes as long as it does. The network serves to monitor the work program as it proceeds to its final destination.

PERT network analysis consists of four steps:

1. Specifying tasks to be completed

2. Sequencing and interrelating work packages

3. Setting up the network

4. Scheduling

The following is a brief description of each of these steps. Moder and Phillips[5] provide more detail and analysis than is offered here.

1. Specifying Tasks to Be Completed ►

Three terms are central to understanding this step: *task*, *event*, and *activity*.

- A *task* is made up of one or more events and their associated activities.

- An *event* is an end item that indicates a condition to be accomplished at a recognizable point in time.

- An *activity* is the work required to complete a specific end item. It is the work processes and the methodology used to finish an event.

Events are connected by activities. Since events are end items, they take up no time, money, or resources in themselves. Activities, however, require time, money, and resources.

In Figure 5, events are shown as circles, and activities are shown as arrows. Suppose, in this figure, that event 1 represents marketing research begun, and event 2 represents marketing research finished. The arrow between these two events would then indicate the activity necessary to conduct marketing research. Task A is seen as two events and one activity; task B is seen as three events and two activities; task C is seen as two events and one activity, but shifted in time phase; task ABC ties together all items that must reach the terminal event 5. Event sequences and priorities of the original tasks have been changed and shifted when integrated in the task ABC network. Development of a new product in the network may now require, in addition to marketing research, a production status analysis, an engineering feasibility study, and a state-of-the-art technological forecast.

5. PERT Sequencing of Tasks

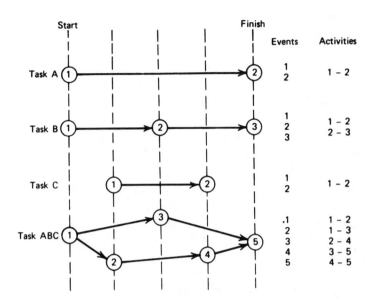

		Events	Activities
Task A		1 2	1 – 2
Task B		1 2 3	1 – 2 2 – 3
Task C		1 2	1 – 2
Task ABC		.1 2 3 4 5	1 – 2 1 – 3 2 – 4 3 – 5 4 – 5

2. Sequencing and Interrelating Work Packages ►

Work breakdown structure, as discussed earlier, makes good use of work packages to reach a set of objectives. The concept of work packages can be fitted neatly into the PERT network by recognizing that just as there are one or more end items in a work package, there are one or more events in a task. Once the component end items or events have been identified, the work packages or tasks can be defined through sequencing and connecting. This is shown in Figure 6.

6. Work Packages in the PERT Network

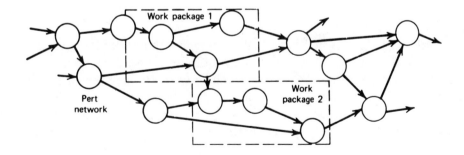

3. Setting Up the Network ►

In a network, several events and activities are combined in such a way that input-output relationships lead to an end. There are no formulas that provide a precise and logical series of steps leading to an excellent and foolproof network. Rather, developing meaningful networks is an art. The following are some suggested guidelines:

- The network should be developed by the individuals familiar with and committed to the objectives and requirements of the program.

- The work breakdown structure, which includes the logical sequence of end items and activities, must be agreed upon by those developing the network.

- The development of the network should start with the ultimate targeted objective and proceed backward to the beginning event. The end objective is constantly and clearly in view, and the network is developed in direct relation to it.

- As the network is developed, a question is asked about each end item: What activities must be completed before this event is completed?

- An activity cannot begin until an event or end item preceding it has been completed.

- Wherever possible, two or more end items and associated activities that can be accomplished concurrently should be set up in parallel paths. This allows a high degree of delegation because of the related parallel efforts.

- A critical path should be identified to discover the longest time it will take to accomplish end items and their associated activities. Increased paralleling will decrease critical path time. Increased sequencing will increase critical path time. (*Critical paths* are defined in the next step.)

- A slack path should be identified to discover the shortest time it will take to accomplish end items and their associated activities. Decreased paralleling will increase slack path time. Decreased sequencing will decrease slack path time. (*Slack paths* are defined in the next step.)

- When an event or an end item holds back two or more activities from starting, there is an event constraint. The offending event should be broken down into smaller events.

- When two or more activities hold back the completion of an end item, there is an activity constraint. The activities should be combined to lead to the end item.

4. Scheduling ►

Once the tasks to be performed have been developed into a PERT network or some related structure, it is necessary for the MBO manager to establish a definite schedule for reaching each end item and an approximate date for starting each activity. By including a schedule as a part of the program for implementation, the PERT plan not only helps keep actions in proper phase, but it also sets target dates for those who are assigned the responsibility for completion. These target dates are based on likely time (t_m), optimistic time (t_o), pessimistic time (t_p) and expected time (t_e).

- *Most likely time* is an estimate of the normal time an activity would take if it were repeated an indefinite number of times under identical conditions. It is the mean time estimate coinciding with the central (most likely) area under a probability distribution curve.

- *Optimistic time* is an estimate of the minimum time an activity will take if unusually favorable conditions are experienced. It coincides with approximately 16 per cent of the area under a probability distribution curve.

- *Pessimistic time* also coincides with about 16 per cent of the area under a probability distribution curve. It is an estimate of the maximum time an activity will take if unusually unfavorable conditions are experienced.

- *Expected time*, which considers the effects of both favorable and unfavorable conditions, can be calculated with the formula shown in Figure 7.

7. Estimating Time for PERT Activities

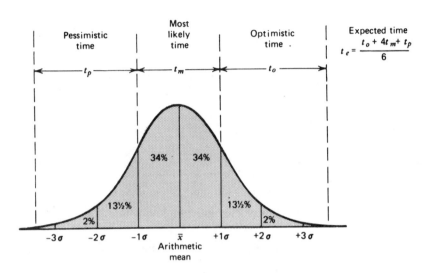

Once the three time estimates are obtained for all the activities of the PERT network, an analysis can be made of the total time required to reach the terminal event. A PERT network having several paths will more than likely have different cumulated time estimates for each path. Those paths that have the longest cumulated time are called *critical paths*, because the entire project or program will be held up if they are delayed. Those paths that have the shortest cumulated time are called *slack paths*, because a great deal of slack time occurs in completing their chain of events. To estimate the probability of meeting the schedule of events or work packages entailed in the completion of an objective, the critical path must be calculated.

_V_Checkpoint: PERT ————————————————————————

Indicate true (T) or false (F).

1. PERT is valuable for dealing with problems of a nonrepetitive nature.____

2. One of the limitations of PERT is that it does not permit work packages to be interconnected to form a network of objectives.____

3. An event is an end item.____

4. There are rigid formulas for establishing networks.____

5. The network should be developed by individuals familiar with and committed to the program.____

Fill in the correct answer.

6. _____ are made up of one or more events and their associated activities.

7. _____ are the work required to complete end items.

8. _____ indicate conditions to be accomplished at recognizable points in time.

9. _____ time considers the effects of both favorable and unfavorable conditions.

10. _____ time is an estimate of the normal time an activity would take if it were repeated an indefinite number of times under identical conditions.

● Checkpoint Answers

1. T   2. F   3. T   4. F   5. T   6. tasks   7. activities   8. events   9. expected
10. most likely

MODEL MANIPULATION AND REVIEW

Thus far, this chapter has provided several types of models the MBO manager may use to simulate, within certain confidence limits, a real situation. How close to reality a model can be is subject to a number of constraints, among them information, time, cost, experience, and simplicity. Once the model is constructed, experimentation and manipulation can be done to determine consequences of changes, faults, and variances. Once an MBO manager has developed a work breakdown structural model, he should manipulate it in several ways to validate important considerations in his objective program. There are four steps in this process.

1. Using the Checklist for Work Breakdown Validity ►

☐ Check to see that the totality of work needed to complete an objective is included.

☐ Check the logic of the divisions and subdivisions.

☐ Check that no subdivisions are left out of the flow from major levels to sublevels.

☐ Check and assure that end items are feeder-objectives in the flow.

☐ Check accountability assignments of each end item.

☐ Check for accuracy of time estimates of each work package.

☐ Check work descriptors for sufficient depth in detail, accuracy, and completeness.

☐ Check participation of management in feeder objectives.

☐ Check for accuracy of cost estimates of each work package.

☐ Check total cost estimate against results of the objective.

☐ Check total time allotment against results of the objective.

☐ Check reliability of risk factor assignments of each work package.

☐ Check total risk against results of the objective.

☐ Check organization chart against the total objective network.

2. Manipulating the Work Breakdown Structure ►

The value of any model lies in the ease with which one can manipulate its variables to acquire a greater understanding of potential problems in the real situation. As Figure 8 shows, the work breakdown structure can be manipulated in a number of ways. Rotation of the structure 90 degrees clockwise with the parts shifted and connected in time phase converts it to a PERT system. Rotation of the structure 90 degrees counterclockwise with the parts used as decision nodes and branches converts it to a *decision tree*. Rotation of the structure 90 degrees counterclockwise with end items displayed as cells develops a *work descriptor and accountability matrix*. Conversion of the structure with levels and parts simulating a management system establishes an *organization chart*. Conversion of the structure into an objective network with subobjectives and feeder-objectives assures *management coordination and interlocking*. Conversion of the structure into an objective network with cost flow levels assures *total costs in getting results*.

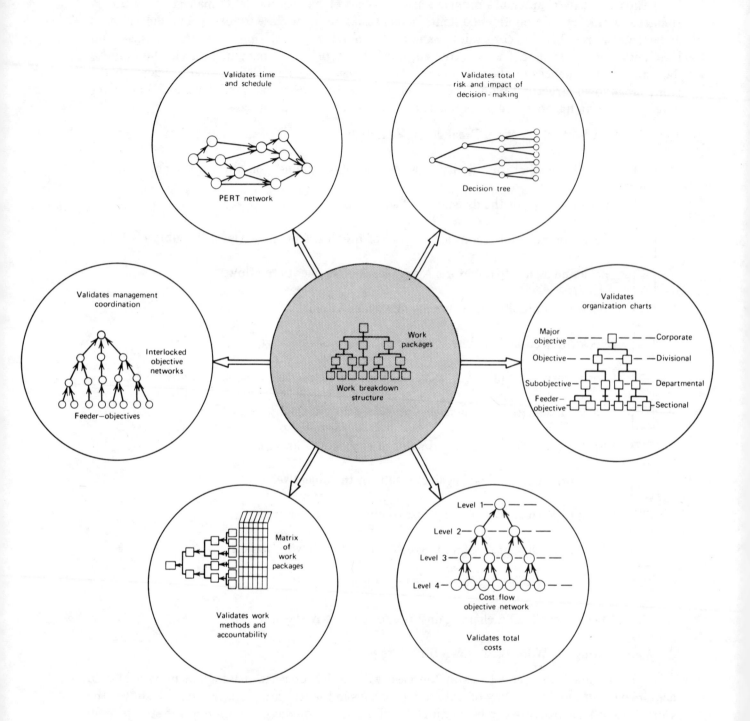

3. Establishing Trial Review Criteria ►

An MBO manager should submit his objective program to a series of reviews and analyses, so that he may assess conflicts and barriers that may arise. A procedure for submitting the proposal to a trial review must meet the following criteria:

- *Is the plan complete*? The manager should ask if everything that needs to be included is included.

- *Is it attainable?* Commitments to the completed plan are made on the basis of two assumptions: that the amount and type of resources allocated are available, and that specified target dates for accomplishments have been set and aligned with other work commitments. These two assumptions should be challenged during an intense review. None of the committed MBO managers can deliver if men, materials, and money cannot be made available within the time specified; validating objectives assures that they will be.

- *Is there managerial support?* A basic premise for the entire MBO strategy is the involvement and support of top management. The authority necessary for the implementation of the plan must be delegated to the individuals who will work to make it a reality. Furthermore, compatibility and harmony must exist between the proposed plan and existing organizational policies. If a conflict arises, one can be sure that a group or an individual will challenge and block the entire proceedings.

- *Will the plan bring about improvement*? The whole point of managing by objectives is to make a significant contribution to the entire organization. The targeted objectives, when reached, should bring about improved conditions in the organization. There must be high confidence in this expectation. Furthermore, the objective program designed to make the departments and individuals strive for higher levels of achievement should be of permanent and lasting benefit to the organization in its future work. Finally, there must be a careful evaluation of the value of the contribution sought relative to money expended and resources utilized. This last point is the most important criterion in the trial review evaluation.

- *Does the plan make the entire flow of events visible*? Visibility means foreseeing the flow of events from start to finish. It permits management to focus on some part of the entire program or to enlarge the scope of the entire plan.

- *Is the plan reliable*? The whole system is no better than its weakest element. Forecasting all the events in a logical sequence goes a long way in improving reliability.

- *Are the objectives interlocked*? Management by objectives is a systems approach. The MBO manager should verify that input/output elements are tied together for cost flow, sales, profits, time, and so on. He should check to see that interfaces are defined and managed for changes and priorities.

4. Applying Trial Review Criteria ►

These criteria form important guidelines to evaluate the validity and feasibility of targeted objectives. Some suggestions on how to apply the criteria are the following.

- Each committed MBO manager can make a presentation in conference with other committed managers to defend and support his role in the plan. These presentations provide a view of each part as it fits into the program as a whole. This step-by-step unfolding of the program will reveal neglected factors in the whole. Conferees will criticize each manager's presentation to uncover weak points and identify deficiencies.

- A "fresh" committee of noncommitted managers and supervisors can review and criticize the proposed plan. Any suggested weaknesses or deficiencies should be explained or adjusted by the committed managers.

- A quantitative model of the plan can be developed and programmed for computer manipulation. Variables in the plan, such as time, can be forced to extremes to demonstrate the effects on the entire plan. Through this computer manipulation, the facts of the situation can be better seen and described.

- Management can make pilot runs of subparts of the plan. These pilot runs would be, in effect, controlled experiments. The results might be useful in making generalizations about the entire plan.

- Simulated runs between two competing groups can be set up — one in favor of the plan and one against it. Each group, according to its position, will work as hard as it can to implement the plan or to assure its defeat. This activity will uncover relationships between various parts of the program that may not be apparent in the original. It also allows consideration of all major variables acting simultaneously. After the simulated runs, both groups discuss the features that appear to be weak and make suggestions for their correction.

COMMITMENT TO DELIVER RESULTS

Setting objectives is deciding firmly on fixed expectations, even though objective statements can be reconsidered, renegotiated, and revised in the light of new information and needs. However, for the most part, the statement is a pledge or promise that is binding. Management is neither hoping for delivery nor gambling on it; it *will* deliver and seals its pledge with a commitment. Managers at the various levels of the organization whose effort and cooperation will be required must understand the anticipated results to be achieved and their own high accountability for delivering these results. With this understanding, all those managers involved take on a commitment to work and strive as a team. The involvement and participation of large numbers of people tend to reinforce the permanent quality of commitments since so much timing and coordination is required. Once a commitment is made, through the validation procedure, all concerned juxtapose their roles in a time sequence for a management systems operation.

Commitment is a process locking all feeder-objectives together for a period of time in a prescribed direction with all management personnel. Commitment is not equivalent to support, nor is it an expression of loyalty. Both support and loyalty are desirable attributes usually found in company personnel. Commitment, however, goes beyond support and loyalty. Once a decision is made, everyone carries out the decision and makes happen what is expected to happen. Questions, disagreements, and disputes are allowed, welcomed, and aired prior to commitment. Discussions of loyalty, personal relationships, and personal likes and dislikes are brought to the surface prior to commitment. However, once a commitment is made, questions of support, loyalty, and the like become less relevant. Release from commitment is always possible if new factors appear in a changing situation. It is distressing to observe companies still striving doggedly to fulfill their commitments when the situation has changed significantly enough to warrant redefinition and redirection. This condition constitutes one of the major difficulties in the practice of managing by objectives. It will be dealt with in greater detail in Chapter 7 in the section on troubleshooting.

◄ SUMMARY ►

In setting objectives, an MBO manager faces an uncertain future; he deals with risk. To reduce risk as much as is feasible, he should engage in a validation procedure. This chapter describes several methods for translating a tentative statement of objective into a validated statement of commitment.

---

1. Two thought-provoking articles on decision trees are the following: John F. Magee, "Decision Trees for Decision Making," *Harvard Business Review,* July-August 1964, p. 126; Jerome D. Wiest, "Héuristic Programs for Decision Making," *Harvard Business Review,* September-October 1966, p. 129.

2. Robert W. Miller, *Schedule, Cost and Profit Control with PERT,* McGraw-Hill Book Company, New York, 1963, pp. 65-67; 98-100; 152-153.

3. Phil Carroll, *Profit Control*, McGraw-Hill Book Company, New York, 1962, pp. 10-16.

4. The network concept has developed in an evolutionary way over many years. It appears that project networking was formally defined by two research teams, one developing PERT and the other CPM. See M.R. Walker and J.S. Sayer, "Project Planning and Scheduling," *Report 6959,* E.I. duPont de Nemours and Company, Inc., Wilmington, Delaware, March 1959.

5. Joseph J. Moder and Cecil R. Phillips, *Project Management with CPM and PERT,* Reinhold, New York, 1964.

Chapter 5 Review

Answer briefly.

1. How do validated objectives help to mimimize risk?

2. What is a decision tree?

3. On what two bases are probability assignments made?

4. What is a work breakdown structure?

5. What are the items in a work package?

_____

_____

_____

_____

6. In PERT, what are the advantages of a network?

_____

_____

_____

_____

7. List the four steps in PERT.

_____

_____

_____

_____

8. What is a critical path? A slack path? Why are they so called?

_____

_____

_____

_____

9. What different estimates of time are considered in PERT scheduling? Define each.

_____

_____

_____

_____

_____

10. What are the criteria for trial review?

_____

_____

_____

_____

_____

11. Discuss two ways that trial review criteria can be applied.

_____

_____

_____

_____

_____

- Doublecheck Answers

1. The process of validating objectives involves relating resources in specific areas of action to the desired objectives. Thus in validating such objectives, the MBO manager investigates areas of uncertainty and areas where contingency plans should be prepared. This helps to minimize the risk of surprises and of finding out too late about potential difficulties.

2. A decision tree is a graphical representation of a series of uncertain events and decision alternatives. It helps the manager to evaluate the likelihood (probability) of a certain sequence of events and actions occurring. The technique also allows alternative decisions for accomplishing objectives to be compared on the basis of their expected value.

3. Probability assignments can be made either based on subjective managerial judgments or on the basis of empirical (historical) data. While historical data allows certain statistical techniques to be used, often the situation is new or sufficiently different from the previous experiences that trained management judgment is the only way to obtain reliable probability estimates.

4. The work breakdown structure is a tool for linking objectives with resources and activities by logically separating the total work required to achieve an objective into related levels and functions. This structure ranges from identifying the total effort required at top levels of management, subdividing into end items the smallest divisions of work that can be assigned.

5. A work package is a work unit to be completed in accomplishing a specific objective. The package consists of several related items — an end item, an accountability assignment, a specified time to complete the package, a work description (or a method to implement the package), a cost estimate, and a probability factor.

6. A PERT network traces the development of all of the work activities (and their sequence) necessary to reach final objectives. The network provides an overview from start to finish, clearly indicating the steps that must be taken before the end objective is reached. Through the graphical representation, the MBO manager is able to identify alternative sequences of tasks and the impact of delays in specific tasks on the total accomplishment of objectives.

7. The four steps included in PERT are:

   a. Specifying tasks to be completed

   b. Sequencing and interrelating work packages

   c. Setting up the network

   d. Scheduling

8. The *critical path* is the path through the network that takes the most time to complete. Thus the critical path determines the shortest time possible in which the entire objective can be accomplished.

   A *slack path* is a path that is not on the critical path, although it does parallel the critical path. Reducing the time on a slack path will not affect the overall completion time for the objective. It is only by reducing time on the critical path (when that does not create a new critical path) that the total time for accomplishing objectives can be reduced.

9. Four different estimates of time are defined for each activity or work package in PERT. Three of these must be provided by the MBO manager. These are the *pessimistic time* for completion, the *optimistic time* and the *most likely time*. Finally, the PERT time is computed based on these three estimates and can be thought of as a smooth value representing the most likely time for that package.

10. The procedure for submitting the objective program to a series of reviews and analyses should meet the criteria of completeness, obtainability, managerial support, improvement possibilities, visibility, reliability, and interlocking objectives.

11. Some of the ways that trial review criteria can be applied include the following:

    a. Each committed MBO manager can make a presentation in conference with other committed managers to defend and support his role in the plan.

    b. A "fresh" committee of noncommitted managers and supervisors can review and criticize the proposed plan.

    c. The quantitative model of the plan can be developed and tested through computer manipulation.

    d. Management can make pilot runs of subparts of the plan.

    e. Simulated runs between two competing groups can be set up — one in favor of the plan and one against it.

6. IMPLEMENTING OBJECTIVES ———————————————————

Key Concepts

- *Planned Motivation.* This concept enables one to deal with motivators and demotivators in a systematic manner. It represents a motivational strategy for finding the best fit among organization objectives, employee needs, and the job situation.

- *Hierarchy of Human Needs.* The basic drives that impel people to act to meet personal needs help explain the reasons people perform as they do. These needs can be arranged in a heirarchy of several levels. Once needs associated with basic levels have been met, the higher levels become the key motivating factors.

- *Coaching and Persuasion.* These are key concepts in the development of planned motivation. They are aimed at guiding and encouraging employees in such a way to motivate them to implement objectives.

Learning Objectives

After you have completed this chapter, you should be able to

- Understand how planned motivation is central to the implementation of MBO objectives.

- Describe how needs drive behavior.

- Describe the roles of coaching and persuasion in planning motivational strategies.

- Plan motivational strategies to implement MBO objectives.

PLANNED MOTIVATION

This chapter will introduce a methodology for implementing objectives — the fourth of the five MBO steps. Central to this methodology is the manager's use of planned motivation.

Definitions ►

Motivating is the skill of a manager in arousing enthusiasm among employees for achieving an objective. It is the work a manager performs to encourage and persuade others to take required action. It is the process of getting employees to reach for organization goals. *Motivators* are those conditions or agents within a job that cause employees to act. Motivators are job factors that give employees satisfaction. *Demotivators* are those conditions or agents within a job that give employees dissatisfaction. Demotivators are job or environmental constraints that will inhibit an individual from reaching an objective. They tend to retard action toward a purpose or a goal. It would be a simple process to formulate a list of motivators and demotivators to be employed when the situation warrants. But such a list is not practical. There is a delicate balance between motivators and demotivators. Too much or too little of a motivator will turn it into a demotivator, particularly in a given labor market, a given industry, a given profession, or a given period of time. For example, challenge is now regarded as one of the most potent motivators a manager can use to incite action. Yet too much challenge or too little will render it a demotivator. There is an amount that is just enough.

> *Planned motivation* is a concept for dealing with motivators and demotivators in a deliberate way. It is a motivational strategy for finding the best fit among organization objectives, employee needs, and the job situation.

Variability of Motivators by Individual ►

The problem of motivation troubles management personnel everywhere. The search is on for a magic formula that will arouse within employees the desire to work for organization objectives while meeting their own personal needs. A practical problem that must be taken into account in this search is that what motivates one person may not motivate another. The use of Herzberg's[1] motivators and demotivators has different effects on different individuals. Motivators that work well with one individual are completely useless with another. Additionally, what motivates an individual one day might not be effective the next. What is needed is a workable scheme for relating important motivators in varying combinations and proportions, while avoiding demotivation. This scheme should be set down in an implementation schedule similar to production schedules. Change any one of the factors and the motivational pattern will change. Similarly, individual variations will effect the type and degree of demotivators that a person will tolerate on the job. A recognized demotivator for one individual may not be a demotivator for another. Motivators can become demotivators with the passage of time.

Variability of Motivators by Job Level ►

Planned motivation gives different amounts of attention to the needs of people at different levels of the organization, since self-motivation varies from low to high as one goes up the organizational ladder. Additionally, planned motivation varies conversely from high to low. This is illustrated in Figure 1. In higher levels of management, because of their position of responsibility, individual managers are able to build motivators into their own work. While planning and organizing his work, a higher-level manager can arrange future commitments in such a way that his personal needs are taken care of. Very little job planning has to be done for him because he does so much for himself. For a higher-level manager, self-motivation is high and planned motivation is low.

1. Relationship of Motivation to Job Level

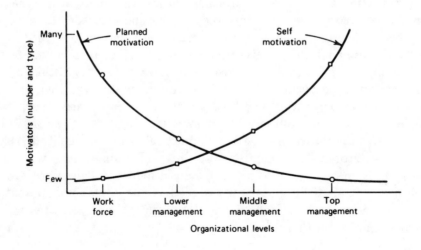

In lower levels of management, however, an individual manager does not have the same opportunity, because his job responsibilities are more restricted. On this level, job planning must fit into a strategy organized from higher levels. Thus, unlike his counterpart on higher levels, the lower-level manager cannot arrange future commitments in such a way that his personal needs are satisfied. Motivators must be planned for him and applied in a deliberate way. For a lower-level manager, self-motivation is low, so planned motivation must be high.

Some motivators are common to all levels, but many are different for each level. It is unfortunate to see managers at middle levels using the same motivators for the work force that they use for lower-level managers. For example, a computer firm that employs a number of professional people in the work force tends to motivate these people and their professional supervisors with the same motivators. Recognition of position is far more potent as a motivator for first-line supervisors than for the working staff. Job enlargement is far more potent as a motivator for the working staff than it is for first-line supervisors. The computer firm ignored this differentiation and found the working force motivated but the supervisory level demotivated and dissatisfied. The firm failed to plan and use motivators for specific management levels. Management should have at its disposal a broad list of motivators. The list should be varied and at best represent potential motivators. They become actual motivators when they are applied properly at the right time to the right person on the right level.

Multiplicity of Motivators ▶

Planned motivation involves the use of multiple motivators. To get an employee from point A to point D, for example, could mean using motivators at points A, B, and C. This is because of the diminishing effects of motivation over time. The diminishing can result simply from conditions on the job or from unforeseen pressures.

Traditional Motivation Versus Planned Motivation ▶

Planned motivation differs from traditional in that the former is systematic, and even scheduled, in the same manner as budgets, capital outlays, new products, and promotions. A contrast of the traditional motivational practices with the planned motivational concept follows.

Traditional Motivational Practices	Planned Motivational Concept
Starts with people in jobs	Starts with system's objectives and feeder-objectives
Single or few motivators	Multiple sequentially related motivators
Through the work	Through the work toward objectives
Day-to-day chance	Motivators are time scheduled
Meets the needs of employees	Finds best fit between organization objectives and employee needs
Applies motivators in existing job classification	Jobs are enlarged, enriched, simplified, or standardized to meet best fit between organization objectives and employee needs
Gives responsibility and control for own work	Fits responsibility and control within commitments of the system
Gives job freedom and additional authority	Fits freedom range and authority within management system
Applies motivators to all levels and all groups	Applies motivators in a schedule by levels within an organization
Waits for diminishing effect before applying new motivators	Anticipates diminishing effects and schedules intensification with new motivators

The problem in planning motivation is not managing work but managing the desire of men to work toward objectives. The MBO manager must identify the work situation, along with its respective variables, before selecting a motivator. Working conditions such as noise, light, other workers, equipment layout, union climate, and organization policies are but a few of these variables. Personal needs and motives for working must also be considered, in order to identify any that might interfere with an MBO program. A motivator is selected as a potential causative agent for action because it best fits three variables: the objective, the work situation, and the needs of the individual. These three variables are closely interrelated; they must all be channeled in the same direction.

The basic idea of managing by objectives is not only to get results but to get results within a certain amount of time. Once an objective has been set, the MBO manager must specify within individual work plans the demotivators to be avoided and motivators to be implemented within a time framework. This is accomplished under a motivation planning schedule. Work plans, needs of employees, motivators, and demotivators are directed toward organizational results and employee satisfaction. An anticipated and planned best fit among all these elements is sought in the schedule, which sets the time and pace not only for the execution of work plans but also for motivators.

V Checkpoint: Planned Motivation Defined

Fill in the correct answer.

1. _____ is the skill of a manager in arousing enthusiasm among employees for achieving an objective.

2. _____ are those conditions or agents within a job that cause employees to act; they give employees satisfaction.

3. _____ is a strategy for finding the best fit among organization objectives, employee needs, and the job situation.

Indicate true (T) or false (F).

5. What motivates one person may not motivate another. _____

6. The variability of motivators from one individual to the next prohibits the development of schedules for implementing objectives. _____

7. The need for planned motivation is the same for employees at all job levels within an organization. _____

8. Traditional motivation starts with people in jobs. _____

9. Planned motivation starts with the system's objectives and feeder objectives. _____

10. Planned motivation generally applies motivators in existing job classifications. _____

• Checkpoint Answers

1. Motivating   2. Motivators   3. Demotivators   4. Planned Motivation

5. T   6. F   7. F   8. T   9. T   10. F

THE RELATIONSHIP OF NEEDS TO MOTIVATION

The basic drives that impel people to act to meet personal needs help explain the reasons people behave and perform as they do. Their striving after things is largely determined by their needs. Each person's particular course of action has been adopted because, in some way, it provides him with satisfaction. Maslow's theory of needs[2] gives great insight to the levels and types of needs that drive people. It is the best explanation for the reasons that people work. A needs hierarchy exists for each individual, and his behavior is determined to a great extent by what these needs are. According to an adaptation of Maslow's concept, man's needs may fall on five levels of variability, as illustrated in Figure 2.

2. Human Needs Drive Human Behavior

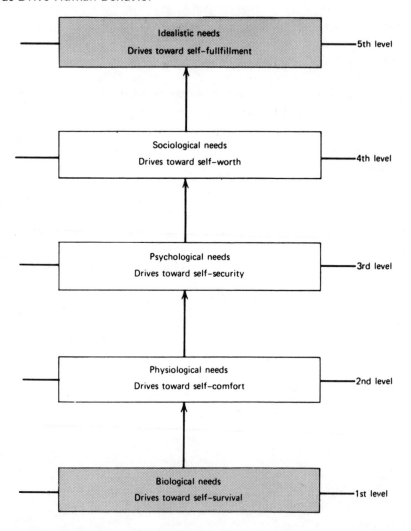

First-level needs are the basic biological needs that preserve the human organism. These are the strong drives for self-survival. They pertain to the biological processes without which we could not exist as humans. Examples of these drives are hunger, thirst, breathing, sex, and sleep. These needs are instinctive and on-going. Satisfaction of these needs can be only temporary since they occur repeatedly from birth until death.

Second-level needs are the physiological needs, the strong drives toward self-comfort. They pertain to the physiological processes that support our metabolisms. Examples are the needs for exercise, shelter, rest, transportation, clothing, and freedom of motion. These are vital in their support of the human organism's life processes. They are not as urgent as the first-level drives but become more urgent when the first-level needs have been satisfied.

Third-level needs are the psychological needs, the strong drives toward self-security. They pertain to the psychological processes involved in the emotional well-being of the individual. Examples of these drives are avoiding threat, danger, tension, and deprivation, and striving for job security, work satisfaction, intellectual challenges, and economic security. These are vital in their support of the mental and emotional processes of the human organism. These needs are culturally influenced. They appear early in life and vary in strength during different phases of life.

Fourth-level needs are sociological, or the strong drives for group acceptance. They pertain to man as he relates to his social environment. Examples are needs for participation, group membership, status, activity, and advancement. These needs are vital to man in the way he relates to other humans and to his environment. The drives toward self-worth are those that make a person wish to feel important and to be accepted by family, friends, church, and community. In an affluent society, these drives are very active. Groups, organizations, and the government are highly influential on the strength and duration of these drives.

Fifth-level needs are the idealistic needs. These are the strong drives toward a sense of self-fulfillment. Examples are the need for beauty, wealth, humanity, fame, creativity, and religion. These needs are vital to the individual in terms of what he wants from life, or what he wishes to become. Occasionally, these needs are simply wishful thinking, as, for instance, when they involve wanting to be a great author, a painter, the president of an organization, a millionaire, or an early retiree. These needs are private, and the individual is likely to share them with few others. To some individuals, these needs are strong and urgent.

Human behavior is a result of the individual's attempting to meet some felt need. These needs vary in type, level, intensity, and duration. Managers can affect the behavior of employees through blocking or supplying employee needs within the job context. Needs and behavior can be related as follows:

1. Lower-level needs will tend to displace higher-level needs in priority when there is conflict. For a hungry person, the drive for food will always displace the drive for participation in a community group.

2. The individual tends to strive to meet his idealistic needs. He moves to higher levels as he satisfies the needs of previous levels.

3. A man's response to being motivated is dominated by the level of need in which he finds himself. Examine a man's behavior and it is quite possible to determine the need he is trying to meet. Conversely, to know a man's need helps one predict what his future behavior will be.

4. Man's needs are on-going. He will always be seeking to satisfy some need at some level.

5. Deprivation of need fulfillment by a supervisor, an organization, or the government will generate behavioral consequences. In a nonaffluent culture, generally speaking, the lower the level of the need deprivation, the more serious and violent the reaction. The higher the level, the less serious and less violent the reaction. To block the drive for food in a society where hunger is common is to generate a serious situation. In an affluent culture where the basic needs such as food and water are readily met, lower-level needs in conflict with higher levels will not generate a serious reaction. In affluent cultures, it is more commonly the blocking of higher-level needs that generates strong reactions. Highly rebellious political behavior may result when these higher-level needs are thwarted or frustrated.

6. Intensity of striving will be greatest at that level to which each individual assigns a high priority. It appears that all humans have needs on all levels. Yet each individual places a priority on the level and type of need he wishes to fulfill. Since each individual will

assign a different priority, a very complex set of priority patterns will emerge. These priorities will change with time.

The striving to meet wants and needs is motivation. Behavior or performance is directed and determined by needs. This provides a fundamental clue to the MBO management of people. If the manager assesses the needs of people as carefully as he does their goals, and if he can align them with organization objectives, strong motivation will result. (The reader is reminded of the disparity angle, described in Chapter 2, which explains this alignment.)

It was mentioned earlier that the needs hierarchy provides a clue to a man's behavior. Basically, the individual strives to meet his own needs first and those of the organization second. Still, the motivational processes are so complex that a man seems to be striving to meet several needs simultaneously. The processes become even more complex when we note that some needs have short time spans while others are of longer duration. A complex fluctuation pattern may be conceptualized for each individual as he meets his needs on the five levels over a period of time. This is suggested in Figure 3.

Since motivators are causative agents that help an individual identify and meet a need, the MBO manager would do well to acquire an insight into the needs of his subordinates and identify motivators that will aid in fulfilling them. Similarly, he will do well to recognize demotivators as causative agents that keep a subordinate from satisfying a need. Avoiding practices that demotivate will go a long way toward removing dissatisfaction.

3. Fluctuating Nature of Human Needs

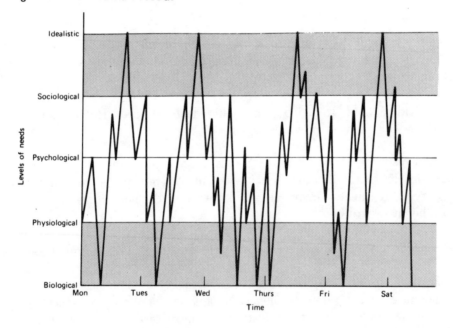

√Checkpoint: Needs and Motivation ──────────────────────────────

Indicate what position each kind of need occupies on Maslow's hierarchy of needs by filling in the numbers 1 (for the lowest level) through 5 (for the highest).

1. Physiological needs ─────

2. Psychological needs ─────

3. Biological needs─────

4. Idealistic needs ─────

5. Sociological needs ─────

Draw lines to match each specific need in the first column with the general class of need in the second column.

6. Need for Status   a.   Biological Need

7. Need for Job Security   b.   Idealistic Need

8. Need for Food   c.   Psychological Need

9. Need for Shelter   d.   Physiological Need

10. Need for Beauty   e.   Sociological Need

THE ROLE OF COACHING IN PLANNED MOTIVATION

Coaching is the guiding and encouraging of employees, in order to motivate them to implement objectives. It is an on-going process and not a periodic event. The best coaching technique is the one that fits the situation. These techniques will vary with the objectives to be implemented, the jobs to be done, and the relationship between the supervisor and the subordinate.

Effective coaching is time consuming. The tendency of some supervisors is to shift or delegate coaching responsibilities to another because of these time demands. Such a shift often results in an inferior and ineffective coaching process. The manager who takes time to consult with his subordinates and to help them overcome problems instills in them his own confidence that the work will be completed.

Do's of Coaching ►

Almost every organization can identify one or more managers who have been quite effective in guiding and stimulating subordinates to complete their objectives. An examination of each of these effective coaches reveals that they use different techniques to deal with different situations. However, some suggestions can be drawn from observing these managers and their methods. The following guidelines are but a few that one may glean.

- A manager must have daily face-to-face, two-way interactions with subordinates on work progress and individual growth.

- A manager must use good timing in offering correction and suggesting improvement in performance.

- A manager must not excessively criticize or discipline so that a subordinate is fearful of moving ahead.

- A manager must recognize the expenditure of effort that yields good results for the organization immediately following the expenditure of the effort.

- A manager must set up and control the situation to allow a subordinate to perform without excessive interference.

- A manager will limit his coaching aims to a specific few but important areas needing change or improvements.

- A manager must confine his coaching to the work and the subordinate's ability to accomplish it.

- A manager must make subordinates feel responsible and accountable for bringing work to a successful end.

- A manager must show a keen and sincere personal interest in a subordinate to help him with his difficulties.

- A manager must allow a subordinate to express his individuality in his work by letting him do the job in his own way.

Don'ts of Coaching ►

In addition to following the principles described above, an MBO manager can improve his coaching ability by recognizing the most common reasons for failure. The following list suggests some of the pitfalls to avoid.

- The manager should not be excessively active himself nor permit his subordinates to be excessively active. The failure to set priorities and assign weights to the many activities required in day-to-day work for reaching MBO objectives will eventually cause scheduled deadlines in the objective plan to be missed. In fact, a tough attitude must be maintained if the many trivial activities that consume valuable time are to be avoided. A good coach will not delegate key responsibilities to subordinates any more than he will allow himself to be victimized by time-robbing trivialities on the job. He will help his subordinates separate essentials from nonessentials and be able to cut corners where possible. Practicing managing by exception, where attention is given to the extraordinary rather than to the ordinary, might be very useful here. Some of the time-robbing activities are too many meetings, inefficient and drawn-out conferences, social conversations, reading long reports, poor information retrieval methods, excessive work, and time given to personal matters.

- The manager should not restrict the climate. A climate that does not allow individual ingenuity to solve problems as they develop will bring the MBO objective plan to a halt. Policies, directives, and attitudes that set undue constraints will eventually force personnel into apathetic conformity. A good coach develops open-mindedness and encourages a spirit of creativity in discovering new and better ways of coping with responsibilities. He will examine existing policies and other regulatory rules to determine if they have a stifling effect on the performance of individuals. This open-mindedness also allows an open door policy; employees will feel freer to consult with their manager if and when they need work clarification and counsel.

- The manager should not allow activities to go uncoordinated. MBO strategy requires a high degree of coordination among employees. Poor human relationships and faulty communication patterns will tend to cause wide differences and disruptions in the diversified activities required to get things done. A good coach will seek out, uncover, and correct feelings of dissatisfaction. He will find the focal points of trouble. He will reconcile differences among the various individuals and groups through repeated emphasis on the prime importance of the whole plan, in comparison with the secondary importance of each component of the plan.

- The manager should not allow problems to go unsolved. Half-solved problems will tend to crop up repeatedly to harass efforts for completing the MBO plan. A good coach solves problems so that they stay solved. He is careful of writing off or discarding small problems that can grow into larger and more complex ones through neglect. He demonstrates to his subordinates a sensitivity for prevention of unexpected incidents that block efforts to operate the plan.

- The manager should not allow performance to vary. Neglect in approaching and dealing with organization politics, grapevine rumors, unethical behavior, job obsolescence, and work conflicts can cause variabilities in performance that make completion of the MBO plan a chance occurrence. A good coach has the courage to get the job done under any condition of stress. He has the backbone to hold back the forces that threaten to distort, distract, or deviate his planned course of action.

- The manager should not coach at the wrong time. Too much coaching can be as damaging as too little. Nothing is more annoying to an employee than to get coaching and a run-down of errors long after the fact. On the other hand, an employee may not appreciate being alerted to traps too far in advance. Warnings about possible errors and guidance around the traps are most effective just before the performance is to be executed. This is the basic reason that coaching is a day-to-day process. A coach's log is a very useful device for providing a system of regular reminders of what has occurred in relation to MBO objectives and what corrective actions must be taken. In this log are recorded deviations or difficulties experienced by subordinates as well as proposed remedial actions. If the log is regularly and faithfully kept, the coaching process is assured a major day-to-day role in the activities of a supervisor. The log for each subordinate should be developed to fit the situation of each manager. Generally, it should contain log entries of work to be done in relation to objectives committed, work now in progress and under schedule, and work completed as part of the work package of a feeder-objective. The log is useful as a source of information if it contains supervisory notes on critical performance incidents, both favorable and unfavorable; past verified accomplishments in the objective program; evaluation notes on subordinates' ability to perform the work in the period ahead, with caution and pitfalls identified; a list of supervisory actions that are likely to pay off in improved employee performance; and a personal sketch of each member of the coaching team in terms of skills, background, past assignments, personal history, strengths, and weaknesses. The coach's log is not only a document for improving the performance of subordinates; it can also be the basis for setting future objectives with the same group of people.

THE ROLE OF PERSUASION IN PLANNED MOTIVATION

In the planned motivation of employees to implement MBO objectives, the manager's ability to articulate instructions and ideas with persuasiveness and conviction can be essential. Force and threats of force in an MBO program are open denials of the essence of the entire program. In its broadest philosophical view, managing by objectives is a motivational strategy whereby people work because it is satisfying. Authoritative methods are signs that the program is being misapplied.

Understand Why Persuasion Is Needed ►

Employees sometimes tend to pull away from commitments they have readily accepted. These human tendencies are so ingrained that employees may not even be aware of them. They form barriers to getting a job done. When he becomes aware of them, the MBO manager is wise to employ a series of skillful persuasive maneuvers to put the subordinate back on the right track. Some of these barriers are:

- Effects of prior habits

- Effects of failure

- "Silent" bosses

- Doubting conversations

One reason why many individuals in an MBO program tend to function less than required or differently from what is expected is that they are victimized by old habits. Prior experience and previous training tend to create set patterns of thought. Bellows[3] refers to these states of mind as regulators of behavior. These habits stifle innovation. Since objective setting is formulating new directions, the danger of individuals following habitual grooves is very real. To offset these habits, management can use the objective-setting participative processes and the coaching given by the supervisor. A spirit of group activity usually prevails in an objective program, and this spirit encourages and sustains an individual in ignoring habits of the past and in relating new work methods to the demands of the objectives. The coach often finds himself persuading the employee to decondition himself, to root out the restricting effects of habits.

Failures in reaching goals in the past are another cause of discouragement toward trying for future goals. Many of these failures in an objective program have resulted from the tendencies of some managers to overchallenge subordinates. For example, an employee who proposes to reduce costs by 10 per cent finds that his supervisor is not only receptive to the idea, but that he even encourages him to go for 20 per cent, a figure that may not be realistic. The failure of the employee to attain the overchallenging target creates self-discouragement that undermines future initiatives on his part. The MBO manager is wise to generate self-confidence in the employee by keeping the objective in the challenge region and by being there to help his subordinate if he stumbles. Persuasively, the manager develops a sense of trust and confidence within the subordinate that the fear of failure is only a resistance to change from the known to the unknown. He instills the idea that progress is made only when there is a performance stretch.

> There is nothing that spurs employees on to implement innovative objectives so much as when management gives help, praise, and recognition on a face-to-face basis. Yet, managers who are quite active and involved with employees in setting objectives, sometimes withdraw from the scene once these objectives are finalized.

When managers wishdraw from a personal position to an impersonal one of reviewing the scoreboard without reviewing those who are making the scores, encouragement to get the job done is lost. Managers should still be active on a face-to-face basis with their sections and departments during the long and arduous period of implementation.

An employee is also highly influenced by the thoughts, feelings, and responses that come from conversations among members of a group. Doubts often emerge for an employee when he hears the irritations, worries, and criticisms of others. His response will be a composite reaction to all these influences both around and within him. Persuasion consists of instilling and strengthening a positive response toward an objective to counter the negative responses acquired from others. Implanting such a response is important in making the person's activities purposeful and in raising his confidence about getting the job done.

The persuasive skills are many and varied. Developing receptivity, or readiness to get the job done, is one. Asking a thought-provoking question is another persuasive skill. Questions can expose positions, arguments, and faulty attitudes. When the subordinate sees all the facets of a problem openly, he takes a more objective view of the matter. Still another skill is the ability to explore thoroughly the spectrum of possibilities and to lead the subordinate to recognize the soundness of certain alternatives and the weakness of others. Doubts can be reduced when alternatives are compared in this way.

The ability to foresee the barriers that may inhibit the implementation processes of an MBO program forms the basis of the manager's understanding of why he must be active day to day, face to face with his subordinates. The persuasive skills he uses to counteract these barriers and to keep subordinates heading in the committed direction is important in getting the job done. The following guidelines, taken from Abelson's research[4] on how opinions and attitudes are changed, may be useful in developing such skills.

Dealing With Arguments in Implementing Objectives ►

Are more employees persuaded by hearing both sides of an argument or one side only? When group members are generally friendly, when your position is the only one that is being considered, or when you want immediate, though temporary, change, one side of an argument should be considered. However, when the group starts out disagreeing or when it is probable that the group will hear another argument from someone else, it is better to bring out several sides to the argument in a manner most favorable to your position. Do it your way.

When both sides of an argument are to be considered, which should be considered first? When opposite views or arguments are considered one after another, the one considered last will probably be more effective, better remembered, and more persuasive.

In arranging a series of arguments, should the more important ones be considered first or last? If the group is initially not very interested in the issues, the important arguments should be presented first. Where interest is high, save the most important for last.

Will a subordinate's opinion be changed to agree with your own if you state your conclusions or if you let him draw his own? If you want the subordinate to change his opinion, lead him up to the desired change, but let him take the last step himself. People seem to be more easily convinced if they think they make up their own minds.

Allowing Groups to Influence and Change Individuals ►

Are employees in a section persuaded more by the section they are in or by an individual supporting an issue? An employee's opinions and attitudes are strongly influenced by the groups to which he belongs and wants to belong.

What control does a section exercise over its members' opinions when the supervisor wants those opinions changed? The employee is rewarded for conforming to the standards informally set up by the section but often punished for deviating from them.

Which member of a section or group is hardest to persuade? Employees who are the most strongly attached to a group are probably influenced least by the supervisor or organization if its views conflict with the established group norms.

Is it easier to change an attitude that has been stated publicly or one that is held privately? Attitudes that employees make known to others are harder to change than attitudes that they hold privately.

Will you be more persuasive if you get subordinates involved in the issues of an argument? Subordinate participation helps to overcome resistance to change. Receptivity is developed, since ideas and facts help to expose the strengths and weaknesses of an argument.

Understanding the Persistence of an Opinion ►

How long does an existing opinion last? An opinion can remain long after a communication has been forgotten. Almost anyone can marshal, on short notice, any number of sound arguments to support his convictions. A newly adopted attitude remains with its host as long as it continues to provide satisfaction for him. It is probably fair to say that an attitude is adopted in the first place because it answers to some need, such as making a subordinate acceptable to the group he works with.

Does repeating a communication make it more effective? Repeating a communication tends to prolong its influence. Frequent reminders of an original commitment tend to keep alive the commitment in the subordinate's mind.

Is opinion change at its highest point right after the persuasive communication has ended or sometime later? Desired opinion change may be more measureable sometime after exposure to the communication than right after exposure.

Appealing to Individuals ►

What programs and instructions do subordinates tend to look for from supervisors? A great amount of evidence can be cited to show that subordinates look for the programs and instructions that support their attitudes and beliefs, and that they tend not to expose themselves to communications that conflict with their own viewpoints.

Is it best to tailor your appeals to the intelligence levels of your subordinates? Yes. Subordinates with high intelligence will tend — because of their ability to draw valid inferences — to be more influenced than those with low intellectual ability when exposed to persuasive communications that rely primarily on impressive logical arguments. Subordinates with high intelligence will tend — because of their superior critical ability — to be less influenced than those with low intelligence when exposed to persuasive communications that rely primarily on unsupported generalities.

In order to change a subordinate's opinion, what do you have to know about why he has that opinion? When the factors underlying attitudes are taken into account, persuasion is more likely to be successful. Successful persuasion depends on an understanding of why a subordinate should accept your point of view, buy your argument, or reach for stated goals.

What characteristics of subordinates make them more easily influenced by persuasive communications? There seem to be no general susceptibility to persuasion. Rather, subordinates with certain specified personality traits are likely to be more readily persuaded by certain appeals and modes of involvement.

Becoming a Persuader ►

Does an employee have to believe in the persuader before he accepts his arguments? There will be more opinion change as a result of persuasion in the desired direction if the supervisor has high credibility than if he has low credibility.

When is belief in the persuader less important in changing opinions? High credibility sources may be important if the persuasion attempt is designed to get immediate results (signing a document, starting resistance, taking a vote). However, if the aim of persuasion is long term, then the believability of the supervisor may not be such a crucial issue.

Do the persuader's reasons for wanting to change opinions have an effect on how successful he will be? The motives attributed to a supervisor may affect his success in influencing subordinates. If a supervisor does not believe and accept his own argument, his persuasive skill will be weakened.

Is what group of subordinates thinks of a supervisor interrelated and influenced by his message? A supervisor's persuasiveness is increased if he expresses some views that are also held by his subordinates.

Should a persuading supervisor try for a maximum of opinion change or a minimum of opinion change at a specific time? The greater the opinion change desired, the less likely the change will occur.

Indicate true (T) or false (F).

1. Coaching is the guiding and encouraging of employees, in order to motivate them to implement objectives. _____

2. Effective coaching techniques will vary with the objectives to be implemented, the jobs to be done, and the relationship between the supervisor and the subordinate. _____

3. One mark of the success of coaching is the speed with which it can be done. _____

4. A manager must have frequent face-to-face interaction with his subordinates up to the time when they start to implement objectives. _____

5. Effective coaching can be done at any time at all. _____

6. Force and threats of force are open admissions that an MBO program has been less than successful. _____

7. One reason why many people in an MBO program tend to function less than required is that they are victimized by their own old habits. _____

8. Habits are regulators of behavior that can stifle innovation. _____

9. Persuasion consists of instilling and strengthening in a subordinate a positive response toward an objective to counter the negative responses he acquires from others. _____

10. In trying to persuade subordinates, it is always advisable to tell them both sides of the argument. _____

11. An employee's opinions are strongly influenced by the groups to which he belongs and wants to belong. _____

12. A great amount of evidence can be cited to show that employees look for the communications that support their attitudes, and that they tend not to expose themselves to communications that conflict with their attitudes. _____

13. All employees are equally susceptible to persuasion. _____

14. The greater the opinion change desired, the less likely the change will occur. _____

15. There will be more opinion change as a result of persuasion in the desired direction if the supervisor has high credibility than if he has low credibility. _____

● Checkpoint Answers

1. T   2. T   3. F   4. F   5. F   6. T   7. T   8. T   9. T   10. F   11. T
12. T   13. F   14. T   15. T

THE APPLICATION OF PLANNED MOTIVATION

Today, there are many motivational principles[5] useful in increasing employee commitment to organization objectives. These principles often fail in actual practice, however, not so much because they are faulty in themselves, but because management lacks the ability to translate and implement them in a manner consistent with the overall structure and needs of the particular organization.

The complexity of motivational problems is caused by the effects of a whole array of factors demanding optimization. Solutions require that no one factor be entirely neglected or left to chance or considered singly. Rather, a planned, combined, and select fit approach should be used in a progressive manner. In order to discover how they can implement motivational principles, management must

1. Be able to analyze organization objectives, task assignments, work packages, or problem situations as to their technical, financial, and human relations requirements.

2. Recognize the disparity that exists between organization expectations and employee expectations.

3. Acquire an insight into the "whys" of employee behavior and needs and work toward developing the skills to narrow the disparity, using the MBO Rule for Aligning Divergent Objectives.

4. Plan the selection, use, and application of motivators to work assignments or problem situations.

The manager's choice of approach and skill in implementing these processes in a useful strategy determine to a large extent the type of motivational response he gets from his subordinate. The following are the specific procedures an MBO manager should follow to institute planned motivation:

- Build motivators into statements of objectives.

- Examine existing jobs for feasibility of reaching objectives.

- Acquire insights into subordinates' needs.

- Develop a list of potential motivators.

- Apply motivators as a "best fit" toward objectives.

Building Motivators Into Statements of Objectives ▶

Planned motivation begins with the structuring of a formal statement of commitment. The whole motivational strategy begins with objective setting. Getting participation and involvement of those to be committed is a process of relating people meaningfully to their future. The give and take during this phase is an expression of employees' reaching for both organization and individual future needs. It is during this phase that the disparity between the organization and the individual is lessened and goals are brought into greater alignment. The objective network approach and the feeder-objective concept create a system of expectations that the employee not only understands but helps to formulate. Direct employee participation and involvement in decision-making about organization objectives or feeder-objectives provide a strong base for applying additional motivators.

With objectives clearly in view, jobs and job groupings must be examined to determine where additional motivators can be inserted and applied meaningfully. An attempt should be made to avoid demotivators, even if job changes must be made. It is inconceivable for an organization to pursue a set of new objectives and still hang on to old jobs. An organization that embarks on an objective program must be prepared to make job changes to reach its objectives. The creation of a management system requires that jobs and job elements align themselves with the expectations set up by objectives. There are four basic and systematic ways to change a job for motivational purposes, and the MBO manager must be prepared to carry them through. These are illustrated in Figure 4.

4. Ways to Restructure Jobs to Meet Objectives

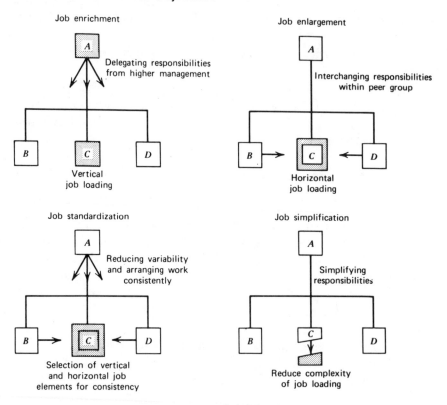

Job enrichment[4] is restructuring an existing job by including a number of duties that the employee finds personally rewarding because they meet many of his higher-level needs. Duties and responsibilities of higher management, when delegated or assigned to subordinates, fall in the enriching category. These are found by allowing the subordinates themselves to identify the enriching elements. In order to fulfill his need, the employee must be convinced that he is doing the work of higher management. This process is known as *vertical job loading* and can be employed in a practical way. As an example of job enrichment, a supervisor might allow his subordinate to help him prepare the annual budget for submission to higher management.

Job enlargement[5] is restructuring an existing job by expanding it to include task elements from other employees' jobs to make it more varied and more meaningful. It meets the employee's needs by eliminating monotony. This process is known as *horizontal job loading*, because it attempts to interchange tasks among a peer group. Horizontal job enlargement tends to counteract oversimplification and gives the worker a whole natural unit of work. As an example of job enlargement, a supervisor might allow his drill press operator to run the miller and sanding machines in addition to the drill press.

Job standardization[6] is the restructuring of an entire job by reducing variety and establishing consistent routines to meet the commitment demands of a feeder-objective. Job standardization may be carried out on the basis of standardized tasks from the higher management level, as well as standardized tasks from the employee's own level. An an example of job standardization, consider the machine operator who runs many different types of machines with varying degrees of skill and productivity, and who also performs a variety of operations with each machine, the particular type of operation changing from day to day. The supervisor standardizes this operator's job by limiting the number of machines he operates and operations he performs from day to day. The supervisor establishes a consistent routine for the operator's daily work.

Job simplification[7] involves reducing a number of task elements or duties within his job that the employee finds personally annoying or difficult. Many employees favor job simplification, since it gives them a high degree of specialization and meets their need to be experts. Less capable subordinates are not given work that overwhelms them. This reduces the amount of support they need from their supervisor and promotes independent action. An example of this is the personnel administrator who is expected to perform a number of personnel functions: to recruit, interview, train, test, counsel, discipline, and discharge. The supervisor simplifies his job by reducing the number of duties he is expected to perform in the personnel department. He may have the personnel administrator specialize in recruiting, interviewing, and hiring.

The manner, method, and time for changing jobs for motivational purposes must be carefully chosen. Several criteria must be used to justify the change. For example, cost of the change must be weighed against increased value of performance. Demotivator effects on group attitudes must be considered before one individual job is altered. Job change must mean greater productivity to a planned and stated objective.

Acquiring Insights Into Employee Needs ►

Motivating employees starts with real insight into their needs. The identification of apparent needs is a part of the planned motivation approach. Having checklists of these needs, such as the following, is helpful. The MBO manager should develop his own list for each individual, as well as for his entire group.

Self-Survival Needs (Biological) ———————————————————————

☐ Needs minimum wage sufficient for biological requirements

☐ Needs food during working hours

☐ Needs protection from dangerous working conditions such as noise, temperature, fumes, dust, and chemicals

☐ Needs water during working hours

☐ Needs rest periods during arduous work

☐ Needs shelter against the weather

☐ Needs to work in an unpolluted environment

☐ Needs regular and sufficient sleep

☐ Needs periodic examinations to assure his survivability

☐ Needs clothing for protection of the body

Self-Comfort Needs (Physiological) ――――――――――――――――――――――

☐ Needs freedom of motion to relieve muscular fatigue

☐ Needs transportation aids to avoid fatigue

☐ Needs facilities to arrange for working conveniences

☐ Needs clean surroundings

☐ Needs an optimum length of working hours

☐ Needs additional wages to make life outside work comfortable

☐ Needs working conditions that will not place undue strain on health

☐ Needs to have work station arranged for ease in carrying out work

☐ Needs exercise to feel healthy

☐ Needs periodic relaxers like coffee and doughnuts

☐ Needs a work atmosphere in which work can be carried on for some time

☐ Needs facilities and equipment for personal habits

☐ Needs housing for opportunity to make a home

Self-Security Needs (Psychological) ――――――――――――――――――――――

☐ Needs security of employment and income

☐ Needs to have supervisor periodically assure him he is needed

☐ Needs to feel protected against unknown future with all types of insurance and a pension

☐ Needs a safe work station

☐ Needs additional wages to provide for bank balance to handle any emergencies

☐ Needs to feel his opportunities do not lead to a dead-end street

☐ Needs to feel he is learning and growing on the job in terms of job requirements and job security

☐ Needs to feel his company is putting into effect quickly his acquired skills in education and training

☐ Needs work that fascinates and generates intense interest

☐ Needs to have his ideas, suggestions, and proposals heard and discussed

☐ Needs to feel his company is growing in capability to secure his future

☐ Needs to feel he has a chance to find his own niche

☐ Needs to feel his company pays salaries as good as or better than other companies

☐ Needs to learn for himself

☐ Needs to know and to be assured periodically where he stands with his supervisor and his company

☐ Needs help to recall or remember facts and procedures not frequently practiced

☐ Needs level of training to achieve what is expected of him

☐ Needs to feel fairness of wages, promotion, and task assignments

☐ Needs clear understanding of the requirements of the job

☐ Needs impartial treatment from supervisor

☐ Needs to know what is going on and why

☐ Needs to know how outside conditions may affect his job

☐ Needs to avoid boring and monotonous routines

☐ Needs to understand company policies as they relate to him and his job

☐ Needs to feel there is justice in management

Self-Worth Needs (Sociological)

☐ Needs to engage in responsibilities that family, relatives, friends, peers, and community think important, significant, and complex

☐ Needs to feel he can do things others cannot

☐ Needs a high salary to feel his "worth" (money is a scorekeeper)

☐ Needs to win among those who are trying to win

☐ Needs to feel he is a future management prospect

☐ Needs to feel the location of the company is valuable for recreation, sports, cultural activities, and friends

☐ Needs to feel the image and reputation of the company are accepted by friends and the community

☐ Needs to talk to people to feel his own individuality

☐ Needs some freedom for individual judgment in doing work

☐ Needs to display company-wide status symbols that convey accomplishment and value

☐ Needs recognition of an individual contribution

☐ Needs to have his ideas, suggestions, and proposals accepted and implemented

☐ Needs opportunity to participate in group activities

☐ Needs to have everyone know that he is steadily progressing and developing

☐ Needs acceptance by his group of peers in intellectual and work activities

☐ Needs to have his opinion treated with respect

☐ Needs to be identified by name

☐ Needs to be involved and participating in decisions affecting his job or other jobs with which he is connected

☐ Needs to know relationship of the job to the finished product

☐ Needs to know relationship of the job to the supervisor's job

☐ Needs to know relationship of his job to those of others in the group

☐ Needs to feel and understand that job change is change upward

Self-Fulfillment (Idealistic) —————————————————————————————

☐ Needs to have life goals respected and accepted in such areas as religion, art, fame, beauty, and humanity

☐ Needs to feel he is a counselor with plenty of available good advice

☐ Needs to feel great rewards await him as recognition of his achievements and contributions

☐ Needs to feel more important than his supervisor

☐ Needs to do increasingly more different work toward great achievements

☐ Needs to feel his experiences are broadening; that is, while in production, he deals with personnel problems; while in engineering, he deals with finances; while in marketing, he deals with manufacturing

☐ Needs to feel that job assignments are meaningful milestones of progress in a great career

☐ Needs to feel someday he can be president of the company

☐ Needs to feel that if he wishes, he can be a consultant to many companies

☐ Needs to have plans for and confidence in a bright future

☐ Needs a sense of outstanding citizenship in the community

☐ Needs to be recognized for religious values

☐ Needs to feel there is a future life and that death does not end all

☐ Needs to display company status symbols among his peers, to show them that he is rising in the organization

☐ Needs to feel he can retire in a manner that meets his retirement needs

Developing a List of Potential Motivators ►

In applying the planned motivation concept, the MBO manager not only acquires an insight into why people work and what the effects of needs on behavior and performance are, but he also formulates a list of motivators that are potentially capable of connecting the needs of employees with the needs of the organization. Having a list of these motivators is helpful. The manager should be aware, however, that they will not work all the time with all people. They are, rather, potential sources of motivation that may work if the conditions are right and if they are applied skillfully. It should be kept in mind that they could become demotivators if improperly used under unfavorable conditions. The following list is broken up into two parts: nonfinancial motivators and financial motivators.

Nonfinancial Motivators

Arrange work for performance stretch. The most effective effort is put forth by employees when they attempt tasks that fall in the range of challenge — that is, not too easy and not too hard — where success seems quite possible but not certain. High performance can never be achieved without high standards. The very process of determining what constitutes challenge and setting objectives accordingly, if done with the employee and not for him, is a potent motivator for getting him to act. Possible challenges lie in increasing the number of assignments performed by any one employee and shortening the time in which a set of assignments is to be completed.

Acknowledge performance accomplishments toward objectives. If a good job performance is recognized and rewarded, it is more likely to recur. The type of performance most likely to emerge in any situation is that which the subordinate found successful or satisfying previously in a similar situation. The supervisor who plans and provides for a steady, cumulative sequence of successful performance experiences toward attainable objectives will bring the subordinate to a high level of motivation. Such a supervisor will see that subordinates get recognition for those accomplishments that both he and the employee consider important or substantial. He will give a feedback to the individual on what he has or has not accomplished, both positive and negative.

Allow participation in the job itself. Employees are more apt to throw themselves whole-heartedly into a work assignment if they themselves have participated in the selection, planning, and decision-making involved in the work packages. A subordinate should become involved and make as many decisions as necessary about the work he is to do. He should be given as much responsibility as he can and will take. Genuine participation, not pretended sharing, has been found to increase the desires to produce, learn, and excel.

Arrange and give promotional opportunities. Avenues of advancement should be provided for all employees, regardless of sex, age, and length of service. Paramount in the minds of employees is the question, "How can I get ahead?" A supervisor who provides these opportunities for advancement immediately after a job well done will find they have more influence on a subordinate than any big promotion that comes much later. In fact, promotion, to be most effective to an employee or to his on-looking peers, should almost immediately follow a desired performance and be clearly connected with that performance in the minds of all employees.

Enlarge, enrich, simplify or standardize jobs. Monotonous, mechanical effort causes most employees to become dullards on the job. Opportunity for fresh and stimulating experiences is a kind of reward quite effective in motivating. Job enlargement and enrichment with varied or innovative experiences provide a stimulus to the employee. Complicated work tasks should be made simpler and easier to understand. Special projects, unusual assignments, and working with other groups on new responsibilities are some of the ways to do this. Job changes must be legitimate changes in the minds of subordinates, which often means rewriting position descriptions.

Develop and train subordinates. When a subordinate experiences discouragement and failure in his work assignments, his self-confidence, level of aspiration, and sense of worth are likely to be damaged. The employee who sees himself at his worst at work is liable to place little value on his job. Conversely, an employee who sees his supervisor take a personal interest in his acquiring new skills and knowledge is likely to spur his performance to greater levels.

A supervisor must be a motivational example. Employees learn much from seeing and observing their supervisor and fellow workers accomplishing their tasks. Subordinates' attitudes are heavily influenced by preferences of their group and supervisor. There is nothing quite so effective as for the supervisor to be an example of what he requires.

Provide better than minimum working conditions. An employee's reaction to such things as poor working conditions — noise, faulty equipment, or distractive conversations, for example — is likely to be apathetic conformity, defiance, scapegoating, or escape. The existence of working conditions below what is regarded as minimum for doing a job provides the basis of dissatisfaction. The supervisor should help the employee in his day-to-day accomplishment by controlling unfavorable working surroundings. This will remove demotivators or dissatisfiers.

Invite inventiveness and creativity on the job. Employees' reactions to excessive direction and autocratic demands lower the stimulation to think, learn, and suggest. An employee who has been working at a job for a period of time will often find better ways to do that job. The supervisor should be receptive at all times to ideas and suggestions for working more efficiently and productively. He should ask subordinates for their opinions and suggestions.

Show employees' contributions to the "big picture." Every employee wants to know where he fits into the organization. The supervisor should explain to him why his job is important in relation to the entire enterprise. There is a great transfer value to an individual situation through collecting and seeing other situations. Whenever possible, a supervisor should share with subordinates the exciting plans and programs for the future. Other motivators:

- Give knowledge of progress performance in getting results.

- Arrange periodic face-to-face meetings for open discussion (president—supervisors; supervisor—his group).

- Show employees what other employees can do and are doing.

- Set up a pride system for meeting targets.

- Delegate responsibility early and encourage rapid promotion.

- Show personal interest in the employee's knowledge, skills, and progress on the job.

- Provide informal coaching and teaching on the "whys" of the job.

- Allow some freedom for individual judgment when making work assignments.

- Provide for competition with others through self-determined standards.

- Involve employee in broad-range goal setting for the organization.

- Provide access to information as related to job requirements and needs.

- Create an atmosphere of positive attitudes and approval.

- Assign employee to influential group of workers with positive attitudes and high standards.

Financial Motivators

Relate wages and salaries to MBO productivity. Annual salaries established at levels on a par with similar positions in the industry and the labor market can no longer be considered effective for motivational purposes. An accountant working in an insurance company and making a fairly typical amount a year will not be financially motivated to transfer to an advertising agency at the same rate of pay. To use wages and salaries as a motivator, the level of dispensation must be higher than that available in the labor market. When the advertising agency offers a substantial increase, the accountant may have the incentive to transfer. Additionally, to use increases in wages and salaries as a motivator, the increases must relate to results the employee obtained on the job. It should be made clear to all that rewards and remuneration should be clearly granted on MBO productivity. The whole process of relating MBO productivity and financial rewards is accomplished with the formal commitment to measure performance against objectives, as worked out and validated between a supervisor and his subordinate for a specified time period.

Give favorable edge to fringe benefit program. Standard fringe benefit packages can no longer be regarded as important for motivational purposes. Such items as vacations, life insurance, travel benefits, and accident, hospitalization, and retirement insurance are now expected norms in many jobs. An organization must provide an exceptional benefit in its fringe package, a benefit offered by no other organization in the same labor market. Some examples of outstanding fringe benefits that support MBO productivity are bonus vacations for increased productivity; educational tuition abatement for favorable performance review; organization-sponsored travel for reaching and exceeding targeted objectives; and use of organization facilities and equipment when results and performance have reached specified levels.

Make effective use of financial incentives. Financial incentives intended to improve the manager's or subordinate's economic status and to give tangible recognition of his effort can be potent motivators. Incentives falling within this category include expense account allowances, annual bonuses based upon operating results, and use of organization owned or leased resort facilities.

Set up attractive deferred compensation programs. Compensation programs that contain provisions creating deferred compensation for the individual while immediate tax deductions can be taken by the organization are as follows: pension plans, profit-sharing plans, stock-option plans, retirement plans, production profit plans, phantom stock plans, and thrift plans. The decision as to their use will depend upon conditions specific to the organization and comparable costs of the programs. Plans that provide opportunities for ownership, such as the stock option, create a sense of partnership and are most potent as motivators. Deferred compensation rewards should be set up to fall within short periods for younger employees and longer periods for older employees.

Case Examples ►

The following case examples illustrate the use of planned motivation to align the needs of the organization with organization objectives in such a way that both are implemented within an expected time.

Problem Situation	Employee Needs	Potential Demotivators	Potential Motivators	Best Fit Application
Problem: unable to get and keep employees working in the foundry	Foundry Worker	Foundry hot, dirty, smelly place to work	Make work desirable and safer	Install fans, safety devices, showers, and lockers
Objective: reduce foundry turnover 10% within 12 months	Needs protection from dangerous working conditions	Many safety hazards exist	Keep environment clean	Automate foundry processes where possible; encourage foundry workers to operate equipment
	Needs to work in an unpolluted environment	Low company image to work in foundry	Raise value of job equal to or better than other job classifications	Allow shower time within working day
	Needs job with good image to family, peers, and community	Low community image to be foundry worker	Provide automated working conditions where possible	Redesign job in order to raise wages to other job classifications
	Needs facility aids for working conveniences	Lowest wage classification in company	Provide privilege for foundry workers not found in other jobs	Match workers' attitudes and temperament to job requirements
	Needs to see value and importance of foundry work	Dead-end job — no transfers in or out	Build up image of foundry jobs in the community	Build up image and importance of jobs in foundry throughout company
			Encourage transfers to other jobs for qualified individuals	

Motivational Problem Situation	Employee Needs	Potential Demotivators	Potential Motivators	Best Fit Application
Problem: low productivity	Jerry Daniels			
Objective: increase productive output 15% within next 4 operating quarters	Needs and wants job security since loyalty to family strong	Work routine and boring	Enrich job for variety and interest	Provide face-to-face discussions to collect ideas on how to improve productivity
	Needs to do quality work; takes pride in finished product	Indifferent climate prevails: high performance not recognized, low performance not corrected	Arrange some challenges for performance stretches	Discuss possible job transfer to an area of low productivity requirements
	Needs no accumulation of money	Supervision pushes quantity at the sacrifice of quality	Assure family-connected deferred compensation normal	
	Needs to be involved because of high capacity and ability	Work simple and task elements few in number per employee	Recognize performance for both quality and quantity	Enrich job with responsibility to conduct informal on-the-job training and indoctrination of new emploees
	Needs to feel he is a counselor with plenty of available good advice	Work situation stifles human individualizing	Allow participation in parts of job planning	Set up "pride" system of meeting targets of both quantity and quality

Motivational Problem Situation	Employee Needs	Potential Demotivators	Potential Motivators	Best Fit
Problem: employee at the top of pay scale and unable to get merit increase	Peter Kyle			
	Needs to accumulate money	Company's principal method of getting and holding employees has been with financial motivators	Arrange training and developing experiences for higher classifications	Enrich job with leadership and supervisory responsibilities
Objective: to retain in employment ambitious and outstanding employee	Needs opportunities for growth and advancement			Enroll in presupervisory training and development
	Needs to feel his company is growing	Company's wage structure has fixed limits to wage levels	Enrich job with additional responsibilities	Redesign job to enlarge tasks from peers and obtain new classification
	Needs work challenges			
	Needs to learn new things on the job	Limited participation in departmental planning and decision making	Involve in broad-range goal setting of department	Allow some freedom to set self-determined standards
	Needs to feel his job does not lead to a dead-end street		Assure merit-rating limit. Explore adjusting merit structure upward	Encourage ideas for improvement of company or department

8. Planned Motivation Schedule: Case Example 4

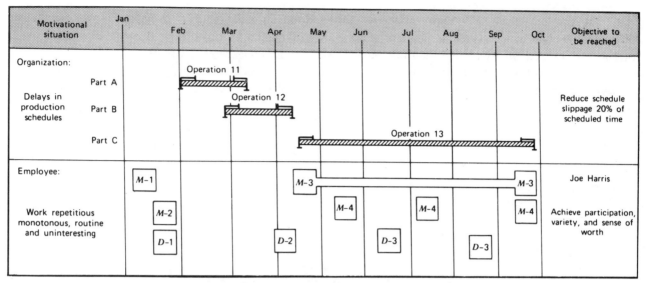

M—1 Arrange face-to-face discussion to collect ideas on how to avoid delays
M—2 Allow Harris to suggest ideas on how to handle customer changes
D—1 Avoid schedules "mysteriously" set by outside person
D—2 Avoid unsatisfactory working conditions
M—3 Enlarge job to include dispatching responsibilites conditional to completing operation 13
M—4 Show performance progress toward targeted dates
D—3 Allow Harris to suggest ideas for automating repetitive routines

9. Planned Motivation Schedule: Case Example 5

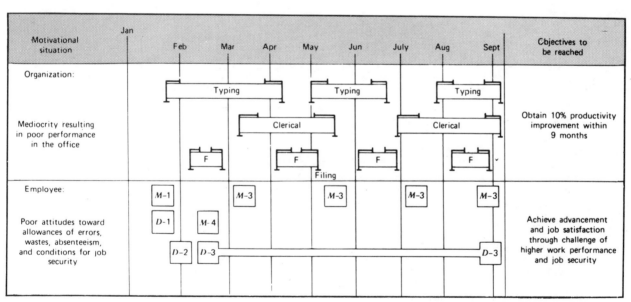

D—1 Provide conference and group discussion on factors for job security
M—1 Institute standards of performance in wastes, absenteeism, errors, and connect to income progression
D—2 Identify and control causes of poor attitudes and interruptions
D—3 Create climate of improvement through supervisory and employee examples
M—3 Show periodic high personal interest in performance improvement, provide coaching and training
M—4 Institute rotational scheme or transfers among employees in similar jobs to avoid job mismatch

◄ SUMMARY ►

The implementing skill required to get things done on a day-to-day, program-to-program, objective-to-objective basis is the heart of successfully managing by objectives. It is the true mark of the MBO manager. By using this implementing skill, the manager gets employees to participate in objective programs because they want to and not because they are driven to. Planned motivation is the core of this objective implementation, and coaching and persuading are key motivational devices.

1. Frederick Herzberg, "One More Time: How Do You Motivate Employees?" *Harvard Business Review,* January — February 1968, pp. 53-62.

2. Abraham H. Maslow, *Motivation and Personality,* Harper and Brothers, 1954.

3. Roger Bellows, *Creative Leadership,* Prentice-Hall, Englewood Cliffs, N.J., 1959, p. 178.

4. Herbert I. Abelson, *Persuasion,* Springer, New York, 1959.

5. Many perceptions of the motivational processes are available in the literature. The reader interested in pursuing these ideas is reminded of the following: S. W. Gullerman, *Management by Motivation,* American Management Association, New York, 1968; F. Herzberg, B. Mausner, and B. B. Snyderman, *The Motivation to Work,* John Wiley, New York, 1965; D. McGregor, *Human Side of Enterprise,* McGraw-Hill Book Co., New York, 1960; V. H. Vroom, *Work and Motivation,* John Wiley, New York, 1964.

6. Frederick Herzberg, William J. Paul, and Keith B. Robertson, "Job Enrichment Pays Off," *Harvard Business Review,* March—April 1969, pp. 61—78.

7. *Ibid.*, pp. 61—78.

8. Benjamin W. Niebel, *Motion and Time Study,* Richard D. Irwin, Homewood, Ill., 1967, pp. 348—371.

9. Gerald Nadler, *Work Simplification,* McGraw-Hill Book Co., New York, 1957, pp. 124—141.

Chapter 6 Review

√√Doublecheck

Draw a line to match each term in the first column to its element in the second column.

1. Job Enrichment   a.   Horizontal job loading

2. Job Enlargement   b.   Reducing variety and establishing routines

3. Job Standardization   c.   Vertical job loading

4. Job Simplification   d.   Reducing number of tasks

Indicate true (T) or false (F).

5. In applying the planned motivation concept, the MBO manager formulates a list of motivators that are potentially capable of connecting the needs of employees with the needs of the organization. _____

6. The whole motivational strategy begins with objective setting. _____

7. All motivators are financial in nature. _____

8. Employees are more apt to throw themselves whole-heartedly into a work assignment if they themselves have participated in the selection, planning, and decision-making involved in the work packages. _____

Answer briefly.

9. What are motivators? Demotivators?

    _____

    _____

    _____

    _____

    _____

10. List five nonfinancial motivators.

    _____

    _____

    _____

    _____

    _____

•   Doublecheck Answers

1. c.   2. a.   3. b.   4. d.   5. T   6. T   7. F   8. T

9. Motivators are those conditions or agents within a job that cause employees to act. Motivators are job factors that give employees satisfaction. Demotivators are those conditions or agents within a job that give employees dissatisfaction. Demotivators are job or environmental constraints that will inhibit an individual from reaching an objective. There is a delicate balance between motivators and demotivators. Too much or too little of a motivator will turn it into a demotivator. For example, challenge is now regarded as one of the most potent motivators. Yet too much challenge or too little will render it a demotivator.

10. To provide nonfinancial motivation, a manager can 1) arrange work for performance stretch, 2) acknowledge performance accomplishments toward objectives, 3) allow participation in the definition of the work package, 4) arrange promotional opportunities, 5) develop and train subordinates.

A major firm in the field of industrial machinery fabrication is planning to launch a massive campaign to push the sale of a recently developed item of industrial hardware. You are asked to prepare the arrow diagram from which schedules for the campaign preparation can be developed. You have available the information listed in the following material. The number in parentheses following the description of each activity indicates the estimated time required for its accomplishment. In general, the project may be broken down into three major categories:

1. Training of sales personnel

2. Consultation with and training of marketing personnel

3. Preparation of the necessary advertising and instruction material for the campaign

SALES

In order to save time on the sales side, it has been decided to prepare phase 1 of the training program for salesmen. (8)

At the same time, the sales managers are selecting the sales personnel who are to be trained. (2)

Both of these activities will therefore begin at the start of the project.

Following their selection, the chosen sales personnel must be relieved of their responsibilities in their areas and sent to the company's training center in the home office. (4)

Obviously it would be foolish for the salesmen to arrive before phase 1 of the training program is ready for them. When phase 1 of the program is prepared, the salesmen will be trained in this part of the program. (10)

While the salesmen are being trained in phase 1 of the program, phase 2 will be prepared. (9)

As soon as the salesmen's training in the first phase is completed and phase 2 of the program has been completed and approved,[2] sales training in the second phase can commence. The second part of the program will take (12).

At the conclusion of the two major phases of their training, the sales personnel will be issued "Customers Instruction Manuals" on the new machine and will spend a short time at the home office becoming familiar with them. (5)

When the salesmen are familiar with the manuals, they will return to their respective territories ready to begin their effort simultaneously with the national advertising campaign. Getting back to their territories should take (1).

---

[1] Copyright © 1973 by the President and Fellows of Harvard College. Reprinted by permission.

[2] Approval cannot be given until the General Marketing Approach (see "marketing" section) has been determined.

I. Personnel

The first step in the project for the marketing side will be the determination of the general marketing approach. (10)

When this has been arranged, the necessary marketing personnel will be selected (4) and brought into the home office. (2)

Following the determination of the general marketing approach, and while the marketing trainees are being selected and brought in, specific training plans for the marketing personnel will be consolidated. (2)

After these plans are consolidated, a familiarization course for these personnel will be designed. (8)

When personnel and course are ready, the training of marketing personnel will proceed. It is estimated to take (8).

II. Advertising

Immediately after the general marketing approach has been determined, advertising plans must be consolidated ("firmed up" in the jargon of the trade). (6)

When this consolidation is complete, a paper is to be *prepared*, (6) and *printed* in a professional journal. (8)

Also immediately following the consolidation of advertising plans, national advertising must be prepared, (10) approved, (4) and distributed to the proper media. (2)

Not until the *marketing* people are trained, the professional paper published, and the advertising distributed, will the national advertising be released and carried by the media involved. The release and preparation to carry the national advertising will take about (2).

It is not planned to proceed further with the national advertising campaign until the salesmen have returned to their territories.

III. Printing

As soon as the advertising plans are consolidated, (the first step under "Advertising" above) a general brochure will be drafted and approved. (4)

Following the approval of the brochure, a *layout* must be designed (5) and the brochure *printed*. (3)

As soon as the brochure is approved, a "Customer's Instruction Manual" will be prepared. (3)

The Instruction Manual in its turn must be approved (1) and printed. (2)

Copies of the Instruction Manual alone will be sent to the training center (1) where the Manual will be utilized in completing the training of the salesmen.

As soon as both the brochure and manual are printed, they will be packaged together and delivered to marketing for general distribution. The packaging and delivery together should take about (8).

Actual implementation of the campaign (which may be regarded as the termination of this project) cannot begin until the salesmen are in their territories, the national advertising campaign released, and the proper brochures and manuals have been received by marketing.

Assignment

Prepare the arrow diagram for this project and select the critical path or paths.

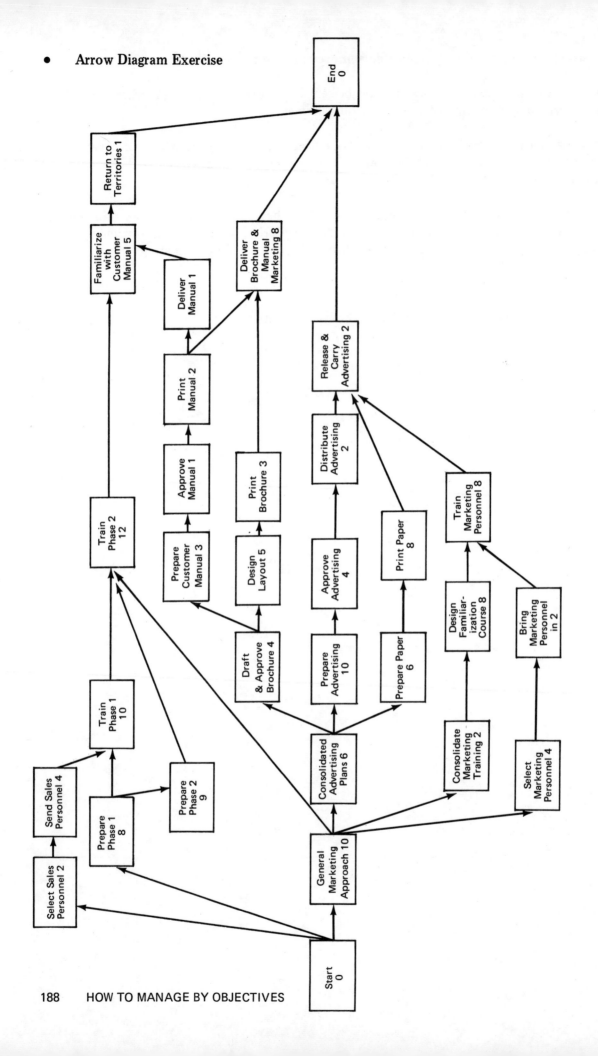

IV. CONTROLLING AND MAINTAINING MBO PROGRAMS

IV
CONTROLLING AND
MAINTAINING MBO PROGRAMS

SELECTED READINGS

7. Controlling and Reporting Status of Objectives

Allen, Louis A., *The Management Profession,* McGraw-Hill Book Co., New York, 1964.

Kellogg, Marion S., *What To Do about Performance Appraisals,* American Management Association, 1965.

Kepner, Charles H., and Benjamin B. Tregoe, *The Rational Manager,* McGraw-Hill Book Co., New York, 1965.

Lindberg, Roy A., "Operations Auditing: What It Is? What It Isn't?" *Management Review,* December 1959.

Lindberg, Roy A., "The Unfamiliar Art of Controlling," *Management Review,* August 1969.

O'Brien, James J., *Scheduling Handbook,* McGraw-Hill Book Co., New York, 1969.

Rowland, Virgil K., *Managerial Performance Standards,* American Management Association, New York, 1960

Tosi, Henry L., and Stephen J. Carroll, "Managerial Reaction to Management by Objectives," *Journal of the Academy of Management,* vol. II, no. 4, December 1968.

Van Valkenburgh, J. F., T. B. Nooger and K. P. Neville, *Basic Synchros and Servomechanisms,* vol. 2, John F. Rider, New York, 1955.

8. Training and Developing MBO Managers

Fryer, Douglas H., Mortimer R. Reinberg and Sheldon S. Zalkind, *Developing People in Industry,* Harper Brothers, New York, 1956.

Kellogg, Marion S., *Closing the Performance Gap,* American Management Association, New York, 1967.

Odiorne, George S., *Management by Objectives,* Pitman Publishing Co., New York, 1965.

9. Improvement Applications

Astor, Saul D., "Plant Security," *Handbook of Business Administration,* McGraw-Hill Book Co., New York, 1967.

Barnes, Ralph M., *Motion and Time Study,* John Wiley & Sons, Inc., New York, 1966.

Bradhurst, Murphy W., "Cutting Costs: Get Everyone in the Act," *Cost Control and the Supervisor,* American Management Association, New York, 1956.

Bursk, Edward C., and John F. Chapman, *Modern Marketing Strategy,* New American Library, New York, 1964.

Carroll, Phil, *Profit Control: How to Plug Profit Leaks,* McGraw-Hill Book Co., New York, 1962.

Ferrell, Robert W., *Customer-Oriented Planning,* American Management Association, New York, 1964.

Hanson, Kemit O., and George J. Brabb, *Managerial Statistics* Prentice-Hall, Englewood Cliffs, New Jersey, 1955.

McCay, James T., *The Management of Time,* Prentice-Hall, Englewood Cliffs, New Jersey, 1959.

Nichols, Ralph G., and Leonard A. Stevens, *Are You Listening?* McGraw-Hill Book Co., New York, 1957.

Parkinson, C. Northcote, *Parkinson's Law,* Houghton Mifflin, New York, 1967.

Peter, Laurence J., and Raymond Hull, *Peter Principle,* Bantam Books, New York, 1969.

Rose, Homer C., *The Development and Supervision of Training Programs,* American Technical Society, New York, 1964.

Staley, John D., *The Cost-Minded Manager,* American Management Association, New York, 1961.

Updegraff, Robert R., *All the Time You Need,* Prentice-Hall, Englewood Cliffs, New Jersey, 1958.

IV. CONTROLLING AND MAINTAINING MBO PROGRAMS

Key Concepts

- *MBO Control.* The purpose of control is to keep activities and efforts on a prescribed course of action. Effective control involves measurement, evaluation, and action and must be real time so that performance variation can be acted on in time to still achieve stated objectives.

- *Status Reporting.* An effective status reporting system is designed to inform all members of management of those items, relevant to their areas of responsibility, that require attention. The system itself must have a definite, logical action pattern and provide timely feedback. When handled effectively, the system provides the MBO manager with a set of working tools for effecting the best possible action at the best possible time.

- *Performance Appraisal.* Such an appraisal serves as a basis for evaluating both individual and organizational performance. The key to successful performance appraisal is tying it to clearly stated performance objectives that are oriented toward job requirements and results rather than toward personality traits or general descriptors.

Learning Objectives

After you have completed this chapter, you should be able to

- List the guidelines for controlling and reporting MBO objectives.

- Summarize the systems concept of objectives status control.

- Describe the advantages of MBO performance appraisals.

- Describe some basic MBO-system trouble spots and suggest remedies for them.

CONTROLLING AND REPORTING: DEFINITION AND GUIDELINES

Controlling and reporting the status of objectives is the fifth and last of the five MBO steps. This chapter will describe how this step is taken, both as an integral part of the first four MBO steps and as a follow-up of implementing objectives. Control should not be treated as a separate function, but as part of the total objective-setting and implementing process. Planning and controlling are inseparable. Control begins with planning by building control points into the objective program. The MBO manager assesses and regulates work in progress with these points, to make sure that what is happening is what he wants to happen. Then, after the objectives have been implemented, he appraises the results to ensure that what is intended to be accomplished is accomplished within defined boundaries, or standards. The boundaries are many, but four commonly stand out:

- Quantity (How much?)
- Time (When accomplished?)

- Quality (How good?)
- Cost (What expense?)

Controlling consists of keeping work activities within specified performance standards such as these. The standards guide the individuals and activities toward the objectives. Comparing actual performance with predetermined standards and ascertaining the difference, if any, is the core of keeping the implementation processes on course toward targets. Such comparison will help the MBO manager avoid overshooting and undershooting of standards. As illustrated in Figure 1, overshooting and undershooting may result in wasted time, money, effort, and material.

1. Met and Unmet Performance Standards

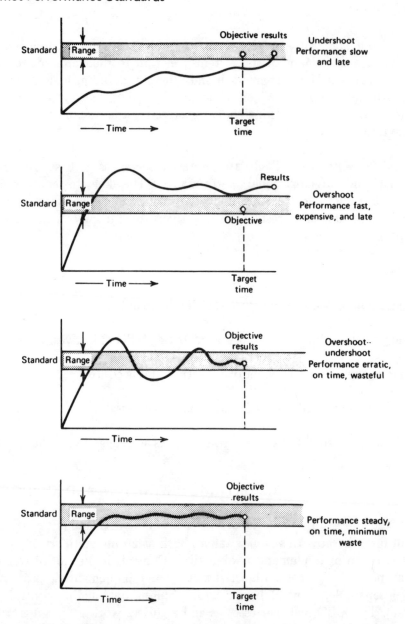

The MBO manager, then, must see that neither too much nor too little is produced; that costs and quality of performance are neither too high nor too low; and that objectives are reached on time, without slippage in either direction. To these ends, the following are some useful guidelines.

Assuring That a Control System Exists ►

One disadvantage of the MBO system is that an unrecognized problem, if allowed to get out of control, can conceivably create a chain reaction that will seriously delay or even halt the entire objective program. To overcome this disadvantage, a system of controls must be incorporated into the MBO system. Key elements of this control system must be identified, coordinated, and made to act in unison. Control points or standards should be identified and ranked for importance in keeping the objective program on course. Greatest control effort should be concentrated at the points of action and decision-making. The further away from a point of action the control effort is made, the less effective the control. Control should be focused where problems are generated, since nipping problems in the bud will eliminate a host of secondary and tertiary effects.

Scheduling Controls ►

The importance of putting the control system on a real-time basis cannot be overstressed. The MBO manager must control his program in such a way that objectives will be reached on schedule. Some objective programs can be computerized, thereby providing variance returns within the time period, to effect a correction for targeted time. Noncomputer timing techniques — such as control charts, Gantt charts, PERT networks and other schedules — are very useful for handling performance measurement with regard to target time and standards.

Real-time control means that performance variances must be identified and given to the manager in sufficient time for him to make corrections necessary for reaching the objective by the targeted date. In some cases, day-to-day surveillance and control may be necessary. In other cases, week-to-week or month-to-month control may suffice.

Using Performance Standards ►

A performance standard gives employees a guideline for differentiating acceptable intensity of work from unacceptable intensity of work. It also serves as a springboard to higher standards for the future. The standard defines a range of output, from minimum level to maximum level, that will eventually lead to a targeted objective. For example, the MBO manager must assure quality to a minimum level or run costs beyond those expected in the commitment. The range between these two levels has to be defined as the intensity of performance just right to meet the objective.

A performance standard gives the criteria by which progress can be measured and evaluated. If the standards are understood and accepted by both supervisor and subordinate, then both need only concern themselves with variances from the standard. These variances give an idea of the corrective action that needs to be taken to get results on a short-range, day-to-day basis. Programs, schedules, and budgets should be defined and arranged in terms of the intensity of work required to achieve objectives.

Setting up Performance Measures ►

Performance measuring is the work an MBO manager does in recording and reporting work in progress and work completed. Recording and reporting involve evaluating and checking the performance against planned action and conveying this information to all concerned. Measurements are made to answer such questions as: How long will it take? Are we doing the work that is needed? Do we need more manpower? Can we interchange work tasks among two groups? In order to make measurements, suitable units of measure must be built into standards. When we ask how long something will take, we expect an answer that will tell us how many days, weeks, or hours. Similarly, when we ask whether we need more manpower, we must use units of measure to give us answers in terms of more or less manpower. When units of performance measurement are carefully identified and built into objectives, all that is needed is careful reading and reporting. Evaluating work performance in progress, for example, requires comparing actual performance with expected performance. This evaluation cannot take place unless performance measures are used that variances are collected and conveyed to those who can execute a correction.

Providing Audit and Inspection of System ►

The MBO manager should always be observing, reviewing, and inspecting to see that the control system is functioning as intended. Periodic audits are one way to assure this. The audit inquires into the accuracy of the records and the results reported. It goes into the adequacy of the management system as well. A good audit should be carried through all phases of the MBO strategy. The baselines described in Chapter 1 are documentation points for collecting information and making decisions. Changes are made to and from this point. The audit very often can use these decision modes to verify practice and performance against what was agreed upon in the baselines. Unsatisfactory items in the audit are referred to the responsible members of the organization for immediate action.

The reader can readily see that auditing should start with the individuals involved in the work. It should be an act of self-evaluation and self-correction. The manager may find it a good idea to allow an outside group with an objective view of matters to analyze the program to be sure it is moving in the directions expected.

Indicate true (T) or false (F).

1. Controlling and reporting status of objectives, the last of the five MBO steps, only becomes important after the other four steps have been completed. _____

2. Controlling consists of keeping work activities within specified standards. _____

3. When objectives are either overshot or undershot, wasted time, money, effort, and material may result. _____

4. In status reporting, the MBO manager need not be concerned with costs. _____

5. Control should be focused where problems are generated, since nipping problems in the bud will eliminate a host of secondary and tertiary effects. _____

6. Real-time control means that performance variances must be identified and given to the manager in time for him to make corrections necessary for reaching objectives by targeted dates. _____

7. Day-to-day surveillance is always necessary. _____

8. A performance standard may serve as a springboard to higher standards for the future. _____

9. The MBO manager cannot evaluate work in progress without performance measures. _____

10. An audit, which inquires into the accuracy of records, should be carried through all phases of the MBO strategy. _____

─────────────────────────────

● Checkpoint Answers

1. F   2. T   3. T   4. F   5. T   6. T   7. F   8. T   9. T   10. T

The Nature of Status Reporting ►

An effective status reporting system is a system designed to keep all levels of management completely informed on the status of the objectives being implemented. Status reporting must be an integral part of the total information flow in the organization; emphasis must be on reporting in time for decision-making and correcting. Record keeping, follow-up reports, and status information on results should be the MBO managers working tools for effecting the best possible action at the best possible time with the responsible personnel.

Status reporting involves organizing information so that it reveals changes that are needed to remove barriers to reaching an objective. Giving too much, too little, or the wrong kind of information must be guarded against. Every effort must be made to relieve the MBO manager of having to wade through data to extract meaningful information. The concept of status reporting is illustrated in Figure 2.[1]

2. Systems Concept of Objective Status Control

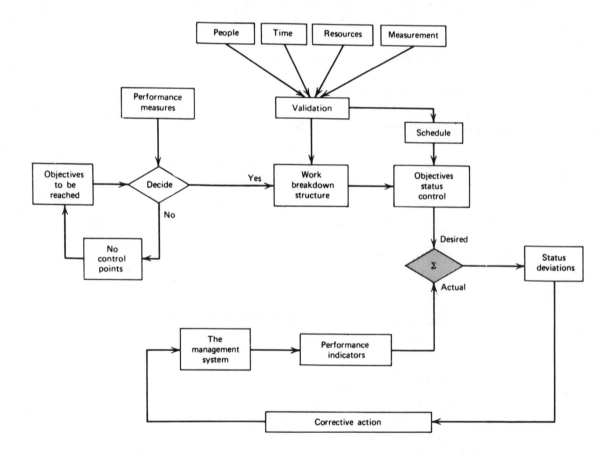

Status control of objectives requires a set of procedures that provide continuous feedback to the manager. There is no reason why accounting information and existing reports cannot be used for this purpose. These documents need to be placed in a status reporting format that is, above everything else, aimed at stimulating needed action toward accomplishing objectives. A good objective status control system focuses on deviations from objectives set for each manager for a particular period. It is the examination of results for that period. A status report for that period would be sent to the responsible manager, outlining the status of his activities.

Perfect progress should not be expected in any status reporting system. The most one can realistically aim for is a minimum number of status deviations and a minimum number of corrective actions. That perfection is not achievable is largely due to the conflicts that arise between individuals' interests and the organization's requirements. The status control system must sense the deviations of targeted progress from actual progress and assure that these fluctuations remain within acceptable limits. A "down" in one period must be compensated for by an "up" in the next period.

Ordinarily, an objective status control system is a total system in the sense that it embraces all aspects of organization commitments and activities. It needs to be a total system to ensure that all activities are proceeding as intended and are in balance with each other. With this total view, management can review the manner in which each part is progressing in relation to the whole. For this reason, the objective status system must be interlocked into the MBO system. All performance indicators and progress measurements must be related and structured into this system. This is not to say that each manager cannot set up his own objective status system in order to have fingertip control of his program and his progress. He can tailor fit his own control system to meet the needs of his group. However, he must be sure that his individual status control system is compatible with that of the whole organization.

This overall objective status control system has two essentials: a definite logical action pattern and a feedback reporting time matrix. In the logical action pattern, certain steps are taken in a prescribed sequence so that status deviations are easily revealed and corrective action indicated. The feedback reporting time matrix relates the expected activities on a time scale with appropriate dates. A PERT network system is a natural means for measuring actual time against expected or estimated time. A status control structure is suggested in Figure 3.

3. Status Control Model

Report Period

Department

A	B	C		D	E
Targeted Events	Key Control Points	Activities and Schedule (Milestones of Progress)		Status Deviations	Corrective Action Responsibility
		Ja Fe Ma Ap Ma Ju Jy Ag Se Oc No De Ja Fe Ma Ap			
End item 1	Progress standard				
	Actual performance				
End item 2	Progress standard				
	Actual performance				
End item 3	Progress standard				
	Actual performance				
End item 4	Progress standard				
	Actual performance				
etc.	etc.				
	etc.				

Column A. This column lists targeted events, or end items, found in the work breakdown structure, that require critical control. Each MBO manager must analyze the network to determine the critical events that require careful surveillance and status reporting, particularly in critical paths and related paths to other networks.

Column B. Measurement presupposes a series of key points or performance indicators to collect information and data on expected progress against actual performance. Quantitative standards or judgmental statements that are indicators of performance are identified for each of the major events. (A sample listing of quantitative measures that can be used as performance indicators appears in the next section.)

Column C. On the principle that time is the essential dimension for comparing expected activities with actual activities, a schedule is utilized in the comparison. On the schedule, one can readily contrast progress of work.

Column D. Status deviations are immediately apparent at the control point. Status deviations are identified as failures or deficiencies in terms of what is expected within the status reporting period.

Column E. Corrective action responsibility is the identification of the individual or section that will be responsible for following up measured deviations with plans for corrective action to eliminate or minimize the deviations.

MBO managers are increasingly operating their objective programs out of sight of their superiors and other managers. An overview of the entire program is thus difficult to obtain. Even traditional forms of status reporting are being overworked in the attempt to supply this total overview. The growth of information management is a symptom of this. The larger the organization practicing management by objectives, the greater its need for managers to be knowledgeable and effective in areas beyond their direct observation. Operations auditing,[2] a new management technique, has come into existence because of this need. Operations auditing is particularly critical for top management personnel who are involved initially in the objective-setting and validation processes but who withdraw during the implementation and control phases. Status reporting, which is a form of operations auditing, should give top management a quick overview of progress.

Status Control Performance Indicators ►

Since control consists primarily of measurement, it is necessary to adopt a basis of measurement that will qualitatively and quantitatively disclose actual progress in relation to expected progress. It must be remembered that the basic purpose of MBO strategy is to yield results, to get things done. The MBO manager must identify performance indices that are useful in giving feedback on his progress toward reaching planned objectives.

Ratios and index numbers can be the basis for making comparisons of actual performance with expected performance. These ratios can be plotted on a graph, diagrammed on a control chart, or tabulated on a matrix, all of which provide an idea of the progress being made. Ratios can also be specially grouped to evaluate the group's progress separately and distinctly from that of other groups. The following is a suggested list of MBO performance indicators.

Profit

- Sales growth rates and profiles

- Customer complaint profiles and rates

- Overhead cost levels and drift ratios

- Net profit as a percentage of sales

- Percentage of increase in dividends

- Sales cost proportion trends and levels

- Frequency and size of sales orders

- Cost of transportation as a percentage of sales level and order

- Mean deviations from standard costs

- Variable cost rates and levels for sales orders

- Percentage of return on investments

- Percentage of share of actual and potential markets

- Current assets to current liabilities ratios

- Accounts receivable trends, rates, and collectibility ratios

- Cost of employer recruitment and placements

- Direct to indirect labor ratios

- Marginal cost trends and ratios

- Profit to total assets

- Ratio of debt to equity funds

- Sales per employee ratios

- Net operating income

- Debt to total assets ratio

Productivity and Schedules

- Inventory correlates with sales levels

- Back order profiles and rates

- Back order correlates with inventory levels

- Frequency and range of missed delivery dates

- Percentage of deadlines met

- Percentage of performance variance against budgets

- Set-up time rates and profiles

- Machine hours per product correlates with process types

- Percentage of utilization of labor capacity

- Output/input correlates between equipment utilization and labor capacity

- Percentage of projects completed against forecasts

- Equipment depreciation and obsolescence trends

- Percentage of time in raw materials availability

- Ratio of experienced production personnel to new personnel hires

- Ratio of farmed-out work to in-company production

- Output per unit of labor input

- Aging of work behind schedule

- Frequency rates for rescheduling

Efficiency

- Percentage of error in filling orders

- Defect correction ratios

- Percentage of scrap and waste

- Mean and range of equipment downtime

- Damage claims as a percentage of sales levels and orders

- Percentage of unit cost in material handling

- Overshipment and undershipment ratios

- Percentage of utilization of capital equipment

- Percentage of utilization of available floor space

- Ratio of inventory to assets

- Traffic intensity ratios

- Task-time completion rates

- Percentage of hand motions

- Queue ratios

- Percentage of items delivered as promised

- Inventory turnover

- Percentage of rework

- Percentage of set-up and preparation time

- Frequency of depletion of safety stock

- Demand time to supply time ratios

- Minimum lead time recorder levels

- Net sales to inventory ratio

- Stockouts to desired service levels

Manpower Management

- Quits and mobility flow rates

- Before and after training scores

- Absenteeism time ratios

- Weed-out and screening profile rates

- Percentage of implementation of performance appraisal recommendations

- Percentage implemented with placement planning charts

- Accident frequency profiles and rates

- Supervisory appointment rate from presupervisory selection and training

- Health profile trends and rates

- Total suggestions submitted and percentage implemented

- Employee transfer requests profiles and rates

- Grievance generation and settlement ratios

- Average tardiness trends and rates

- Number and settlement of disciplinary cases

- Percentage of time allowances for personal needs

- Number of promotions from within

- Overtime deterioration ratios

- Recruitment and placement costs

- Percentage of completed development experiences

Complete each statement by circling the correct letter.

1. An effective status reporting system is a system designed to inform

    a. all members of management

    b. a few key MBO managers

    c. lower-level supervisors only

2. Status reports should give

    a. all available information

    b. enough information to reveal needed corrections

    c. cost data only

3. An objective status control system should have

    a. a definite logical action pattern

    b. a feedback reporting time matrix

    c. both of the preceding

4. For comparing actual performance with expected performance, MBO managers use

    a. ratios   b. index numbers   c. both of the preceding

Indicate true (T) or false (F).

5. Status reporting involves organizing information to reveal changes that will be necessary if an objective is to be reached on time. _____

6. Status deviations are deficiencies in terms of what is expected within the status reporting period. _____

7. Because of the special nature of status reporting, accounting information and existing reports cannot be used in their preparation. _____

8. From any good status reporting system, an MBO manager should expect a perfect match between expectations and results. _____

9. A good objective status control system should offer managers ways to see if all activities are proceeding as intended and are in balance with each other. _____

10. MBO managers are increasingly operating their objective programs out of sight of their supervisors and other managers. _____

————————————————————————

● Checkpoint Answers

1. a   2. b   3. c   4. c   5. T   6. T   7. F   8. F   9. T   10. T

PERFORMANCE APPRAISALS

Performance appraisals not only serve as a meaningful basis for evaluating organization performance but also aid in appraising individual performances.[3] A rater enjoys the opportunity to use accurate data as the basis for his appraisal. The ratee enjoys participation in and commitment to those performance requirements in which he is involved. A strong and impartial attitude toward the appraisal process generally prevails between the two.

The technique of individual performance appraisals has significant advantages over the many other appraisal methods currently employed. The following are some of these advantages:

1. *MBO appraisals relate more closely to the job.* An MBO appraisal is oriented toward job requirements and work results rather than toward personality traits or general descriptors. Specified objectives are highly related to results needed and expected by the organization. Evaluation is tailored to an already well-structured situation. MBO job clarification and responsibility definition make appraising more accurate.

2. *MBO appraisals are more objective.* Supervisors are usually reluctant to cite deficiencies without outstanding evidence. Having reliable and accurate information on performance helps the supervisor to be less subjective. His role as appraiser changes. He does not have to defend his position. The supervisor is on solid ground during a confrontation with employees. He is armed with information which the employee knows and understands.

3. *MBO appraisals are active and positive.* The MBO appraisal involves both the supervisor and the subordinate and thus is not passive. Each is active in a positive way in assessing job performance. There are no unilateral actions, as found in other appraisal systems. This enhances communications and motivation.

4. *MBO appraisals are opportunistic.* MBO appraisals do not have to follow past practices. New opportunities are easily handled within the objective-setting process. The MBO performance appraisal approach avoids slavishly following preconceived ideas and methods. Because the approach is future-oriented, it encourages an employee to innovate.

5. *MBO appraisals encourage performance stretches.* There are many purposes to an MBO appraisal. Chief among them is the stimulation it gives to improving individual performance. The mission of improvement is generic to MBO practice. Level and consistency of effort can be readily evaluated for individuals in the system.

These advantages are not only feasible but are currently enjoyed by organizations using performance objectives methods. In organizations that have reported use of this technique, there is conviction that exceptional results are experienced in terms of improved performance.

The ways in which individual organizations are using performance objectives as appraisal systems vary. This lack of uniformity is the result of the organizations' various reasons for using the system. Some use an appraisal system to determine annual salary increases; this is commonly known as *merit rating.* Others use appraisal systems to identify and develop promotable managers. Still others use appraisal systems to stimulate, motivate, and encourage improved performance. In actuality, the MBO appraisal system can combine all these reasons, since each relates to concerns and accountability of managers. Performance appraisals are part of the entire managing process and can include virtually all elements of managing: organizational planning, delegation, evaluation, control, communications, development, motivation, and coordination.

Whatever the goal, a most important guideline is building the performance measurement or indicator into the statement of objective. Without this quantitative indicator, progress toward results becomes merely a matter of interpretation. Performance standards for the activities are developed to indicate the level or intensity of effort that is needed to achieve the objectives. Prior agreement is obtained on these performance standards and evaluation is made on this basis. The job or position descriptions can be useful if they are written to incorporate both objectives and standards. If not, new appraisal forms should be developed. Samples of such forms are illustrated on the following pages.

These forms are used for annual review. The underlying value of annual performance review is the opportunity it affords to gain feedback about results achieved. The annual cycle is convenient because of other annual instruments, such as budgets, profit statements, and forecasts. In this annual review, the MBO manager summarizes individual achievements and suggests ways to improve in subsequent years. Causes for lack of progress or achievement are brought out at this time. There is a meaningful exchange between supervisor and subordinate.

Performance Objectives Appraisal

Name		Date	
Position	Dept	Division	

Step 1.   Priority   List Objectives   Start Date   Complete Date   Give Performance Standards

Step 2.   Comment on results achieved for each objective listed in step 1:

Step 3.   Improve individual's performance: Where performance is weakest
             Where performance is strongest

Step 4.   Specific plans to improve:
             Actions and Activities   Responsibilities   Dates

Supervisor	Date	Next higher supervisor	Date

Results Planning and Appraisal Report

Name _____ Department _____ Date _____

Results expected: Performance standards:

1. _____   1. _____

   _____   _____

2. _____   2. _____

   _____   _____

3. _____   3. _____

   _____   _____

Approved: _____ Date _____   Coordinated with _____ Date _____

Planned activities: Schedule

1. _____   Start   Complete

   _____ |—|—|—|—|—|—|—|—|—|—|—|—|

2. _____

   _____ |—|—|—|—|—|—|—|—|—|—|—|—|

3. _____

   _____ |—|—|—|—|—|—|—|—|—|—|—|—|

4. _____

   _____ |—|—|—|—|—|—|—|—|—|—|—|—|

Evaluation of results: Tentative objectives for next year:

_____   _____

_____   _____

_____   _____

_____   _____

_____   _____

Evaluation approved:

_____   _____   _____   _____
Reporting Manager   Date   Coordinating Manager   Date

Cost Reduction Performance Appraisal

Objective: _____

_____

_____

_____

_____

Target: $ _____

Activities: _____

_____

_____

_____

_____

_____

_____

Results: _____

_____

_____

_____

_____

Percent of Objective	Jan	Feb	Mar		Apr	May	Jun		Jul	Aug	Sep		Oct	Nov	Dec	
150%																
125%																
100%																
80%																
60%																
40%																
20%																
0%																

✔ Checkpoint: Performance Appraisals ───────────────

Fill in the correct answer.

1. An MBO performance appraisal is oriented more toward _____ than toward personality traits or general descriptors.

2. MBO performance appraisals serve as a meaningful basis for evaluating both

   _____ and _____ performances.

3. An MBO performance appraisal actively involves both the _____ and

   the _____ in a positive assessment of job performance.

4. Without _____ , progress toward results becomes merely a matter of interpretation.

5. Appraisal forms should indicate both _____ and _____ .

───────────────

● Checkpoint Answers

1. job requirements and work results   2. organizational, individual   3. supervisor, subordinate
4. performance indicators   5. objectives, standards

208 HOW TO MANAGE BY OBJECTIVES

TROUBLE SPOTS AND SUGGESTED REMEDIES

Having completed our coverage of the five MBO steps, we will now turn to a discussion of MBO trouble spots and suggested remedies for them. First, let us review some of the benefits of the MBO system:

- The MBO system increases profits by orienting employees to get results.

- It brings clarity and precision to jobs, programs, and planning.

- It heightens motivation to make performance stretches.

- It brings organizational clarity through elimination of misfits and redundancy.

- It promotes coordination through interlocking and alignment.

- It makes compensation allocations easier by evaluating employees in terms of the results they achieve.

- It encourages management development through performance stretches and objective performance evaluation.

- It improves supervisor-subordinate communication.

- It provides definition and clarification of problem areas.

- It builds confidence in commitments.

In spite of benefits such as these, management by objectives is not without its problems and troubles.[4] Following are some of the trouble spots that have been identified and some suggested remedies for them.

Trouble Spots	Remedies
1. Targeted objectives are persued even though a change or desist is indicated.	Cease implementing objectives when unexpected changes render objectives unfeasible, irrelevant, or impossible. Select alternatives or contingencies from a situation action model and set up a desist time schedule. Revalidate. Communicate change to all participants.
2. Targeted objectives are persued even though an unexpected opportunity arises.	Reanalyze payoff of existing objectives in light of the new opportunity. If utility and value will be substantially greater, permit new targets to be set in lieu of prior commitment. Shorten time-span commitment if new opportunities arise frequently.

3. The achieving of targeted objectives is emphasized at the expense of unspecified results.

Targeted objectives must be significant, critical, and high in priority. Keep the number of these objectives at a minimum and make it clear that unanticipated routine work must be completed. Routine work can be set up and written in terms of maintenance objectives or can be handled in a traditional way.

4. Targeted objectives are expected in an unfairly short, or even unattainable, amount of time

Hold frequent progress conferences to clarify difficulties and reset levels of challenge. Hold frequent meetings for the purpose of removing obstacles to accomplishment. The MBO Rules for Stretching Performance and Performance Distribution Within a Group should guide setting the challenge level for attainability.

5. Understanding of managing by objectives only exists on the lower levels of management. Top management gives lip service only to the effort.

Bring in an outside consultant to do an internal selling job. Distribute among top managers articles, studies, and books that deal with the systems approach to the strategy and the need for total management involvement and support.

6. Objectives are written in terms of work activities rather than in terms of work results.

Set up training programs and workshop seminars for practice in writing objectives as results rather than as activities. Develop a manual that illustrates sample objectives similar to organization needs. Show how validation procedure can evaluate the wording of an objective.

7. Compensation is geared strictly to results, regardless of outside influences.

Develop checklist of probable influences that may keep an individual from reaching results. Set up a policy for changing or modifying objectives if circumstances beyond anyone's control occur. Otherwise, compensation should be geared closely to results.

8. Difficulty is experienced in setting measurable goals for staff personnel who assist line people to get their results.

Use two-way or three-way joint feeder-objectives. Objectives set for staff personnel should be set in a line context, and the score of results should be shared by both. Use MBO Rule for Interlocking Functions.

9. Challenge level is juggled, in order to justify pay increases.

Use past records to validate performance stretch. Document performance history for comparison with similar jobs in the future to assure the mission of improvement. The 5 to 15 per cent progressive performance stretch should apply.

10. Individual's or department's objectives are not interlocked with those of the whole organization.	Use concept of feeder-objectives and develop an objective network to show input and output contributions in the total system. Follow MBO Rule for Interlocking Functions.
11. Objectives are not attained, owing to circumstances beyond everyone's control.	Failure to attain objectives can provide useful guidelines for the next round of objective setting. Greater emphasis should be put on level of attainability and the probability of occurrence. Experience with risk factors should provide future guidance. Greater emphasis should be placed on the validation phase (step 3) if an organization is plagued with circumstances beyond everyone's control.
12. Employee participation is not a real commitment.	Allow employee to take an active role in the preliminary phases of decision-making. Identify and clarify his areas of accountability for the objectives set and the responsibilities of his job. Build motivators into areas of accountability.
13. There is an inability to get tough management with die-hard traditional approaches to managing to try managing by objectives.	Carefully select a project that can be set up as an objective program. Get agreement from management to implement the project using the MBO approach. Report the results of the project and contrast the advantages and disadvantages with the traditional way. Use the advantages to convince the previously unconvinced.
14. There is an unmanageable amount of paper work and red tape.	Some paper work must be tolerated. By keeping the number of objectives to the critical few necessary for performance stretches and quantum jumps, the paper work requirements will be kept to a minimum. Paper work shortcuts will develop with experience and knowledge of the system. Follow MBO Rule for Focus.
15. Objective performance evaluation will threaten the use and value of the conventional merit rating system or managerial trait technique.	Objective performance evaluation and merit evaluation serve the same purpose. The former emphasizes results, the latter emphasizes activities or traits. The merit system will be changed if not eliminated entirely. Some trait evaluation will be retained where it is clearly relevant to a manager's ability to get results. The practice of managing by objectives as a new strategy will cause an impact leading to change in existing practices. An organization must be prepared to make these changes.

16. Difficulty is experienced in quantifying targeted objectives; targets are written as traits or duties that merely sound like targets.

Writing good objectives is a skill developed through training and practice. Performance in every job can and must be measured. Skill can be developed through training programs, workshop seminars, and staff coaching. Special examples can be formulated as a guide for those needing special help. A guide manual can be useful.

17. Objective setting does not seem to fit in with highly specialized and technical work.

Objective setting fits into any kind of work package from which results are expected. The claims that a specialized situation cannot be results-oriented is not true; the situation needs to be reorganized and redefined in terms of getting results. This redefinition may involve shifting responsibility to an individual from a department or from an individual to a team or project.

18. There is an inability to get feedback of contributions and measurement of progress.

Feedback under MBO takes three forms. First, the individual observes and knows his own performance in relation to what is expected of him. Second, the individual gets periodic reports with evaluations of his overall performance. Third, the individual gets coaching, counseling, and appraisal reviews from his superiors who have first-hand knowledge from which to assess the work.

19. Objective-setting processes are time consuming and must be done after hours.

Objective setting is not extra work. It is part of the person's job to plan ahead, make improvements, and set deadlines. Time must be found during regular hours. Lack of time may be the result of the manager's setting objectives over too wide a range of job responsibilities. The chief value of managing by objectives is focus and concentration on the three or four areas most critical to the organization. The beginner at using the strategy should learn to crawl before he starts to run.

20. Difficulties arise in determining priority among a multiplicity of possible objectives.

Determine optimum alternatives by using decision matrix and payoff analysis in the situation action model.

21. There is an inability to get total management involvement owing to the fluidity and scattered nature of the organization.

Select task force to create a large matrix of alternatives and criteria. Allow individuals unable to involve themselves in the development of the matrix to select alternatives, and optimize them in terms of the individuals' needs and positions.

22. There is difficulty in deciding on entry points from which to begin the objective-setting process.	First enumerate clearly the many entry points possible for the organization:

1. Five-year profit plan

2. Top-down, bottom-up system

3. Budgetary approach

4. Common objective approach

5. Appraisal by results approach

6. Job descriptions approach

Carefully assess which entry points, either singly or in combination, are most likely to set down roots for the objective-setting process. An outside consultant can help.

23. There is an inability to implement MBO objectives at lower organizational levels.

A philosophy and understanding of the concept of managing by objectives must be provided to first-line supervisors before applied strategy and technique are discussed. They must see and understand managing by objectives as a managerial way of life. Training programs, seminars, and managerial coaching for first-line supervisors are an absolute must.

24. Management people are too overloaded with day-to-day production necessities to take the time to coordinate with other sections.

Setting objectives is a fundamental act of managing. Second to it is establishing the necessary confidence that reaching for objectives will be successful. Crisis managing develops when coordination with and confidence in other sections does not exist. The MBO Rules for Focus, Balancing Organizations, and Interlocking Functions should be followed. Assure that joint feeder-objectives exist in every department.

25. Objectives are set so low that the benefits do not justify the expenditure of effort and resources.

Estimate cost of reaching objectives and compare with benefits accrued. If benefits are not greater than cost, objective level must be raised for better results. Managing by objectives must exact a performance stretch from all employees.

26. An objective statement does not have a risk value; the degree of confidence in delivering results has not yet been determined.

Risk is high when uncertainty and low confidence prevail. Collect needed and relevant information and set up a decision tree to reduce uncertainty and raise confidence. Use past histories or information from other sources when nothing else is available.

27. Difficulty is experienced in equating compensation increments to basis of achievement.

Objectives having greatest pay-off or utility should be given greatest weight for rewards, both financial and nonfinancial. Subordinates must have in advance a clear understanding of the weight various job aspects will have in a final evaluation.

28. The time span in which objectives are to be achieved is too long to give a feeling of progress.

Using the feeder-objective approach, bridge long-range objectives by creating short-range milestones of progress. Each feeder-objective meets a target date that contributes toward an ultimate set of results. Follow MBO guidelines for long-range, short-range, and immediate-range forecasting for setting time span.

29. Action toward reaching objectives is at a low level and not intensive enough.

Subordinates probably were not involved in the objective-setting process and are most likely pursuing a manager's personal set of objectives. Get a subordinate to feel that a commitment of the organization is partly his doing, a result of his thinking and his decision. This goes a long way in getting him to deliver necessary results.

30. Original objectives are being reached, but there is an inability to deal with the changes that affect the objectives during the time intervals.

Set objectives for shorter periods of time. Forecast the changes that will occur during the time interval and build these into objectives as contingencies.

31. Independent setting of objectives by different departments results in objectives that are overlapping, conflicting, and out of sequence.

Use the validation procedure suggested in Chapter 5 to bring about alignment, interlocking, and network connection. The work breakdown structure serves as a guide to achieve coordination at varying levels.

32. There is difficulty in getting older persons who have been disillusioned in the past by new programs to become involved, participate in, and accept the MBO processes.

Reduce resistance and reluctance to participate by:
1. Developing the climate. Circulate MBO books and magazines; use the organization newspaper; circulate successful cases; hold special presentations on managing by objectives.
2. Providing knowledge and understanding of managing by objectives through training programs, seminars, consultants, an organization MBO manual, and books.
3. Using certain people to set examples. Hire experienced MBO consultants; use managers who show leadership qualities for coaching and persuading.

4. Involving personnel. Allow experimentation and trial of managing by objectives with special projects that pose no great difficulty; allow personnel to try it with good coaching.

33. Objective-setting process seems to be practical only for certain sections or functions of the organization. It has little support in R & D because these groups feel that their creativity must be spontaneous.

The objective-setting process is applicable to areas of responsible creativity. Any R & D effort is intended to support an organization-wide effort to gain new or improved products and services for consumer markets. Responsible creativity is the only justification for R & D organizations. Objective-setting processes are attainable under these conditions.

34. Objectives based on a performance appraisal program achieve neither expected results nor management involvement.

Most appraisal programs are staff-conceived, organization-wide, and personnel-oriented. As such, they never become a significant part of the line managerial process or a managerial way of life. Instead of administrating the MBO program from a staff department, decentralize and administer it among the various line departments.

The organizations that have had successful results with MBO strategy and have overcome trouble spots have done so because their supervisors and managers were not only familiar with the strategy's rationale and procedure, but also were willing to put forth effort and time. needed to make it work.

On the other side of an objective program is a control program. The purpose of control is to keep activities and efforts on a prescribed course of action. Control should not be treated just as a separate function. It is part of the total objective-setting and implementation processes, as well as a follow-up to the other phases of the strategy. Comparing actual status with prescribed standards and ascertaining the difference, if any, is the heart of control. This chapter presented several techniques for keeping status reporting an integral part of the total objective program.

Trouble spots do exist in the practice of managing by objectives. This chapter included a troubleshooting chart that suggested some remedies for typical problems encountered by organizations introducing the strategy. Hard work, new policies, and organizational changes will be required to create a management system ready to produce the type of results for which the system has been created.

1.   J. F. Van Valkenburgh, T. B. Nooger, and K. P. Neville, *Basic Synchros and Servomechanisms*, Vol. 2, John F. Rider, New York, 1955, pp. 1-13, and Charles H. Kepner and Benjamin B. Tregoe, *The Rational Manager*, McGraw-Hill Book Co., New York, 1965, pp. 54-55.

2.   Roy A. Lindberg, "Operations Auditing: What Is It. What It Isn't." *Management Review,* December 1969, pp. 2-10.

3.   Marion S. Kellogg. *What To Do About Performance Appraisals,* American Management Association, 1965.

4.   Henry L. Tosi, and Stephen J. Carroll, *"Managerial Reaction to Management by Objectives,"* Journal of the Academy of Management, Vol. II, no. 4, December 1968, p. 415.

Chapter 7 Review —————————————————————

$V\!V$ Doublecheck

Using the letter, match each MBO trouble spot in the first column with its suggested remedy in the second column.

Trouble Spots	Remedies
1. Targeted objectives are persued even though a change or desist is indicated.	a. Determine optimum alternatives by using decision matrix and payoff analysis in situation action model.
2. Compensation is geared strictly to results, regardless of outside influences.	b. Cease implementing objectives. Select other objectives from a situation action model and set up a desist time schedule. Revalidate. Communicate change to all participants.
3. Individual's or department's objectives are not interlocked with those of the whole organization.	c. Allow employees to take an active role in the preliminary phases of decision-making. Identify and clarify their areas of accountability for the set objectives. Build motivators into areas of accountability.
4. Employee participation is meaningless and not a real commitment.	d. Develop checklist of probable influences that may keep an individual from reaching results. Set up a policy for changing objectives if circumstances are beyond anyone's control. Otherwise, gear compensation closely to results.
5. Difficulties arise in determining priorities among a multiplicity of possible objectives.	e. Use concept of feeder-objectives and develop an objective network to show input and output contributions in the entire system. Follow MBO Rule for Interlocking Functions.

Answer briefly.

6. Explain how overshooting or undershooting will hamper performance in reaching a set of objectives. ·

————————————————————————————————————

————————————————————————————————————

————————————————————————————————————

————————————————————————————————————

————————————————————————————————————

7. List and describe the guidelines for controlling and reporting status of objectives.

_____

_____

_____

_____

_____

8. What is meant by status reporting?

_____

_____

_____

_____

_____

9. What is the value of status control performance indicators?

_____

_____

_____

_____

_____

10. What are the advantages of MBO individual performance appraisals?

_____

_____

_____

_____

_____

1. B   2. D   3. E   4. C   5. A

6. Controlling consists of keeping work activities within specified performance standards. Overshooting or undershooting leads to wasted time, money, effort, and material. Wide swings in performance make it difficult to stabilize at a level that is acceptable and satisfactory to the organization. Instead, undue effort and resources are consumed in simply making the changes necessary to bring performance back into line with the stated objectives.

7. A set of guidelines for controlling and reporting status of objectives might include the following.

   a.   A listing of targeted events or end items that require critical control

   b.   A series of key points or performance indicators for which information can be collected in order to determine progress being made

   c.   Comparing actual performance with planned performance on a time dimension

   d.   Identification of status deviation

   e.   Development of corrective action and assignment of responsibility for taking that action

8. Status reporting is that portion of the total information flow in the organization that emphasizes supplying relevant information for decision making concerning corrective action that is needed. It involves measuring performance, comparing that to stated objectives, and identifying actions needed to reduce deviation and bring performance back into acceptable limits.

9. The main value of status control performance indicators is in providing a basis of measurement that will qualitatively and quantitatively disclose actual progress being made in relation to expected progress. Such indicators serve as key focal points for management attention and quick identification of those sitations that require additional management attention.

10. Some of the advantages of MBO individual performance appraisals are the following.

   a.   Relating performance appraisals more closely to the job

   b.   Making performance appraisals more objective

   c.   Making appraisals both active and positive

   d.   Using appraisals as a means to include new opportunities in stated objectives

   e.   Encouraging performance stretch through the appraisal process

8. TRAINING AND DEVELOPING MBO MANAGERS ─────

Key Concepts

- *MBO Skills.* The effective use of MBO by the manager requires a balance of special skills in the areas of objective setting, objective implementing, and measuring and correcting. An understanding of what these skills are and how they are interrelated is a first step in helping managers obtain them.

- *Teaching MBO.* Even though on-the-job experience is one of the best ways to acquire MBO skills, the teaching process needs to be formalized and should include workshops and seminars. These may be administered on the job by the organizations or off the job by institutions specializing in management education. Their aim is to provide stimulation, influence attitudes, and impart knowledge about the entire MBO area.

Learning Objectives

After you have completed this chapter, you should be able to

- List basic MBO skills.

- Describe several ways of teaching MBO skills and advantages and disadvantages of each.

WHAT ARE THE BASIC MBO SKILLS?

Skill is the ability to apply knowledge effectively and readily in the performance of a particular physical or mental task. Use of a skill can be a vital demonstration of the possession of knowledge. For the manager, this means that, while the understanding of MBO principles is essential, he must still develop the skills appropriate to applying these principles in specific situations. This may turn out to be harder than it seems. Managers may have a thorough understanding of MBO strategy and yet be less than successful at putting this strategy into practice. This often happens with managers who have to adopt a whole new outlook on themselves before they will be truly able to manage by objectives.

Identifying specific skills of successful MBO managers is difficult because of the complexity of the strategy, and because different situations call for different managerial styles, which, in turn, require different skills and characteristics. Yet, there appears to be a common body of specific skills that, once acquired and developed, can lead to successful managing by objectives. These specific skills are given in the following checklist. As you read through this list, you might want to rate yourself on a scale of 10 in order to construct a rough estimate of your MBO weaknesses and strengths.

Objective-Setting Skills ─────────────────────────

☐ Ability to generate alternatives from present and past experiences

☐ Ability to project concerns and desires

☐ Ability to sense and forecast trends

☐ Ability to perceive where improvements can be made in everyday experiences, even outside one's normal province of thinking

☐ Ability to predict outcomes

☐ Ability to see the whole from given constituent parts

☐ Ability to determine appropriate pace and sequence for objectives

☐ Ability to sense, predict, and forecast an accomplishment at a point in time

☐ Ability to see the simple patterns behind complex ones

☐ Ability to focus on the critical

Objective-Implementing Skills

☐ Ability to complete a task through an intensified effort

☐ Ability to sense people's needs and drives and relate them to planned objectives

☐ Ability to foresee barriers and circumvent them

☐ Ability to fit people into proper work assignments

☐ Ability to establish rapport with and gain response from people

☐ Ability to compromise and gain consensus

☐ Ability to articulate and persuade hostile and competing groups

☐ Ability to empathize with and adopt organization life styles

☐ Ability to convey information with clarity

☐ Ability to coordinate various power groups

☐ Ability to move ahead in the face of risk and uncertainty

☐ Ability to align, dovetail, and connect two or more courses of action

Measuring and Correcting Skills

☐ Ability to measure parts and to decide what these measures mean in terms of completion of the whole

☐ Ability to analyze and quantify a complex mass of information

☐ Ability to find measures of central tendencies

☐ Ability to measure deviation, variation, and drift from prescribed objectives

☐ Ability to use sampling indicators to measure progress over time

☐ Ability to initiate feedback corrections or reduce variance

☐ Ability to collect relevant information from probing, questioning, and observing

☐ Ability to schedule interwoven projects

☐ Ability to form judgments and determine trends from statistical data

HOW ARE BASIC MBO SKILLS DEVELOPED?

Development Through Doing ►

Formal education is not sufficient for teaching basic MBO skills to the manager. This sort of education, which provides a breadth and depth of knowledge, does form a basis from which skills can develop, however. It must be accompanied by on-the-job experience, where basic MBO skills can be applied. Such a down-to-earth approach must be well structured and must focus on responsibilities to be carried out from day to day. The individual who is to be trained must practice the strategy in his own job. He can be encouraged to absorb himself in the strategy. Top management must encourage this approach by its participation in and use of basic MBO skills.

The emphasis in this approach is on the individual rather than on a group. The individual should be given the latitude to restructure delegated assignments in an objective. In other words, the individual, when first asked to complete a project, should be allowed to participate in setting the objective, relate the targeted results to existing commitments, and proceed to validate and to implement. This process enables careful analysis of activities, authority, and the work situation to predict accomplishment of the assignment within a specified period of time.

A perfect solution for training MBO managers has not yet been found and probably never will be. Success in many organizations, however, seems to follow from this general pattern:

1. Find the way in which managing by objectives works in your organization and do more of it. Focus the strategy on the areas of the organization's greatest need. Share with others your knowledge of how managing by objectives will fill this need.

2. Give on-the-job training in basic MBO skills, with the focus on practicing the strategy at all times to get results. Methods employed should involve the trainee's doing as much of the work himself as possible.

3. Develop a guideline manual that sets forth the procedures for a systematic approach to MBO strategy. Specific examples from within the organization, as well as proven policy guidelines and practices, should be included.

4. Do not allow training to be formalized as only a behavioral activity. The soundest approach is to put managing by objectives in a line context for a balanced way of managing. Line managers should use MBO as an integral tool in their planning of the technical, economic, and functional requirements of their product or service as well as in behavioral matters.

5. Establish through policies and examples that managing by objectives is a way of life. Each manager and supervisor develops confidence toward its use when he sees his supervisor, as well as the organization's president, performing in the same fashion.

6. Hire individuals who have successfully practiced the strategy in other organizations and who can wield influence and provide information within the work setting.

7. Key the training of MBO managers to an individual basis. This means the individual must want to develop the skill. He will ask for the assistance he needs because he sees the value of it for himself and for the organization. He should not be forced.

There is no doubt that the most effective training is built into daily on-the-job experience — experience that has been varied in type and level to stretch the individual to new levels of achievement. This is not to say that managing by objectives can be taught in an informal way. On the contrary, in order to provide the best results, it must be carried out with formalized processes of relating, involvement, and commitment. Highly structured training programs that are designed to provide employees with a thorough knowledge of these processes and that are aligned with on-the-job development and practice will truly give subordinates the specific skills necessary to MBO practice. Such training programs, which may take the form of workshops, are most useful in the areas of providing stimulation, influencing attitudes, and imparting knowledge. Open resistance to managing by objectives can be brought out in an open forum with experts and peers. Real understanding of the MBO philosophy can be acquired in a give-and-take discussion. Trainees would be informed as to the potential MBO benefits, the problems associated with its use, the means to overcome these problems, and the techniques for applying the strategy. Through discussion of difficulties, training programs can help employees avoid getting off on the wrong foot. Specific skills can also be acquired in these workshops. The first and most obvious of these skills is the ability to write a formal statement of objectives.

On-the-job workshops can be augmented by workshops conducted off the job. Several institutions specializing in management education offer such MBO workshops. Of course, an organization does not have control over the course content and must rely on the participating individual to relate and transfer as much as possible to his on-the-job needs.

Outside programs make available valuable experience and discussion that can be very beneficial. Getting away from the immediate job to see things from a distance with others who are doing the same thing helps people to clarify the particular problems facing them. Questions raised by other participants often enable one to study a point of view that otherwise would go unrecognized. When these two advantages are combined — the exposure to other viewpoints and a perspective on one's own organization — an individual can get some meaningful guidance for his own development.

Organizations that can provide in-plant programs to supplement outside professional assistance can provide a more meaningful experience than can outside seminars and workshops alone. Particularly useful is the participation of line managers in presenting the program to subordinates. This has a twofold advantage. First, it forces the line manager to analyze his own understanding of managing by objectives in preparation for conducting the program. Second, it places the line manager in the true position of a coach. This reinforces the subordinate's relationship with and respect for his supervisor.

To assist an organization that wishes to set up an in-plant MBO training program for managing by objectives, a seminar workshop has been organized, and suggested outlines are given in the following pages.

MBO SEMINAR-WORKSHOP OUTLINE

I. Preliminary (2 weeks before seminar)

1. Study *Manual for Developing Individual Objectives*

2. Study definitions of all terms

3. Read two books from list suggested in "Reference Reading"

4. Prepare solution to organization case

II. First day

1. Managing by objectives
   a. Concept of getting results
   b. Traditional methods of managing compared
   c. Organizational barriers to getting results
   d. Organization purpose and MBO philosophy

2. Finding the objectives
   a. Trends, errors, forecasting disruptions
   b. The mission of improvement
   c. Situation action model
   d. Assessing managerial performance stretches

3. Objective setting processes
   a. Establishing and writing performance objectives
   b. Objective networks and feeder-objective modules
   c. Organizational entry point
   d. Interlocking and weighting objectives for optimum results

4. Workshop: Participants make a situation analysis and write a statement of objectives for their respective departments. Critiques and analyses will be offered by participants to improve the skill of setting objectives. (Personal plan for practicing managing by objectives is initiated.)

III. Second day

1. Work breakdown structure
   a. Organizing programs to deliver results
   b. Work breakdown matrix
   c. Networks and project systems
   d. Interlocking through objective networks

2. Validating objectives
   a. Work packages and risk factors
   b. Decision trees and PERT networks
   c. Trial run of programs
   d. Venture analysis and simulation

3. Workshop: Participants will continue with personal plans to validate their anticipated objectives by organizing and developing resources. Potential problems analyses and trial run of programs will be conducted.

IV. Third day

1. Techniques for implementing objectives
   a. Planned motivators and the motivational process
   b. Releasing individual potential through coaching
   c. Techniques of persuasion
   d. Completing work packages

2. Objective status control systems
    a. Status control model
    b. Appraisal systems and performance indicators
    c. Diagnosing troubles and suggesting remedies
    d. Personal performance appraisal

3. Workshop: Participants will analyze a developed plan for implementation to detect trouble spots and problem areas. Remedies and contingency actions are proposed and analyzed. A personal plan for managing by objectives is completed.

4. Summary and conclusions
    a. Strategies to obtain performance improvement
    b. Competitive edge
    c. Objective-oriented organizations and individuals
    d. Management practices of the future

GUIDELINE MANUAL FOR DEVELOPING INDIVIDUAL OBJECTIVES

I. Organization's purpose for managing by objectives

II. Brief theory of the management concept

III. Summary of objectives procedure in organization

IV. Procedure in detail
1. Finding objectives
2. Setting objectives
3. Validating objectives
4. Implementing objectives
5. Status reporting and progress reviews

V. Questions and answers

VI. Organization case history

VII. Personal plan

VIII. Additional reading

✓Checkpoint: MBO Skills

Indicate whether the following skills are objective-setting skills (S), objective-implementing skills (I), or measuring and correcting skills (M).

1. Ability to predict outcomes _____

2. Ability to use sampling indicators to measure progress over time _____

3. Ability to coordinate various power groups _____

Indicate true (T) or false (F).

4. Formal education is not sufficient for teaching basic MBO skills to a manager. _____

5. The MBO trainee should not be permitted to participate in the restructuring of delegated assignments in an objective. _____

6. There are rigid guidelines for training MBO managers. _____

7. MBO training should be formalized only as a behavioral activity. _____

8. The most effective MBO training is built into on-the-job experience. _____

9. Open resistance to managing by objectives can be brought out and modified through an open forum with experts and peers. _____

10. MBO training courses offered by institutions specializing in management education have the advantage of taking the trainee away from his immediate job, so that he may evaluate his organization's situation from a distance. _____

● Checkpoint Answers

1. S   2. M   3. I   4. T   5. F   6. F   7. F   8. T   9. T   10. T

REFERENCE READING

Additional reading resources for the development of skills for practicing the strategy of managing by objectives are given below.

Batten, J. D., *Beyond Management by Objectives*, American Management Association, New York, 1966, 140 pp. Drawing on his knowledge of management methods and practices, the author claims that many objective programs lack one vital element, one intrinsic power that makes things happen: motivation. Without motivation, or personal involvement, an MBO program may never pay off. The author shows how many managers install a so-called MBO program with its apparatus of goals and required results, and then they sit back and wait for great things to happen. But merely establishing the machinery is not enough: it is only when employees from top to bottom are motivated and see the importance of an all-out effort both to themselves and to their organizations that objectives are reached and organizations come alive.

Drucker, Peter F., *Managing for Results*, Harper and Row, New York, 1964, 240 pp. The effective business, the author observes, focuses on opportunities rather than on problems. How this focus is achieved in order to make the organization prosper and grow is the concern of this book. Drucker takes a hard look at products and services to see how many qualify as tomorrow's breadwinners. Only when an executive has an accurate picture of realities is he able to make his business effective. The book combines specific economic analysis with entrepreneurial forces for business prosperity.

Hughes, Charles L., *Goal Setting*, American Management Association, 1965, 157 pp. This book explains in meaningful practical language how to recognize the needs for self-fulfillment and job satisfaction and how to stimulate goal-seeking behavior in all employees — how, in short, to make managing by objectives a reality. The author describes how overall objectives can be broken down into subgoals that managers and employees at all levels can readily grasp, associate themselves with, and work toward, creating both individual and organization success. Effective performance and organization survival and growth depend on the validity of the goals and the goal-setting processes.

Howell, Robert A., *Management by Objectives — Should It Be Applied?* doctoral dissertation, Harvard University, Cambridge, Mass., June 1966, 269 pp. This is a research report of the findings of nearly a year's organizational study aimed at determining how the application of an actual MBO system compares with a theoretical model structured after a budgetary system. The organization studied is a large U.S. corporation that has utilized managing by objectives for all its supervisory personnel for about 5 years. The study shows the strong correlation that exists between managing by objectives and organizational structure, activity usage, and activity morale.

Killian, Ray A., *Managing by Design*, American Management Association, New York, 1968, 369 pp. Effective management performance is no accident. It is the result of a calculated plan for achievement formulated by the executive who aims for success and gets it. The author offers practical guidelines to get favorable results in the job. He gives techniques for setting up plans and following through, for keeping operations moving with problem solving, for channeling organization resources in directions offering greatest benefits, and for finding ways to communicate with subordinates.

McConkey, Dale D., *How to Manage by Results*, American Management Association, New York, 1965, 144 pp. This book is for those executives who are vitally concerned with profits and the day-to-day realities of obtaining tangible results. The author provides a thorough explanation of what is meant by management by results. He summarizes the whole approach in a few guidelines and offers pertinent facts for developing and initiating a results program. The author provides useful charts to help implement an organization's program and includes case studies from United Air Lines, Monsanto Company, State Farm Insurance, and other leading organizations.

McGregor, Douglas, *The Human Side of Enterprise*, McGraw-Hill Book Co., New York, 1960, 244 pp. In formulating Theory X and Theory Y, the author opened up new vistas for others to reflect upon. Theory X and Theory Y are essentially ways of describing how a manager feels about people and their normal reaction to work. They are two extreme ends of a management point of view; in practice, a manager may fall somewhere in between. The author identifies the assumptions each of these theories contain and how these assumptions determine how well managers handle people. This book has significant implications for getting results through understanding and motivating employees.

National Industrial Conference Board, *Managing by and with Objectives*, Study No. 212, National Industrial Conference Board, New York, 1968, 77 pp. This report deals with the concept of management by objectives and the practices followed by organizations to implement the concept. It concentrates upon the experience of firms that use management by objectives as a general approach to the task of managing the business rather than for some other more limited purpose. The report discusses the procedures used to determine objectives, the degree to which objectives are quantified, and the mechanisms used to ensure that the objectives of one manager do not conflict with those of others. It examines the case of objectives in controlling business operations and in appraising managerial performance. Five case studies of companies using this approach to management illustrate the key elements of the technique.

Odiorne, George S., *Management by Objectives*, Pitman Publishing Corp., New York, Toronto, and London, 1965, 196 pp. The author shows that only the precise definition of both organization and personal goals can produce effective management today. He describes a system of management that defines individual executive responsibilities in terms of organization objectives. He shows how managers jointly identify organizational goals and define major responsibilities in terms of the results expected of them. With management by objectives, accountability is established and a team effort, which does not eliminate individual risk taking, becomes possible.

Odiorne, George S., *Management Decisions by Objectives*, Prentice-Hall, Englewood Cliffs, N.J., 1969, 252 pp. The author provides working managers with tested scientific methods that will dramatically improve their decision-making and problem solving ability. Emphasis is placed on making sophisticated mathematical and behavioral techniques intelligible and useful. These are also brought to bear on crucial areas of costing, sales, production, and planning. He presents models of every type of decision facing management. Models are analytically treated for input, action, output, and feedback in the objective approach.

Schleh, Edward C., *Management by Results*, McGraw-Hill Book Co., New York, 1961, 251 pp. The unique results system successfully used by the author for more than 20 years gives a fresh practical insight into solving management problems. The author shows how his technique is applicable to every level of responsibility—how jodgment, ingenuity, and initiative are maximized. Broad in scope, the book carries the reader through all types of management problems from the simplest type of delegation from one man to another through the application of results management.

Steward, Nathaniel, *Strategies of Managing for Results*, Parker Publishing, West Nyack, N.Y., 1966, 213 pp. The author uses examples from actual experiences to show exactly where things went wrong in many organizations and how executives took steps to correct them. He points up blind spots of middle management and how these can impair the future. These blind spots concern people, ideas, values, handling of problems, realities, and so forth. He indicates symptoms of these blind spots and countermeasures that overcome them. The author shows how to indoctrinate people in the art of diagnosing and reports on some of the managerial morale situations growing out of troubleshooting experience.

Valentine, Raymond F., *Performance Objectives for Managers*, American Management Association, New York, 1966, 208 pp. The author characterizes the MBO concept as a style of thinking and demonstrates how managerial efficiency can be increased by following logical techniques. The author explains the use of a quantitative approach that deals with actual results rather than with traditional behavior ratings, and shows the advantages of a performance objectives program in upgrading the capability of the managerial force. He shows how many current methods of measuring managerial performance are neither fair nor objective. He describes practical methods for performance appraisals and tells how performance objectives are meaningful in appraisal systems.

◄SUMMARY►

This chapter discusses some of the basic MBO skills and some of the basic ways for developing these skills in prospective MBO managers. Because the main usefulness of these skills is in applying MBO strategy, on-the-job experience is one of the best ways to acquire them. This is not to say that managing by objectives can be taught in an informal way. The teaching process should be formalized, and it may include workshops and seminars. These workshops and seminars, which may be administered on the job by the organization or off the job by institutions specializing in management education, are most useful in providing stimulation, influencing attitudes, and imparting knowledge.

Chapter 8 Review

Answer briefly.

1. Why would it be difficult for a manager to acquire MBO skills without help or practice?

   _____

   _____

   _____

   _____

   _____

2. Explain how MBO skills are developed through on-the-job experience.

   _____

   _____

   _____

   _____

   _____

3. Explain the usefulness of workshops and seminars in developing MBO skills.

   _____

   _____

   _____

   _____

   _____

4. Why should the teaching of MBO skills be formalized?

   _____

   _____

   _____

   _____

5. Why is it difficult to generalize about the MBO skills of different managers who have successfully applied MBO strategy?

_____

_____

_____

_____

_____

● **Doublecheck Answers**

1. Identifying and acquiring MBO skills without help or practice would be extremely difficult because of the complexity of the MBO philosophy and the range of situations which are faced by the typical manager. Thus it is extremely hard for a single manager to generalize from his diverse set of experiences as to the appropriate skills and focus for effective MBO management.

2. A general pattern that seems to have been effective in developing MBO skills through on-the-job experience involves the following.

   a. Finding the way in which MBO works best in the organization and then doing more of the same

   b. Focusing on practicing the strategy of MBO at all times, with the trainee doing as much of the work as possible

   c. Developing a guideline manual that sets forth the procedures for a systematic approach to MBO with specific examples from within the organization

   d. Using MBO not only in behavioral matters but in matters related to the product or service as well

   e. Supporting MBO as a way of life through policies and examples

   f. Keying the development of MBO skills to the specific situation and requirements of the individual manager

3. Seminars and workshops as a part of developing basic MBO skills are most useful in providing stimulation, influencing attitudes, and imparting knowledge. For example, real understanding of the MBO philosophy can be acquired through a give-and-take discussion among the trainees and leaders in such a setting.

4. The teaching of MBO skills should be formalized in order to reduce the duplication of effort in searching for what constitutes the most important skills. Also, since those skills will be required by all managers in the organization, it is much more efficient to teach those systematically and through formalized procedures than it is to expect them to be discovered on an individual basis.

5. Probably the most important reason for the difficulty in generalizing about the MBO skills of different managers who have successfully applied MBO strategy is the fact that MBO is really a philosophy of management. As such, it must be tailored to the individual management style of the manager. Thus, there is no single set of skills or outline procedure that will lead to an effective MBO philosophy for every manager. Rather it is necessary to teach each manager the essence of MBO strategy and then allow him to adapt it to his own situation, needs, and preferences.

9. IMPROVEMENT APPLICATIONS ─────────────

Key Concepts

- *Profit Plan.* The profit plan is an active, viable strategy for obtaining profits through contributions from all segments of the organization. Such plans should be organized around objectives rather than around organizational functions.

- *Time Analysis.* A key aspect of improvement applications is the more effective use of management time. Through the analysis of the present use of time, the manager can determine where his time could be spent more profitably and which items should be either delegated to others or simply discontinued.

- *Methods Improvement.* This technique involves a systematic study and analysis of existing work methods and procedures in order to discover new or perhaps better methods for accomplishing work. While the technique has long been used by industrial engineers, its concepts are applicable in all areas of management.

Learning Objectives

After you have completed this chapter, you should be able to

- Give reasons why an organization should constantly be planning and executing improvement programs.

- Outline improvement programs in the areas of profits, sales, costs, management time, communications, methods, and training.

INTRODUCTION

The elusive competitive edge that every organization should attempt to maintain can be thought of in terms of the mission of improvement. The continuous performance stretch for more and better results is the competitive edge an organization has. As long as the organization embarks on aggressive improvement programs, competitors will find it difficult to keep up unless they make the same performance stretches. The MBO manager must assume primary responsibility for the mission of improvement to provide this competitive edge. He must develop the skills to achieve improvements for the enterprise. The plan for these improvements should permeate the entire organization, so that the leap forward is natural and expected. As a beginner, the MBO manager may experience minimal results. With time, growth, and experience, however, improvement is likely to become a way of life.

The critical point of any organization is usually at the end of the introduction, growth, and saturation phases. At this point the manager has three alternatives to choose from: do nothing and experience, before very long, an abort or bankruptcy; put out a minimum of effort, and experience a general decline or obsolescence; or execute repeated thrusts in performance as required by MBO practice. These alternatives are illustrated in Figure 1.

This chapter deals with some of the key areas of an enterprise that can undergo improvement. These areas are

Profits	Management Time	Training
Sales	Communications	
Costs	Methods	

1. Improvement Requires Repeated Thrusts in Performance

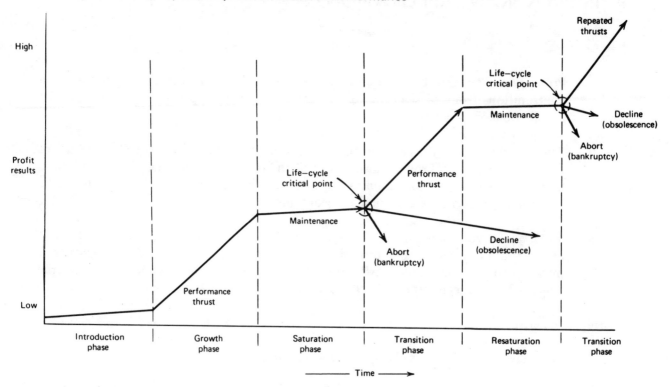

PROFIT IMPROVEMENT[1]

Successful managers hit profit targets more often than their unsuccessful colleagues, because they plan their profits and keep their operations pointed in that direction. They recognize that profits do not just happen; they are caused. Profit improvement is establishing profit objectives in a profit plan and organizing all efforts to reach these objectives. The objective-setting processes of MBO strategy make the planning and organizing for profit systematic and deliberate.

Annual Profit Improvement Plans ►

The following are four ways to improve profits.

- Increase sales volume

- Increase price margin

- Reduce capital investments

- Reduce costs of operating

The profit improvement plan should be organized around these four major objectives rather than, as traditionally, around organization functions. The 5-year profit plan described earlier is a progressive forecast and connects both long-range and short-range targets. Each part of the plan includes a forecast, objectives, means for reaching the objectives, and provisions for making adjustments when changes occur. The annual profit plan contributes to the long-term future of the enterprise, just as the individual manager's objectives contribute to the organization's annual plan. The future commitment of an organization is balanced with its present needs, and the organization meets those needs in the light of its future commitment. An outline of the more important aspects of an annual profit improvement plan is given in the following table.

Annual Profit Improvement Plan

A. Profit objective

   1. Total capital to be used
   2. Return-on-investment objective after taxes
   3. Profit objective for 19XX

B. Sales improvement

   1. Marketing forecast, planning, and strategy
   2. Requirements and alternatives for sales volume
   3. Sales volume objective contributed by:
       a. Sales and contracts feeder-objective plan
       b. Engineering feeder-objective plan
       c. Research feeder-objective plan
       d. Public relations feeder-objective plan
       e. Quality control feeder-objective plan

C. Price margin improvement

   1. Competitive analysis, pricing review, and discounting practices
   2. Requirements and alternatives for percentage of market share
   3. Price margine objective contributed by:
       a. Sales feeder-objective plan
       b. Finance feeder-objective plan
       c. Production feeder-objective plan
       d. Accounting feeder-objective plan
       e. Legal feeder-objective plan

D. Capital investment improvement

   1. Facilities analysis, cash flow, equipment utilization
   2. Requirements and alternatives for capital additions
   3. Capital improvement objective contributed by:
       a. Production feeder-objective plan   d. Research feeder-objective plan
       b. Finance feeder-objective plan   e. Legal feeder-objective plan
       c. Accounting feeder-objective plan

E. Cost improvement

   1. Cost effectiveness, cost control, cost avoidance
   2. Requirements and alternatives for cost reduction
   3. Cost improvement objective contributed by:
       a. Production feeder-objective plan   d. Personnel feeder-objective plan
       b. Purchasing feeder-objective plan   e. Accounting feeder-objective plan
       c. Quality control feeder-objective plan

F. Changes in annual profit plan

   1. Authority for initiating and approving changes
   2. Procedure for effecting changes

A profit plan is an active, viable strategy for obtaining profits with contributions from all segments of the organization. When sales and profits are below the expected level in a fiscal period, an intense effort should be organized to make up for these losses in the succeeding period. Measuring, correcting, improving, and ultimately achieving are the essence of the profit plan.

Profit and Loss Statements ►

A profit and loss (P & L) statement is a vital indicator of the health and position of the organization. The statement not only pinpoints the profit and loss for each product line, as well as for the entire operation; it also breaks down profit and loss on each item for the current period, as well as cumulatively to date. Comparing the P & L statement with those of other periods and other organizations provides a form of measurement to determine the action necessary to handle variances.

From a single month's profit picture of what has happened and what is likely to happen should emerge certain trends. Thus a downward trend can be controlled and redirected before it gets out of hand. Records of sales and costs over past months and years can provide a useful measure for making improvement forecasts for coming months and years. This was described earlier in the discussion of improvement forecasts. The most reliable and meaningful way to predict the future is to extrapolate from the past.

Profit Improvement Analysis ►

The MBO manager must strive each year for higher sales volume at lower cost. He sets objectives and plans accordingly to get a percentage increase in sales volume from the previous year. Similarly, he sets objectives and plans accordingly to reduce his operating costs by getting a percentage decrease in operating costs from the previous year. It is useful to organize one's thinking about profit improvements in a logical form. Comparisons made from year to year yield a profit improvement analysis, as illustrated in Figure 2.

2. Trend Analysis for Profit Improvement

Comparing Fiscal Years

Objectives	19__	% Change	19__	% Change	19__	% Change	19__	% Change
Sales volume	—							
Returns & allowances	—							
Cash discounts	—							
Net sales	—							
Total costs	—							
Direct labor	—							
Direct material	—							
Overhead	—							
Taxes	—							
Profit amount	—							
Profit percentage	—							
Return on net worth	—							

A feel for changes over the years, months, or weeks helps minimize the risks one should take. It builds confidence that the objectives set for the coming period will be reached. For example, a profile trend of how payroll is increasing or decreasing in relation to total sales helps the manager intuit the percentage level that should be targeted for the next period. Or he might make his judgment on the basis of an examination of the total number of payroll hours worked by all employees against total sales. To the manager the foremost question should be, "How does the most recent fiscal period compare with the period immediately preceding it and the period prior to that?"

Overall Profit Improvement Network ►

In summary, profit improvement begins by targeting percentage increases in sales volume and price margin and percentage decreases in capital outlay and operating costs. A strategy is set up that involves all members of the organization and focuses their activities, efforts, and resources to these ends. Through the performance and implementation stages, the targets that must be hit are never lost sight of, and day-to-day operations are pointed in that direction. The objective network concept described in an earlier chapter not only structures the involvement and contributions but suggests the alignment and orientation that must be maintained, as illustrated in Figure 3.

SALES IMPROVEMENT[2]

A manager trying to get sales improvement using the MBO approach must know where he has been, where he is going, and how the marketing effort relates to the total organization. With this strategy, he sets his sales volume targets, validates them, organizes his work packages, and proceeds to implement them. If he runs into problems, he has the contingency plans and personal experience to formulate a new plan to enable him to move ahead, even if at a slower pace.

Sales improvement is another way of saying that the organization plans to increase the number of customers ordering, the size of orders, and the frequency of repeat orders. With this in mind, the MBO manager needs to focus on customer needs and wants. He needs to understand how these needs change and what competitors offer.

> An organization that has its sales effort centered around customers is an organization properly directed toward sales improvement. This seems to be a simple and naive statement. The fact is that many organizations give only lip service to the principle of customer orientation.

The function of marketing planning includes activities for generating strategies through which to create new markets or enlarge existing markets. A major difficulty in developing these marketing plans lies in laying cohesive plans of action throughout the entire enterprise. Preoccupation with obtaining this cohesiveness often inhibits the plan's polarization toward customers. The following are some guidelines for getting sales improvements through customer orientation.

Treating Customers as Investments ►

Organizations make capital investments in equipment, facilities, land, materials, furniture, inventory, and trained workers—all in order to serve the needs of customers. The fact is that investment does not stop here. It goes right to the customers themselves. Orientation toward customers means the following:

- Customers represent valuable investments of money, time, and effort and should be treated as more valuable than equipment, furniture, and materials.

- Customers should be considered in the long run, as well as in the short run. Customer service should be considered as a deposit on repeat orders.

3. Objective Network for a Profit Plan

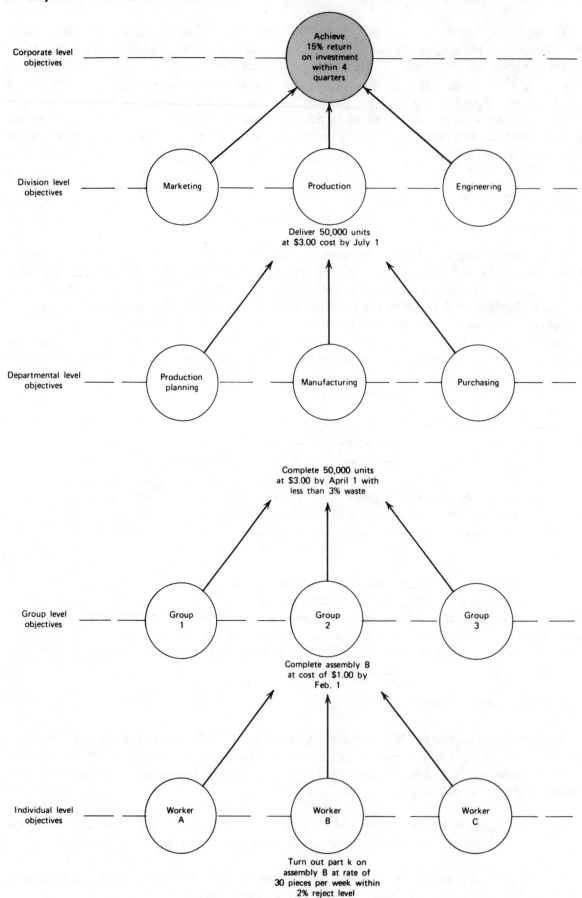

Corporate level objectives — Achieve 15% return on investment within 4 quarters

Division level objectives — Marketing, Production, Engineering

Deliver 50,000 units at $3.00 cost by July 1

Departmental level objectives — Production planning, Manufacturing, Purchasing

Complete 50,000 units at $3.00 by April 1 with less than 3% waste

Group level objectives — Group 1, Group 2, Group 3

Complete assembly B at cost of $1.00 by Feb. 1

Individual level objectives — Worker A, Worker B, Worker C

Turn out part k on assembly B at rate of 30 pieces per week within 2% reject level

- Repeat orders from customers can be viewed as a variable. That is, customers can reorder few times or many times and can buy very little or a great deal. What the customer does depends directly on his degree of satisfaction with previous orders filled.

- Since customers are assets, depreciation, obsolescence, and deterioration are factors an organization must guard against. The MBO manager must strive for the competitive edge.

Developing a Customer-Oriented Organization ►

The conflict between cost and price continues. Under our form of economy it will always continue. Does this mean that the only way we can attract and hold customers is with low prices and low costs? The answer is an emphatic no. Obviously, prices are most important and should be kept competitive. There are, however, other approaches to get and hold customers. One such technique is called *sales sensitivity*. Sales sensitivity requires that all employees of an organization be sensitive to the importance and value of a customer and conduct themselves accordingly. Employees behave and perform their normal duties in such a way as to elicit customer satisfaction; they project a quality image that affects sales favorably. According to this concept, the waitress in a restaurant is first a saleswoman and then a waitress. The guard in a bank is first a salesman and then a security officer. The telephone operator is first a saleswoman and then an operator.

Using Customer Improvement Planning ►

As cited earlier, sales improvement planning is planning to increase the number of customers and the frequency of their orders. The first step of this plan is to set sales improvement quotas or objectives in terms of customers. An evaluation and review of past and present performance form the basis for the sales volume improvement to be achieved. These guideposts help in appraising progress as plans are implemented. They indicate where deficiencies occur and where opportunity exists. These measures are incorporated in the sales improvement chart illustrated in Figure 4.

4. Customer-Oriented Sales Improvement Planning

Sales Improvement Objectives	Last Year	This Year	First Year of Plan		Second Year of Plan	
			Amount	% Improvement	Amount	% Improvement
Total sales volume in market 　Sales volume by districts 　Sales volume by products 　Sales volume by customers						
Total customers in market 　Customers by districts 　Customers by products 　Customers by sales						
Company's share of market 　Percentage sales volume 　Percentage customers 　Customers per product 　Customers per district 　Customers per buyer category 　Customers per salesmen 　Customer profit ratio 　Customer turnover per 　　district 　　product 　　salesmen						

Because of the importance of customers to sales, sales improvement objectives should be specified to

- Increase competitive edge.

- Open new territories and broaden customer base.

- Increase depth of market penetration.

- Focus and concentrate on sales increase of key accounts.

- Increase market occupancy factor.

- Reduce misdirected and wasteful advertising.

- Increase service to meet or better customer expectations.

- Reduce quality or price to fit market demands.

- Increase inquiries through product awareness strategies.

- Increase service time to meet discretionary buying power.

- Increase market segmentation where indicated.

- Make greater number of specific proposals to potential key accounts.

- Reduce interest-arousing effort in favor of increased contact-making effort.

- Maintain present level of customers to assure reorders.

The following sales improvement checklist is made up of questions that many successful MBO managers have found helpful to ask. Check those that seem most important to your own situation.

- [ ] Have you evaluated your situation to find areas for sales improvement?

- [ ] What is the percentage of depth of market penetration?

- [ ] What is the number of total potential customers in the market?

- [ ] Are you competitive in your area with respect to price?

- [ ] Are you competitive in your area with respect to type, quality, and delivery of service or products?

- [ ] Are your sales (customers) increasing? decreasing? leveling?

- [ ] Do you need new services or products to increase sales?

- [ ] Have you established a plan with objectives for sales improvement?

- [ ] Where are your greatest sales and customer opportunities?

- [ ] Do you have an on-going sales improvement training program?

- [ ] Why do customers buy from you rather than from your competitors?

- [ ] Why do customers buy from your competitors rather than from you?

- [ ] How effective are your promotion and advertising?

- [ ] Do you feel promotions are giving you the depth of penetration you need?

- [ ] Are you using the right media for reaching customers?

- [ ] Is your promotional budget related to objectives for improving sales volume?

- [ ] Do you coordinate promotion outside the organization with sales sensitivity within the organization?

- [ ] Do you treat customers as an investment for repeat visitations and orders?

- [ ] Is the service rendered equal to or greater than customer expectations?

- [ ] Are production and distribution facilities geared to meet the demand resulting from promotional efforts?

- [ ] Is there a follow-up procedure for handling inquiries?

- [ ] Is there a sufficient intensity of persistence in follow-up work?

- [ ] What is the competitive edge of products and services?

- [ ] Is the sales staff trained in time-saving techniques and work planning for sales results?

COST IMPROVEMENT

Profit improvement is the MBO manager's focal point, and the greatest contribution toward this improvement lies in cost control. Controlling costs is not just a matter of setting up a program; it is more nearly a way of managerial life. Its core is acceptance of the idea that whatever an organization does to establish quality, service, and efficient operations, it does with minimal costs. This attitude is often ignored, because costs are usually thought of in terms of figures. But costs are primarily a matter of people. It is people who generate and control costs. Consequently, the MBO manager cannot afford to overlook his greatest prospect for keeping costs down: the way he deals directly with his employees and the way his employees do their work.

Cost reduction and cost control have always been important, but today, in the face of rising prices, spiraling costs, profit squeezes, and lower productivity, they are more important than ever. The days of automatic price increases to recover costs are gone. For some time we have been in a buyer's market. Discount practices and growing competition have become so entrenched that the only solution to rising costs is not increasing prices but planning and organizing activities and efforts aimed at accomplishing cost control.

In the face of all these pressures, cost improvement programs must be deliberately and systematically planned with year-in and year-out consistency. Cost-cutting and last-ditch slashing by panicked management are desperate one-shot cost improvement attempts made because of a lack of foresight and planning. MBO cost improvement is built into the work plan in such a way that the practitioner controls and reduces costs as he moves about completing the technical and functional aspects of his job.[3] Cost improvement is natural to managing by objectives since the strategy's focus capability can lend the cost effort a precision, concentration, and direction not normally offered by other managerial strategies.

MBO cost improvement is a series of targeted objectives designed to effect a favorable change for an organization. The following are some areas in which a manager can set MBO objectives for cost improvement.

Improving Labor Use ►

The use of labor influences the total cost picture greatly. The MBO manager would do well to begin his cost improvement by using his employees to better advantage. Productivity is the term used for the output of an employee toward meeting performance standards, while minimizing the resources consumed in the process. Obviously, any increase in the productivity of substandard performers will raise the average productivity of the entire group or department. Unquestionably, it is better to improve the productivity of substandard performers than to raise the productivity of those who are already meeting the standard.

Careful screening, selection, and orientation of new employees begins the process of better labor use. This is where the proper attitude toward costs should begin to be instilled in the employee. The MBO manager must accept the idea that employees should be trained not only to meet a job performance standard wherever they are assigned, but also to meet it at lower cost and on time. Most employees at the time of hire are not cost conscious. Therefore, the manager must make them cost conscious through training and retraining. This is not a one-shot operation.

Reducing Repeat Work ►

Every time a recycling of work occurs because of human error, labor costs automatically go up proportionately. Material costs also double. The basic — and controllable — sources of human error that cause repeat work are indifference, ignorance, incompetence, and confusion. The following are guidelines to overcoming these sources of human error.

- Tell the individual about his errors, so that he knows what he has done.

- Indicate the cost of error to the individual.

- Original training may not have taken hold. Provide retraining.

- Get people to focus on details. When an employee sees that his supervisor expects attention to detail, he will strive for it. The supervisor should set a good example.

- Watch and evaluate attitudes at the time of hire. Look for such indications of sloppiness or carelessness as poor appearance and tardiness in keeping appointments. An individual's personal attitudes will be reflected in his work.

Reducing Waste ►

Wasted material, idle people, and broken equipment are fundamentally caused by sloppy or imprecise planning. They are the results of the failure to anticipate with greater exactness what is needed and the failure to have a contingency plan to handle overages. Waste prevention and control are not accomplished in one shot. They must be dealt with as a continuing day-to-day task within the work itself. Consider and use the following improvement guidelines:

- Reduce idle time during slack periods. Develop a priority checklist of extra work and set down in advance who will do what.

- Practice and encourage conservation of such resources as water, lights, cutting oils, paper, tools, and pencils.

- Establish waste prevention and elimination projects. Schedule these projects and assign members of the group to implement them.

- Reclaim scrap that can be reused. The reclamation process can be a valuable source of savings provided the cost of reclamation is below the cost of new material.

- Plan for greatest material utilization possible. Design a contingency scheme to carry out when all materials are not utilized.

Reducing Stealing and Pilfering ►

Statistical research[4] has shown that out of every three people who work for organizations, one will never steal, a second will steal every chance he can get, and a third will steal if the opportunity arises and he feels he can get away with it. Thus two out of every three employees are potential problems in security. Their reasons for stealing vary from a need to support extravagant living or pay unforeseen expenses to a feeling that they must make up for insufficient compensation by the organization. But whatever their reasons, they cause American industry to pay 6.5 per cent of its annual gross sales in pilferage. The MBO manager must accept the fact that internal security is an absolute must. He has to set up a system of internal checks that will stop such stealing. For this purpose, he may use the following guidelines:

- Treat the cash register and the handling of cash with greater respect. Follow an operating manual's procedure for cash control, deposits, tapes, safe control, and reports.

- Set up a system of spread control, where one person checks the work, deposits, inventory, and so forth, of another.

- Keep accurate records as described in operating manuals. Money or stock should be checked by a senior employee.

- Practice the surprise audit and be sure everyone knows it. Plan frequent surprise audits of various critical areas where opportunity for defalcation may be high. A changing schedule of surprise audits will keep the potential thief in line.

- Look at recorded percentages to identify leaks of cash, costs, supplies, materials, and tools. The more locked doors, the less leakage.

Improving Overhead ►

Overhead costs in most organizations, if not in all, are usually too high. Basic to overhead improvement is overhead control as a percentage of material and labor. There will always be a proportion of fixed expenses that are not avoidable. The MBO manager, however, sets a target to maintain or reduce, on a percentage basis, overhead costs in the following areas.

- Staff departments

- Maintenance and repair of equipment, tools, and buildings

- Telephone, telegram, and TWX expenses

- Office equipment and supplies

- Employee benefits and indirect compensation

- Paper procedures and records retention

- Utilities and resources

- Data processing and electronic computers

- Personnel processing procedures

- Communications media and newspapers

- Unused space and housekeeping

Following Cost-Reduction Guidelines ►

The following guidelines may suggest ways to reduce costs in your organization.

- Plan to keep employees productive between jobs.

- Give instructions and orders clearly and understandably.

- Provide a full day's work for each employee.

- Understand and know operating procedures.

- Keep tools and equipment in their proper places.

- Avoid overtime.

- Do not allow employees to do less than they can.

- Get advance notice of termination from employees.

- Notify early call-in resources when personnel are needed.

- Write records, requisitions, and orders accurately.

- Do not allow employees to get in the habit of talking, visiting, and killing time.

- Get employees started on time.

- Do not delay in making decisions.

- Investigate immediately when repairs are needed.

- Organize yourself in both time and work.

- Explain the money value of tools, material, and supplies and the costs of waste.

- Watch employees' eyesight and health as possible causes of spoiled work.

- Discourage carelessness and off-quality work.

- Do not take an employee's ability for granted. Make sure he can do the job.

- Listen to what employees are trying to say.

- Encourage employees to offer suggestions.

- Ask advice and opinions of employees on mutual problems.

- Study business methods for efficiency.

- Get from new employees helpful ideas that they may bring from previous employment.

- Take an interest in the troublesome areas of the unit.

- Guard against failure to control turnover of capable employees because of the following:

  a. Not appreciating the direct and indirect costs of labor turnover.

  b. Bossing instead of giving intelligent direction.

  c. Being too strict or too lax in enforcement of discipline.

  d. Not keeping promises that could be kept.

  e. Making promises that cannot be kept in regard to wages, promotion, and so on.

    f.   Discharging employees without sufficient cause; improper use of the discharge slip as a penalty.

    g.   Keeping an employee on a job for which he has a violent dislike.

- Know the right kind of supplies to order.

- Do not order more materials and supplies than necessary.

- See that materials and supplies are stored properly.

- Inspect equipment, machinery, and tools to keep them in good working condition.

- Protect idle equipment from heat, dust, and dirt.

- Provide instruction on the proper use of equipment.

- Do not abuse small equipment by using it for large work.

- Avoid treating one person better or worse than others.

- Never take sides in employees' arguments.

- Never criticize one employee to another.

- Always question employees who leave of their own accord.

- Be sure to interpret management's real aims and policies correctly to employees.

- Do all you can to adjust wages and working conditions fairly.

- Receive new employees in a kindly, helpful manner.

- Provide complete job instruction for new employees.

- Impress upon new employees the necessity for a full day's work and what it consists of.

- Be sure to select new employees with proper qualifications for the work to be done.

- Avoid showing impatience with new employees who learn slowly.

- Get other employees to show a friendly, helpful attitude to new employees.

- Inform new employees as to conditions and regulations, such as those dealing with safety, pay days, lavatories, drinking water, lockers, and washrooms.

- Inform new employees about unpleasant or dangerous parts of their work.

- Commend employees for doing good work.

- Explain as much about the work as possible in order to make it interesting.

- Show interest in employees' progress and personal affairs.

- Be ready to admit a mistake to an employee.

- Pay attention to an employee's ability and temperament in assigning work to him.

- Do not approve the formation of cliques among employees.

- Do not rate employees on any grounds other than competence; avoid such grounds as race and religion.

- Do not permit an employee to remain at work when he is sick.

- Always promote employees when it is possible and advisable.

- Give due consideration to problems affecting wages and working conditions.

- Cooperate with other employees and departments, as well as with customers.

- Understand organization policies thoroughly and explain them to employees.

- Deal sensibly with gossip and tale-bearing.

- Never pass the buck to other employees.

- Be sure to represent the employees adequately to management.

- Do not permit disgruntled employees to agitate against the organization.

- Give full support to unpopular organization regulations.

- Promote friendliness and cooperation among employees.

- Avoid thoughtless criticism of any organization policy or of any individual in the organization.

- Cooperate wholeheartedly with top management.

✓Checkpoint: Profit, Sales, and Cost Improvements ————————————

Fill in the correct answer.

1. A _____ is an active, viable strategy for obtaining profits through contributions from all segments of the organization.

2. A _____ pinpoints the profit and loss for each product line, as well as for the entire operation.

3. A manager uses a _____ to compare profits from year to year.

4. Profit improvement plans should be organized around _____ rather than around organization functions.

5. The four ways to improve profits are to increase sales volume or _____ , or to reduce capital investments or _____ .

6. An organization that has its sales effort centered around _____ is an organization that is properly directed toward sales improvement.

7. _____ should be regarded as a deposit on repeat orders.

8. Under the concept of _____ , a waitress is first a saleswoman and then a waitress.

9. _____ is the term used for the output of an employee toward meeting performance standards.

10. The greatest contribution toward profit improvement today lies in _____ .

Indicate true (T) or false (F).

11. Every time a recycling of work occurs because of human error, labor costs automatically go up proportionately. ____

12. Two out of every three employees may potentially steal from their organization. ____

13. Basic to overhead improvement is overhead control as a percentage of material and labor. ____

14. If he has a proper sales improvement program, an MBO manager does not need a contingency plan. ____

15. The MBO manager must strive each year for higher sales volume at lower cost. ____

———————————————

● Checkpoint Answers

1. profit plan   2. profit and loss statement   3. profit improvement analysis
4. objectives   5. price margin, operating costs   6. customers   7. customer service
8. sales sensitivity   9. productivity   10. cost control   11. T   12. T   13. T   14. F   15. T

MANAGEMENT TIME IMPROVEMENT[5]

Avoiding Time Robbers ►

We often think that time robbers are external to us and that we have little control over them. Careful analysis will show, however, that basically we steal our own time. We allow and engage in activities without regard to managing time. Following is a list of time robbers that, if stopped, will leave us with more time, energy, and money to release into an operation.

- Carelessly done work

- Delayed decisions

- Excessive communications

- Uncontrolled telephone calls

- Casual visitors

A job done hastily, partially, or so carelessly that it must be done over is a monstrous thief of time. Inefficiency probably ranks first among all time robbers. If a job must be done over, the time required for its completion is doubled. Working fast is never the answer if it results in rework. Your first consideration should be to work accurately and completely. Only after you are sure of accuracy should you concentrate on speed.

Another time robber is the failure to make timely decisions. Early decisions can cause some difficulty, but it is well known that delayed decisions can cause even more. Prompt action, when action is needed, is the best way for getting results.

> The MBO manager knows that procrastination can set up a backlog that costs heavily in money. Unless altered circumstances lead you to question your objectives, finish work once you have started it.

In response to the great call for more and improved communications, there has been an orgy of communications that have sapped valuable time. Written reports and memoranda too widely distributed, reading material not relevant to the job, unnecessary outgoing correspondence, and excessively long letters are some of the time robbers participating in this orgy.

Meetings and conferences that ramble for lack of planning are also terrific time wasters. Subordinates should participate only in those meetings that directly affect them; if management requires them to attend other meetings, it is only wasting their time. The following are aspects of good conferences:

- Held only with persons necessary for the discussion

- Agenda and purpose stated and facts ready

- Effective conference leadership provided to keep discussion to the point

- Responsibility affixed for follow-through

The uncontrolled use of the telephone is another devastating time waster. It is hard to find the manager who has clearly thought through his best procedure for maintaining control of both incoming and outgoing calls. Here are some hints for controlling phone calls:

- Group outgoing calls. Get them out at one time, as on a production line. Calling others makes it possible for you to hold your phone conversations at a time of your choosing. When you say "give me a call," you invite interruptions.

- Authorize your secretary or switchboard operator to screen your incoming calls. Make a list of people to whom you will always speak. List circumstances in which you will always wish to be called. Set up a procedure to determine the name of the caller and the purpose of the call, and establish a system for referral to the appropriate person.

For some, the casual visitor may be almost as much of a time robber as the uncontrolled phone call. He may be a fellow manager, a friend, a relative, or an unexpected inquirer. What is your philosophy about such interruptions? They consume time. When an unexpected visitor drops in, it can disrupt an entire day's planning, particularly when there is no time limit set on his visit. The following are possible ways to avoid this:

- Give a friendly word or two suggesting that you get together sometime and indicate that a schedule has been arranged.

- Screen with a secretary or assistant the floaters and drop-ins.

- Close doors if you are in an office.

- Continue your work while the visitor is there. He will get the hint.

Other time robbers include

- People who keep you waiting

- Undelegated responsibilities

- Mediocre personnel who require constant retraining

- Misplaced items and a poor retrieval system

> There is a notion that pressure is a time robber, a notion that if pressure exists, the organization should be viewed with alarm. This notion has now been discarded, since successful enterprises are those whose managers work well under pressure. It is the tranquil and contented organization that is alarming. A manager should not be too easily satisfied with his results.

Improving the Management of Time ►

The first step in getting more time for yourself is to find out how your time is being wasted. Make a checklist of those areas you suspect and carefully evaluate whether any time can be salvaged if they are controlled or eliminated. This evaluation should be carefully set down with a simple time and motion study of your daily activities or a cursory but accurate survey of deviations of planned activities from actual activities. Use a systematic approach to do this, as suggested by the following form.

Next, list the problems you must tackle, setting up a system that separates the critical items you must do from the less critical items that others can do. Do not dilute your effort with trivia. The effective MBO manager organizes his activities to meet his profit plan. He does not, for example, spend many hours scheduling employees only to find in the end that the payroll is too high. Instead of trying to fit the schedule to the employees, he attempts to fit the employees to the schedule.

Your system of priorities should help you get rid of detail that consumes your time. Force yourself to become organized. For example, all management jobs require a certain amount of record keeping. To many managers, this is not only a chore but a bore. Purchase records, personnel records, and the like are usually set aside to be done later. Usually the manager falls behind and later finds he has an even greater problem as the paper work mounts. If he had forced himself to be organized and had made these a part of a morning priority plan, he would be much happier, would make fewer errors, and would be able to cooperate more easily with those waiting for the information.

After you have set your priorities, schedule your daily activities. As soon as you arrive at work, take five minutes to write down what you intend to accomplish during the day. This is managing by objectives in miniature. Do not play it by ear. If you do, you will get only half as far as you want to get. Writing down a schedule forces you to set a timetable for yourself. At the end of the day you will be able to say to yourself, "I accomplished what I was after today." In writing down your intended accomplishments, compress your time — make it count. Force yourself to do larger projects in shorter periods of time. Tackle the tough problems first thing in the morning, when you are fresh and can think clearly.

Keep a record of your scheduling in the past and determine where improvements can be made. Just because a schedule has been used does not mean it cannot be improved upon. Work on maximizing results from your existing schedules.

Other ways to save time are:

- *Learn to say no.* Get into the habit of using the greatest timesaving word in the English language, the two-letter word, "no." Do not listen to discussions of irrelevant commitments and unwanted activities.

- *Carry on two activities simultaneously.* Whenever possible gain time by doing two things at once. We are already practiced in making time serve a dual purpose. For example, we read the newspaper while eating breakfast; we drive a car while listening to the radio.

- *Know when to stop.* Countless hours, days, and weeks are wasted because we pursue a target or execute a plan that is faulty to begin with. Know when to stop and take a different direction.

- *Develop retrieval procedures.* Organize your activities and records in such a way that they can be efficiently retrieved. Do not store unless you know how to retrieve quickly.

- *Listening is a great time saver.* Time is spent, resources are wasted, and employees are lost because a manager has failed to listen to what really happened. Develop your listening skills so that you are alert for factors that affect the operation of a unit. Listen for relevant and pertinent details. You will avoid later rethinking, redigging, and reworking.

Time Analysis for Improving Management Time

Name _____ Dept. _____ Date _____

Time Robbers	Expected Time	Actual Time	Wasted Time (Difference)	Corrective Actions	Improved Time
Repeat work					
Incomplete work					
Delayed decisions					
Telephone calls					
Overcommunications					
Drop-in visitors					
Waiting for people					
Failure to delegate					
Family interruptions					
Retraining					
Misplaced items					
Poor retrieval system					
Coffee breaks					
Reading					

Total time wasted _____   Total time improved _____

Can an MBO manager master time and make it his servant? Sometimes. And he gets greater and greater control over time as he becomes more and more skillful in pinpointing results to be accomplished on a time spectrum. He comes to realize the importance of daily accomplishments as contributions to the larger and more significant programs that affect the organization.

COMMUNICATIONS IMPROVEMENT

Communication is the means by which we get other people to understand us. Speaking and writing are considered by many as the major ways to communicate. But there are other means, as well. The average time,[6] in percentage, devoted to these means by a manager or supervisor in the course of a day is as follows:

Listening	32%
Body language (physical gestures)	30%
Speaking	21%
Reading	11%
Writing	6%

Knowing the Barriers to Communications[7] ►

The following are some of the major barriers to effective communication:

- *Defensive listening.* When we listen defensively, we do not listen at all. When the other person is speaking, we are taking that time to compose our rebuttal. In other words, we have already decided he is confused, misinformed, or stupid.

- *Boss consciousness.* Employees tend to tell their supervisor what he likes to hear: that things are going well. As a consequence, information flowing up through the organization often does not reflect the true state of affairs. A subordinate will sometimes avoid asking for important information, because he feels he may be criticized for not already knowing that information. In somewhat the same fashion, a manager may be reluctant to admit to his subordinates that everything is not going well, because he thinks this might be seen by them as an admission of his weakness.

- *Inability to express ideas clearly and concisely.* It is important to use the concise right word or expression. (The Gettysburg Address contains 266 words, the Ten Commandments, 297 words, but the government's O.P.S. regulation on pricing contains 26,911 words.)

- *Feelings of insecurity.* A manager is sometimes unwilling to pass on his skills and technical know-how to others. He feels that he ceases to be important as soon as there are others who can do his job. He feels insecure if his subordinates are as well informed on some important subject as he is.

- *Failure to select the proper medium.* There are many ways to communicate with people: fact-to-face dialogues, body language, telephone calls, memos, letters, reports, conferences, posters, visual aids, and so on. If an inappropriate medium is selected, the message may not be successfully conveyed.

- *Preoccupation with other parts of the job.* There is poor reception when a supervisor gives an order that an employee has not been conditioned to expect. Subordinates preoccupied with and committed to other tasks are not good receptors.

- *Inability to remember.* The average individual remembers 50 per cent of a message directly after receiving it and only 25 per cent after 2 weeks. All human beings are "leaky vessels." Recognize the fact that subordinates at times will forget.

- *Listening to the grapevine.* One way to get an inkling of what is going on is to listen to the half truths, speculations, and outright lies on the grapevine. Listen to them but never use the grapevine to spread information. The grapevine always exists in the absence of good communications. If your organization does not have a grapevine, the chances are that it has good channels of communication.

- *Misinforming with facts.* Facts are often used by people to distort, misinform, or oversimplify. Statistics have a mathematical base, hence they suggest an accuracy they may not possess.

Improving Your Communications Skills ►

The MBO manager's problems of communication are related to the many in-house groups and individuals that must help him implement his objective programs. These groups are many and varied, as Figure 5 shows.

5. MBO Managers Communicate With Many Groups

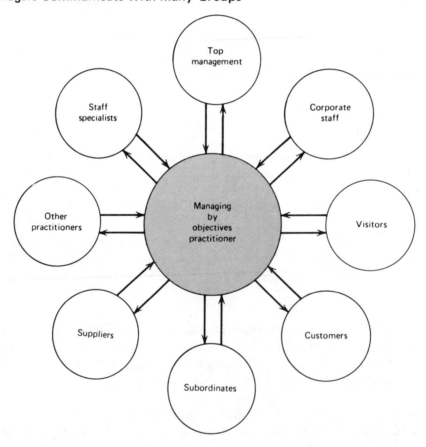

The MBO manager should develop the skills to handle these groups effectively. He will find that applying the following rules in his organization will result in definite progress toward both long- and short-range objectives. He should:

- Tell it right.

- Listen for meanings.

- Plan for communications

- Use sound human-relations techniques.

Telling it right ranks high in getting ideas, directives, and information over to people. Following are some practical guidelines for applying this rule:

- *Tell enough.* Individuals require information in varying amounts. Under the pressure of time, a manager may forget that there are individual differences in know-how and experience. His tendency is to give one message to everyone. A new employee, however, must be told more than a seasoned, senior employee.

- *Tell soon enough.* Do not surprise your subordinates by telling them at the last minute. Telling in advance helps the subordinate to respond to and to accept what you are trying to say.

- *Tell often enough.* New employees must be continually reminded. Older employees must also be reminded. Constant repetition of important matters to new and old employees alike will eventually pay off.

- *Tell everyone concerned.* The often-quoted expression, "Why doesn't anyone tell me?" is too often heard. The MBO manager must be sure to inform all his subordinates of what they need to know.

- *Tell it in the right tone.* The tone of the communication is fully as important as its content. People see and interpret behavior, tone, and facial expressions as well as the content itself. Use tones and body language that fit the content.

- *Tell it in writing.* The chance of confusion or failure to remember is minimized when you give your information in writing.

In the words of Epictetus, "Nature has given men one tongue but two ears that we may hear from others twice as much as we speak." Listening can be developed as a skill for collecting information about what others are thinking and doing. Listening for meanings means listening beyond words, or listening for intent. For example: Your car is stuck in a snow bank and a passer-by finds you looking over the situation. "Having trouble?" he asks. If you were listening beyond words, you would hear, "Can I help?" The situation, the person, and the context should be taken into consideration to discover the underlying meanings of the words uttered. Listening for meanings also means listening for feelings. The emotional component is bound to be tied up in the message content. Be on the alert to detect feelings and handle them accordingly. An outburst over a small issue may mean that the individual is loaded with emotional dynamite. Be on guard for bad listening habits, such as the following:

- *Assuming the communications to be uninteresting.* The good listener is a sifter or a screener, always hinting for something worthwhile that he can store away. People are always trying to say something even though it may seem uninteresting at times.

- *Faking attention.* Subordinates may fake attention to their supervisor when he is telling them something because he is their supervisor. The supervisor must get the attention of his receiver first before speaking. Usually, a short personal dialogue is a good means to do this.

- *Listening only for facts.* When you listen only for facts, you miss how the facts hang together. When you listen, try to get the main idea.

- *Tolerating distractions.* The human ears receive all sounds, some of which are distracting. The more there are of these distractive sounds, the more complicated and difficult it becomes to block them out.

- *Evading the difficult.* People tend to avoid tough, technical, and complicated communications. They prefer to listen to the easy, light, and known sources. Break down a difficult communication into easier component parts.

Before communicating with subordinates, plan what you will say and when and how you will say it. Apply the following guidelines:

- *Plan the media you will use.* Telephone calls, written notes, face-to-face dialogues, body language, group conferences, time cards or schedules, memos, statements of policy, posters, and blueprints are some of the many media that can be used. Select the one most appropriate for conveying the message to people so that they will understand. Avoid the grapevine, channel jumping, hearsay, rumors, and gripes. In the absence of planned media, employees will use their own.

- *Keep the number of go-betweens to a minimum.* Each person through whom a message must pass to get from the teller to the receiver is a potential communications barrier.

- *Plan intershift communications.* Two shifts will be more likely to pull in the same direction if there is a smooth transition between the two. Allow shift overlap; managers of both shifts should be on friendly terms; keep shift notes or a log book of items to be done; do not trust memory; and reserve a time to communicate.

- *Plan what to pass along.* Decide in advance what information to pass along, how it will be passed along, and to whom. Subordinates who must have certain information must be identified in advance.

- *Develop the skill of questioning.* Raising good questions at the right time will facilitate communications.

    Why is it necessary?
    What is its purpose?
    Where should it be done?
    When should it be done?
    Who is best qualified to do it?
    How will it be done?

- *Watch carefully the giving of orders.* Every person has a zone of acceptance of an order from his supervisor. He is likely to comply with orders that fall within that zone and to reject orders that fall outside it. The zone of acceptance is illustrated in Figure 6. Each individual's zone will vary as to what he will or will not do for his boss.[8] This zone is conditioned by needs, desires, experiences, and relationships. Do not assume that a subordinate will do whatever the supervisor asks.

6. An Order Zone of Acceptance

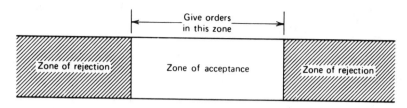

The zone of acceptance can be enlarged if:

1. Subordinate understands that the order is without false implications.
2. Subordinate takes a positive and constructive view of the order.
3. Subordinate sees that the order is consistent with his needs and values.
4. Subordinate can physically and mentally carry out the order.
5. Subordinate sees that the order is compatible with his interest.
6. Subordinate understands that the order will not violate prior conditions of agreement.

• *Set up the conditions for easy communications.* An MBO manager must create an atmosphere in which a subordinate can and will go to him and communicate. A climate in which there is free flow of information and ideas develops when status and bossism are not obstructions, time and media are available, the prevalent policy is to expect communications, personality factors are not allowed to interfere, and listening is regarded as important.

• *Communicate to subordinates in terms of the jobs they occupy.* Know what your employees want from their jobs and give them specific information about the following:

1. What is expected of them and how they measure up to expectation.
2. How their job fits into the organization and their chances for advancement.
3. What the outlook is for the organization and what the prospects are for steady work.
4. How the policies of the organization affect the employee.
5. What the background of the organization is.
6. What changes in methods are being made.

Good human relations can be the key to successful communications. Of the human-relations techniques suggested in the following checklist, mark those you feel might be effectively applied in your organization.

☐ Let each person know where he stands. Do not fail to discuss his performance toward objectives with him periodically.

☐ Give credit where credit is due, that is, give credit commensurate with accomplishments.

☐ Inform people of changes in advance. Information makes people effective.

☐ Let others participate in plans and decisions affecting them.

☐ Gain your associates' confidence. Earn their loyalty and trust.

☐ If a person's behavior is unusual, find out why. There is always a reason.

☐ Instead of giving orders, suggest or ask whenever possible. People generally do not like to be pushed. But do not use innuendo, hint, or implication.

☐ When you make a mistake, admit it and apologize. Others will resent your blaming someone else.

☐ Take every opportunity to demonstrate pride in the group. This will bring out the best in them.

☐ Know all your employees personally. Find out their interests, habits, and sensitivities, and capitalize on your knowledge of them.

☐ Listen to your subordinates' proposals. They have good ideas, too.

☐ Show employees the importance of every job, thus satisfying their need for security.

☐ Criticize constructively. Give reasons for your criticism and suggest ways in which performance can be improved.

☐ Precede criticisms with mention of a person's good points. Show him you are trying to help him.

☐ Do as you would have your people do. The supervisor sets the style.

☐ Be consistent in your actions. Let your employees be in no doubt as to what is expected of them.

☐ Explain the why of things that are to be done.

☐ If one man gripes, find out his grievance. One man's gripe may be the gripe of many.

☐ Settle every grievance, if at all possible; otherwise, the whole group will be affected.

$\sqrt{}$Checkpoint: Management Time Improvement and Communications Improvement ————

Indicate true (T) or false (F).

1. While procrastination may be an inconvenience to a manager, it is not much of an influence on an organization's costs. _____

2. There is no such thing as too much communication within an organization. _____

3. Work pressure can have a positive effect on productivity. _____

4. The first step to getting more time to yourself is to find out where you are wasting time. _____

5. An effective MBO manager is so well organized that he can afford to leave his paper work for his spare moments. _____

6. Most people communicate more by speaking than by any other means. _____

7. To encourage employees to communicate with you, encourage them to be boss conscious. _____

8. Through unwillingness to pass his knowledge along to subordinates, a manager creates a communications barrier. _____

9. When listening to others, listen not only to what is said, but also to what is meant. _____

10. Each person through whom a message must pass to get from the teller to the receiver is a potential communications barrier. _____

————————————————

● Checkpont Answers

1. F   2. F   3. T   4. T   5. F   6. F   7. F   8. T   9. T   10. T

METHODS IMPROVEMENT[9]

To improve methods, the MBO manager must systematically study existing work methods, in order to discover new and perhaps easier ways to get things done. The greatest benefit of this approach lies in improving the organization's operating efficiency or productivity, which is generally measured in output units per time or costs per unit. The interest in methods improvement to gain greater productivity has recently become more pronounced because of the increased size and complexity of organizations, increased worker specialization, increased work and quality standards, increased influence of government, and increased availability of scientific approaches to productivity.

In an earlier chapter, the performance stretch concept was discussed in some detail. Targeting and getting performance stretches is targeting and getting greater productivity. It is possible with good methods improvement to increase individual productivity from 10 to 20 per cent. This increase is obtained through an organized approach to methods improvement.

Objectives and Areas for Improvement ►

The overall objectives of methods improvement are increased productivity and lower operating costs. The degree to which these are met will depend upon successfully meeting the following specific objectives:

- Reduce handling time of equipment, tools, and materials.

- Eliminate all unnecessary activity.

- Decrease time to complete an operation.

- Eliminate duplication of effort.

- Make work safer and less fatiguing.

- Eliminate waste of time, energy, and materials.

- Increase deliveries to customer.

- Decrease paper work.

These objectives are usually sought in work areas where improvement is needed. For example, idle time and job delays are productivity robbers. Waiting for materials, tools, and equipment raises the question, Why the wait? Can the existing methods and procedures be altered to reduce the wait? Excessive handling and backtracking are other examples of productivity reduction. The methods analyst attempts to identify flow processes to see if materials can be made to flow smoothly from job to job through the department. Bottlenecks create another obstacle to productivity improvement. A single element in a series of elements in a job process that delays the whole process can rob the entire department of a higher level of productivity. Still another area that suggests productivity improvement are those jobs or situations in which repetitive volume is greatest. A small savings in time, cost, or material on an operation repeated many times a day can amount to large overall savings during the course of the year. High-cost items often indicate obvious areas for which reduction analysis can lead to savings. These high-cost items are not just materials, equipment, or labor rates; they include equipment set-ups, job changeovers, schedule changes, low production speeds, and poor housekeeping.

Most organizations are engaged in the effort to improve methods. Unfortunately, most of their effort is informal. MBO methods improvement must be formalized, since it requires a series of techniques and procedures as well as a philosophy of work. Setting objectives for methods improvement is the first step in this formal approach. The degree to which an organization is successful in reaching these objectives will depend for the most part on how carefully the objectives are selected and decided upon. The three basic processes of relating, involvement, and commitment described in earlier chapters apply here.

Investigation and Analysis ►

Once the MBO manager has selected an area for improvement, he should go through a methods improvement analysis. This analysis will give him estimates of the costs or time that might be saved by his efforts if the situation is improved. The methods improvement analysis compares what old method values are with what new method values will be when that method is installed. The time and money required to put the improvement into operation are estimated and recorded. To ensure that this is done, it is advisable to set up the analysis in logical steps, using a form similar to that on page 265. Notice that data collected for improving the situation are tabulated so that top management can see the situation at a glance, thus participating in the procedure. This participation is important for the ultimate implementation of the improved procedure.

The flow process chart is a visual tool for recording and observing an operation in the sequence in which it occurs. This arrangement allows the operations to be analyzed systematically and critically. It is helpful for analyzing facts and relationships, in order to develop an improved method. It can assist in communicating to others an understanding of the overall picture. The five basic activities used in flow process charts are operations, transportation, inspection, delay, and shortage. These are illustrated in Figure 7 for a proposed method of assembling pencil slabs. By summing up the types of activities, the distances traveled, and the time consumed, the situation can be more easily grasped. Improvement is attempted through reducing the number of activities, the distances traveled, or the travel time from station to station. In the summary table of the figure, the difference column suggests the improvements possible if the old flow process layout is replaced by the proposed new one.

Work simplification is defined as setting out in an organized manner to find a better and easier way of doing a job. It requires an attitude that always seeks to find a smaller number of simpler motions to execute a job task. It has one vital principle: every detail of a job should be challenged for the purpose of spotting wasted or excessive time, energy, or materials. The questioning attitude and the skills described in an earlier chapter are most important in work simplification. The complacent individual with a closed mind is a major obstacle to simplifying work. Such self-imposed limitations on thinking prevent the emergence of possible solutions.

Work simplification deals with the three basic ingredients of a work flow situation: distribution of work; sequence of work; and volume of work. Methods improvement through work simplification raises questions about job descriptions, job design, and work assignments. Some of these questions are the following:

- Are the duties spread too thin?

- Is the work load evenly balanced?

- Can work operations be reduced? combined?

- Are skills of employees used to best advantage?

- Is there duplication of duties?

- Is too much time being spent on unimportant tasks?

- Is the job too complex?

The questions pry loose facts about the work distribution in terms of activities taking the most time, misdirected efforts, too many unrelated tasks, proper utilization of skills, work load on employee, and conditions that hamper efficiency and enthusiasm. The process chart or systems flow chart can be used as the basis of a work simplification effort.

7. Flow Process Chart for Assembling Pencil Slabs

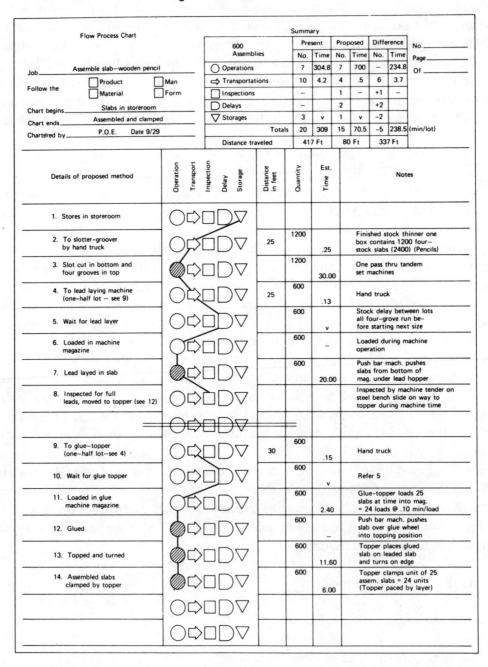

Methods Improvement Analysis

By _____ Dept. _____ Date _____

Dwg. No. _____ Item No. _____

Areas of improvement:

☐ Fewer man-hours

☐ Lower material costs

☐ Increase mach. prod.

☐ Safer operation

☐ Less scrap

☐ Less downtime

☐ Lower overhead

☐ Less turnover

Old Method Description:	Operations	Standard Time	Direct Labor Costs	Materials	Material Costs

New Method Description of change:	Operations	Standard Time	Direct Labor Costs	Materials	Material Costs

Summary	Material Costs	Direct Labor Costs	Overhead	Total
Old method				
New method				
Savings				
Total savings				

TRAINING IMPROVEMENT

Training programs are invaluable for new employees who do not entirely meet the requirements of the jobs for which they were hired and for all employees who are being encouraged to make performance stretches. Consequently, the MBO manager should regard training not as extra chores in his many duties, but as part and parcel of his job. He will find his operations running smoothly, his costs low, and new customers coming when he has a well-trained and skillful staff.

Indicators of the Need for Training Within an Organization

Needs for training vary considerably from organization to organization. The following list of indicators is a sampling.

- Gross sales leveling off or declining

- Material or labor cost percentages rising

- Percentage of overhead expense increasing

- Number and type of customer complaints increasing

- Waste excessive

- Pilferage and stealing high

- Errors in filling orders

- High frequency of bottlenecks and poor storage

- Excessive equipment breakdowns

- Excessive time needed to complete a job

- Excessive absenteeism, tardiness, or resignations

- Repairs continually needed

- Maintenance costs high

- Excessive time needed to take and fill a customer's order

Indicators such as these should flag the MBO manager that something is wrong. Although it might be a number of things, the manager will generally find that people are involved and are probably causing these problems. Providing training to employees may be a solution. The need for training can be discovered through budget and variance reports, operations reports, performance ratings, observations, face-to-face dialogues, and customer complaints.

Once improvement needs have been identifed, actions should be planned to correct and meet these needs. Advantages will be gained for both the supervisor and the employee: for the supervisor, sales targets and cost budgets are met; for the employee, feelings of self-respect and confidence are developed.

The Training Cycle

Training is providing a series of stimulating informative experiences designed to show an employee how to direct his performance toward an objective. The first step is to establish the goal to be reached by training. Subsequent steps are to identify the needs, plan the experiences, conduct the training, evaluate the results, and retrain if need be.

The advantages of a systematic and deliberate approach to training over trial-and-error methods are that it shortens learning time, reduces errors, forces a higher level of achievement, and consequently permits the organization to have more confidence in the trainee. Figures 8, 9, and 10 are some suggested approaches to systemizing the training effort.

8. Determine Organization Deficiencies (Training Needs)

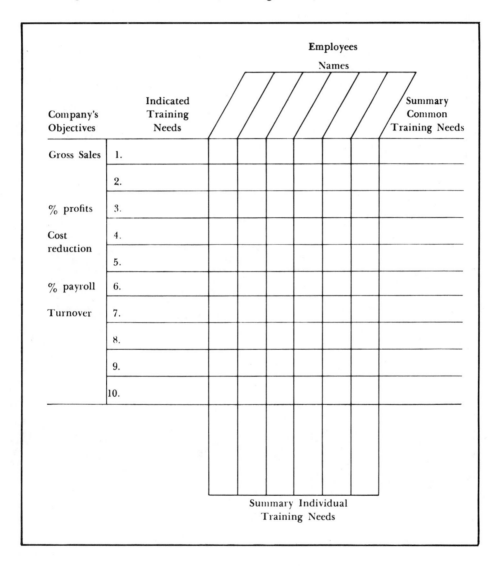

9. Plan and Act on Deficiencies

	Planning Sheet				
Training Project Number	Who Will Be Trained?	What Is Needed?	How Can It Be Achieved?	By What Date? (Completion)	Responsibility Check-off

10. Keep Training Progress and Follow-Up on Individual

	Training Steps	1	2	3	4	5	6	7
Name of Trainee	Target Time							
Job Title								
Date of Entry Entry Test								
Remarks								
Steps Completion								
January							
February							
March							
April							
May							
June							
July							
August							
September							
October							
November							
December							

Most training in organizations is individualized on-the-job training. This has proved to be the most useful technique in teaching a specific job. Job instruction training (JIT)[10] is a formalization of this technique that can be used at all skill levels. The JIT procedure is the following:

1. Prepare

    a. Know precisely what training is required (set objectives).

    b. Set up a training-activity timetable.

    c. Prepare information, procedures, or skills to be demonstrated.

    d. Select training aids most useful for the training.

    e. Decide on where training should take place.

    f. Decide on who will train and answer questions.

2. Get set

    a. Put the employees to be trained at ease.

    b. Emphasize the importance of doing the job correctly.

    c. Arouse the employees' interest in learning.

    d. Control all environmental factors that may distract or interfere.

3. Instruct

    a. Manager explains what is to be done and why. He indicates the key points that make the operation easier and faster.

    b. Manager demonstrates while employees observe. By questioning, make sure the employees are following you. Repeat points that may not be clear.

    c. Manager lets employees try while he observes. He points out mistakes and praises what they do well.

    d. Manager repeats demonstration where employees did not do well. Employees observe and are questioned. Manager repeats points that may not have been clear.

    e. Manager lets employees try again. Avoid proceeding too rapidly. Be patient. Remember, everyone was once a beginner.

    f. Manager puts employees on their own. Let the employees perform at will. Assign a senior fellow employee to help the new employee when the occasion demands.

4. Check and follow-up

   a. Performance results must meet the objectives set in the unit, such as gross sales, customer satisfaction, costs control, and better time utilization.

   b. Manager from time to time checks objectives of his unit with the performance level of employees.

   c. Frequent follow-up of an employee is a must.

   d. Prepare and schedule improvement training.

> The MBO manager should never be satisfied with the level of performance he is getting from his employees. If sales are to grow, performance must grow proportionately. Improvement training is not necessarily for correcting employees. Rather, it is designed to increase the number of results and the frequency of reaching new sets of results.

5. Guidelines for effective on-the-job training

   a. The manager is the best person to conduct training. Employees see him as their superior and regard what he says and does as most important.

   b. To be a good trainer, the manager must first know the content of the job in which the employee is to be trained. Additionally, he must know how to train, as described in the JIT procedure.

   c. The manager must recognize that each individual is different in learning ability. Some will learn fast, some slowly. Learning rates vary with each individual. Give the slow learners time to pick up their training.

   d. The manager should recognize that learning rates vary with the type of tasks involved. Single-skill motor abilities can be acquired in short learning time. Complex skills, both mental and motor, will be acquired at a slower rate.

   e. The manager must recognize the value of motivation in the learning process. When employees understand how and why training will benefit them personally, interest will develop and they will want to learn.

   f. The manager must space the training. Employees will learn more rapidly if their instruction is spaced over several short periods rather than concentrated in one.

   g. The manager will find the employee more ready to learn if the employee feels and understands the need for training.

   h. The manager will find training in one thing at a time best for learning concentration. Stick to a principal training objective until the trainee has learned how to do it.

i.   The manager should let the trainee correct himself. Do not overdo correction. Correction is like seasoning, a little goes a long way and too much spoils the dish.

j.   The manager must train so as to encourage the employee. Do not correct him in front of others. Do not be quick to blame the trainee. Compliment the employee after a performance step has been properly executed.

✓ Checkpoint: Methods Improvement and Training Improvement ────────────

Indicate true (T) or false (F).

1. To improve methods, the MBO manager must systematically study existing work procedures. ____

2. Because of the increased size and complexity of organizations, interest in methods improvement has increased. ____

3. The one overall objective of methods improvement is increased productivity. ____

4. Training programs are invaluable for employees who do not entirely meet the requirements of the jobs for which they were hired. ____

5. Training programs are not likely to be effective means for encouraging employees to make performance stretches. ____

6. Excessive waste is one adequate reason to institute a training program. ____

7. Through systematic training, employees learn faster than they would through trail-and-error methods. ____

Fill in the correct answer.

8. The _____ is a visual tool for recording and observing an operation in the sequence in which it occurs.

9. _____ is defined as setting out in an organized manner to find a better and easier way of doing a job.

10. The first step of the training cycle is to _____ .

─────────────────────

● Checkpoint Answers

1. T   2. T   3. F   4. T   5. F   6. T   7. T
8. flow process chart   9. work simplification   10. establish the training goal

◄ SUMMARY ►

The mission of improvement is generic to the MBO managerial function. Managers should never be content with the state of affairs. They should search for new plateaus of accomplishment. They should recognize a simple truth: even though the future of an organization is uncertain, it must act to make itself better than it has been in the past.

There are many approaches to improvement. Some are primarily concerned with obtaining improvement in the efficiency of using direct labor. Some are primarily concerned with the application of a new technology. Still others are concerned with material utilization and cost. The principal move on management's part is to reach for and achieve improvement where it is needed. Such improvement plans should go on continually.

This chapter dealt with some of the key areas of improvement that an MBO manager may pursue: profit improvement, sales improvement, cost improvement, management time improvement, communications improvement, methods improvement, and training improvement. A unified approach to improvement within an organization is possible with the conceptual strategy of managing by objectives.

1. Phil Carroll, *Profit Control: How to Plug Profit Leaks,* McGraw-Hill Book Co., New York, 1962, pp. 1—17.

2. Edward C. Bursk and John F. Chapman, *Modern Marketing Strategy,* New American Library, New York, 1964, pp. 1—69.

3. Murphy W. Bradhurst, "Cutting Costs: Get Everyone in the Act," *Cost Control and the Supervisor,* American Management Association, New York, 1956, p. 30.

4. Saul D. Astor, "Plant Security," *Handbook of Business Administration,* McGraw-Hill Book Co., New York, 1967, pp. 7; 185—195.

5. James T. McCay, *The Management of Time,* Prentice-Hall, Englewood Cliffs, N.J., 1959, pp. 157—168.

6. Ralph G. Nichols and Leonard A. Stevens, *Are You Listening?* McGraw-Hill Book Co., New York, 1957, p.6.

7. Ibid.

8. The idea of zone of acceptance and rejection has been borrowed from probability and statistical inferences of the normal curve. The range of these zones varies with each individuals. In large aggregates 68,95, and 99 per cent will fall in different standard deviations. See Hanson and Brabb, *Managerial Statistics,* Prentice-Hall, Englewood Cliffs, N.J., 1955, p. 87.

9. Ralph M. Barnes, *Motion and Time Study,* John Wiley, New York, 1966.

10. Homer C. Rose, *The Development and Supervision of Training Programs,* American Technical Society, New York, 1964, p. 253.

Chapter 9 Review ————————————————————

$\checkmark\checkmark$ Doublecheck

Answer briefly.

1. Why should an organization constantly seek improvement?

2. What is a profit improvement plan?

3. What is the relationship between profit improvement, sales improvement, and cost improvement?

4. What are some principal management time robbers?

5. What are the principal ways managers communicate? What is the average time devoted to each?

_____

_____

_____

_____

_____

6. What are some guidelines for good listening?

_____

_____

_____

_____

_____

7. What is "methods improvement"? What is its greatest benefit?

_____

_____

_____

_____

_____

8. For which kind of employees might training be advantageous?

_____

_____

_____

_____

_____

9. List five indicators of the need for training within an organization.

_____

_____

_____

_____

_____

10. What are the steps of the training cycle?

_____

_____

_____

_____

_____

- Doublecheck Answers

1. The continuous performance stretch for more and better results is the competitive edge an organization has. As long as it embarks on aggressive improvement programs, competitors will find it difficult to keep up unless they make the same performance stretches.

2. The profit improvement plan systematically establishes profit objectives and organizes all efforts in order to reach those objectives. All aspects of the organization are brought into play in systematically seeking to improve overall profits.

3. There are four ways to improve profits — increase sales volume, increase price margin, reduce capital investment, reduce operating cost. Sales improvement and cost improvement plans are subplans that can be used to accomplish profit improvement. They are the means by which profit improvement is accomplished.

4. Some of the principal management time robbers are

   - Carelessly done work

   - Delayed decisions

   - Defective communications

   - Uncontrolled telephone calls

   - Casual visitors

5. The principal ways managers communicate and the fraction of their time devoted to each are the following.

   - Listening   32%

   - Body language (physical gestures)   30%

   - Speaking   21%

   - Reading   11%

   - Writing   6%

6. Most of the guidelines for good listening really represent overcoming bad habits that often develop in the area of listening. These bad habits include assuming that communications will be uninteresting, listening only for facts, pretending to pay attention, tolerating distractions, and evading difficult situations.

7. Methods improvement is the systematic study and analysis of existing work methods and procedures in order to discover new or easier ways of accomplishing work. The greatest benefit from applying this technique is in increased productivity and consequent lower operating costs.

8. Training programs are invaluable for new employees who do not entirely meet the requirements of the job for which they were hired. Such programs are also beneficial to all employees who are being encouraged to make performance stretches. Consequently, the

MBO manager should regard training not as an extra chore in his many responsibilities but as a part and parcel of his job.

9. Some of the indicators of the need for training within an organization are the following: gross sales leveling off or declining, material or labor cost percentages rising, percentage of overhead expense increasing, number and type of customer complaints increasing, excessive waste, excessive pilferage, errors in order filling, high frequency of bottlenecks and poor storage, excessive equipment breakdowns, excessive time needed to complete a job, excessive absenteeism, tardiness or resignations, continual need for repairs, excessive maintenance costs, and excessive time to fill customer orders.

10. The steps involved in the training cycle are the following.

    a.   Statement of objectives

    b.   Determination of training needs

    c.   Planning for training (content, methods, experiences)

    d.   Preparation for training (location, climate, timing)

    e.   Training and coaching

    f.   Training evaluation

    g.   Retraining and reevaluation

    h.   Feedback

    i.   Reformulation of training needs

Early one Saturday morning, Carter Jones, the quality control supervisor for Sigma Electronics, was sitting in his office and contemplating the need for doing some planning for his area for the next several months. Although the quality control area was not a critical problem at the present time, he knew that with the continued rapid expansion of the company's activities it would become increasingly important in the future. Thus he wanted to be sure that he had planned his operations in sufficient detail so that all would go smoothly during the coming months.

Sigma Electronics was a small manufacturer of electronic components and finished products. The company was located in the San Francisco area. It had been started by two engineers who wanted to break out on their own and try their own skill at business and the development of new products. During recent months, the company had entered the small hand-held calculator market and had made significant strides in providing inexpensive calculators for large quantity buyers. (Most of these calculators had a wholesale price of less than $60.)

Carter's responsibilities included checking the acceptibility of all finished products before they were shipped to the customer. He also had responsibility for the quality checking of incoming material and parts. While the general corporate objectives relating to his duties stated only that the company wanted to at least meet its competition in terms of quality, Carter realized that the two founding partners were very committed to actually doing better than the competition. When Carter had pushed the sales department to make this general corporate objective more operational, they had stated that the company planned to issue a 90-day warranty on parts and labor within the near future on all calculators and to minimize the number of calculators that were returned due to defects.

The types of problems that existed in the quality control area could be grouped into three categories: electronic failures, mechanical failures, and cosmetic problems. The first category related mainly to the failure of one or more electronic circuits to operate properly. The second category was mainly a physical problem in terms of the calculator case fitting the keyboard and the readout mechanism. (On some of the materials that Sigma had purchased, the openings in the plastic cases were not properly aligned, which made it difficult to use all of the keys when the final unit was assembled.) The final category of quality control problem dealt simply with the appearance of the finished product. Sigma felt that their product should be consistent in terms of color and should match closely the original specifications that had been drawn up by engineering.

While Carter's superior, the vice president of manufacturing, had not detailed any specific assignment for changing and formalizing quality control procedures, Carter felt that it was important to do so at the present time. Presently, there were only three people working under him in this activity. He was certain that with the rapidly expanding sales of calculators this number could quadruple within the next year. As he contemplated the types of procedures that he might adopt, he remembered that the research and development group had offered to design and build any electronic testing equipment that he might need, and he was sure that if he wanted help from the production manager, it would be obtained easily.

With the above thoughts in mind, Carter set out to plan the types of procedures that might be followed, to organize the activities in the quality control area, and to establish his own control system for monitoring that activity.

Assignment

As a first step in applying MBO to Carter's problem, prepare an outline that covers the objectives, the organization of the work, and the establishment of control procedures. Using that outline and assuming Carter's situation, develop as precisely as you can each item in the plan.

- Sigma Electronics: The Functions of a Manager

A.   Apply the systems approach.

   1.   Corporate objective(s). (What are the general corporate objectives that are relevant in this situation?)

      a.   Stated objective: To meet the competition in terms of quality.

      b.   Informal objective: To do better than the competition in terms of quality.

   2.   Formulate policies to carry out objectives. (What are the policies that have been established to help reach these corporate objectives?)

      a.   Offer a 90-day warranty on parts and labor.

      b.   Minimize the number of defective units.

   3.   Short-range plans to implement policies. (What type of plans might be considered in this situation?)

      a.   Set up three separate quality checks, one for each type of defect.

      b.   Have each calculator checked by a single individual.

   4.   Detail procedures for implementing plans. (What are the areas in which procedures are needed in order to effectively implement the quality control plan?)

      a.   Establish acceptable quality limits.

      b.   Determine at what point quality check should be performed and by whom.

      c.   Establish control system so that production can learn from the results of quality control.

B.   Organize the quality control activity.

   1.   Define the work. (What is the nature of the work to be performed?)

      a.   Physical check of a sample from all incoming parts orders

      b.   Cosmetic check prior to assembly

      c.   Electronic check prior to final assembly into plastic case

      d.   Mechanical check of completed product

   2.   Identify the people. (Who will do the work?)

      a.   Quality control people to perform checks c and d

      b.   Order receiving department to perform check a

      c.   Production assembly people to perform check b

3. Define the workplace. (What will it look like?)

    a. a and b will be completely integrated into existing operations and locations.

    b. A quality control area will be physically set aside adjacent to the final assembly and shipping areas.

4. As head of quality control, what will be the limits of my authority, responsibility and accountability, or at least, what would I like them to be?

    a. Authority: to reject all parts and products not meeting specifications; to work with sales in setting specifications; to handle all personnel who work exclusively for quality control

    b. Responsibility: To meet the corporate objectives and policies relating to quality control

    c. Accountability: Accountable to V.P. Manufacturing for the quality of products shipped

C. Establish control procedures.

1. Objectives of this activity

    a. To identify defects at the earliest stage possible

    b. To provide feedback to production on quality standards and performance

    c. To minimize the number of returns (e.g., less than ½ of 1%)

2. Reporting procedures

    a. Approval form to be completed on all incoming orders of parts and material

    b. Periodic report to be made on cosmetic defects

    c. Quality control report to be made on each production batch of calculators, noting types of defects and number

3. Evaluating performance

    a. Standards to be established to determine when special attention is needed

    b. Weekly quality control meeting with production

4. How to take corrective action?

Batches of incoming items or finished products that do not meet standards will be analyzed by quality control supervisor.

5. How will I communicate and educate those who will be involved in this activity?

    a. Written standards will be prepared.

    b. Examples of typical defects will be prominently displayed at quality check location.

    c. Procedures will be defined in writing and demonstrated to all production workers.

    d. Periodic checks of individual performance will be made by production manager and quality control supervisor.

    e. Person doing the actual quality check will be asked to sign off on each batch checked.

PRE- AND POST-TEST

PRE- AND POST-TEST

Write your responses (true or false) on a separate piece of paper. Compare your responses with those on the Answer Sheet and write in your score. Do not refer to the Answer Sheet until you have completed all the questions. Do not refer back to your answers on the Pre-Test until after you have completed the Post-Test and calculated your score.

MANAGING BY OBJECTIVES: AN OVERVIEW

1. In managing by objectives, progress is measured in terms of specified goals rather than time limits.

2. Coordinated decentralization is MBO's historical taproot.

3. The greater the focus on results, the greater the likelihood of achieving them.

4. In an MBO program, all the accountability is at the top.

5. In a well-run MBO system, no time is spent validating objectives.

6. MBO objectives should always spur managers to try to achieve more than they really can achieve.

MBO APPROACHES TO TYPICAL MANAGEMENT PROBLEMS

7. The critical-few objectives on which an MBO manager should focus are always obvious.

8. The MBO Rule for Future Action is a means of minimizing the need for crisis management.

9. Under the MBO Rule for Focus, 80 percent of identified demands should be regarded as critical.

ISOLATING OBJECTIVES

10. Because it is neither rational nor scientific, intuition plays no part in improvement forecasting.

11. Planning improvements means planning improvements in existing capacity.

12. Added capacity is always improved capacity.

13. Immediate improvement forecasts deal with urgent problems covering periods of one year or less.

14. In seeking the best course of action, doing nothing is a valid alternative to consider.

SETTING OBJECTIVES

15. "To improve economic conditions" is a good MBO objective because it permits a sensible range of interpretation.

16. The more concrete the information an MBO manager can build into his objective statement, the more likely it is that those involved will interpret it in a similar manner.

17. Quantified objectives suggest a precision that does not exist.

18. In setting MBO objectives, the challenge to the individual must always fall within a range acceptable to the group.

19. The output of the best performer is roughly twice that of the poorest.

VALIDATING OBJECTIVES

20. The more accurate and complete a work breakdown, the greater the likelihood that the actions necessary to complete the objective will be understood.

21. A decision tree is a shorthand notation for the likelihood of occurrence of each event in a chain of events.

22. PERT is a valuable technique for dealing with problems of a repetitive nature.

23. Tasks are made up of one or more events and their associated activities.

24. Work descriptions are statements of the methods that will be utilized in completing a work package.

25. Time allotments are specifications of time needed to complete a work package.

IMPLEMENTING OBJECTIVES

26. The variability of motivators from one individual to the next does not prohibit the development of schedules for implementing objectives.

27. The need for planned motivation is the same for employees at all job levels within an organization.

28. A manager must have frequent face-to-face interaction with his subordinates up to the time when they start to implement objectives.

29. In trying to persuade subordinates, it is always advisable to tell them both sides of the argument.

30. Habits are regulators of behavior that can stifle innovation.

31. All motivators are financial in nature.

CONTROLLING AND REPORTING THE STATUS OF OBJECTIVES

32. Controlling consists of keeping work activities within specified standards.

33. An audit, which inquires into the accuracy of records, should be carried through all phases of the MBO strategy.

34. In status reporting, the MBO manager need not be concerned with costs.

35. Day-to-day surveillance of status is always necessary.

36. MBO managers are increasingly operating their objective programs out of sight of their supervisors and other managers.

37. An effective status reporting system is a system designed to inform all members of management.

38. Because of the special nature of status reporting, accounting information and existing reports cannot be used in the preparation.

39. An MBO performance appraisal is oriented more toward job requirements and results than toward personality traits.

TRAINING AND DEVELOPING MBO MANAGERS

40. The MBO trainee should not be permitted to participate in the restructuring of delegated assignments in an objective.

41. The most effective MBO training is built into on-the-job experience.

42. Formal education is not sufficient for teaching basic MBO skills to a manager.

43. MBO training courses offered by institutions specializing in management education have the advantage of taking the trainee away from his immediate job so that he can evaluate his organization's situation from a distance.

44. The ability to predict outcomes is an objective-setting skill.

IMPROVEMENT APPLICATIONS

45. Every time a recycling of work occurs because of human error, labor costs automatically go up proportionately.

46. Two out of every three employees are a threat to steal from their organization.

47. Basic to overhead improvement is overhead control as a percentage of material and labor.

48. If he has a proper sales improvement program, an MBO manager does not need a contingency plan.

49. The MBO manager must strive each year for higher sales volume at lower cost.

50. Through unwillingness to pass his knowledge along to subordinates, a manager creates a communications barrier.

• Pre- and Post-Test Answers

1. F	20. T	40. F
2. T	21. T	41. T
3. T	22. F	42. T
4. F	23. T	43. T
5. F	24. T	44. T
6. F	25. T	
		45. T
7. F	26. T	46. T
8. T	27. F	47. T
9. F	28. F	48. F
	29. F	49. T
10. F	30. T	50. T
11. T	31. F	
12. F		
13. T	32. T	
14. T	33. T	
	34. F	
15. F	35. F	
16. T	36. T	
17. T	37. T	
18. T	38. F	
19. T	39. T	

Pre-Test Score ____

Post-Test Score ____

M